An Introduction to Personal Finance

(A Republic of Ireland/ United Kingdom text)

An Introduction to Personal Finance

(A Republic of Ireland/ United Kingdom text)

3rd Edition

Anne Marie Ward

(BA (hons), Macc, FCA, PGCUT, PhD, FHEA)
Professor of Accounting, Department of
Accounting, Finance and Economics,
University of Ulster at Jordanstown

Chartered
Accountants
Ireland

Published by
Chartered Accountants Ireland
Chartered Accountants House
47–49 Pearse Street
Dublin 2
www.charteredaccountants.ie

ISBN: 978-1-908199-17-1

Typeset by Compuscript
Printed by CPI Books UK

LIABILITY

At the outset it is highlighted that the author is NOT a financial adviser. This book and its contents should not be taken as financial advice. Each and every individual is different, their circumstances, needs, objectives, etc., are different. Independent financial advice should be obtained from an appropriately qualified registered financial adviser. It is a criminal offence to provide financial advice if not registered with the appropriate regulatory body.

For my husband

For my husband.

ABBREVIATED CONTENTS

DETAILED CONTENTS

PREFACE

When an individual has a strong awareness of their ability to generate funds, has knowledge of their expenditure and debt commitments (and the associated cost of this debt), has formalised their financial objectives, considered their financial responsibilities for dependants and evaluated their retirement needs, then they are in a strong position to have financial control over their lives. Having financial control means not being financially dependent on others, including relatives and/or the Government. By preparing a financial plan, individuals can carefully manage their income and expenditure, can identify their financial risk and take steps to minimise it, can target bad, expensive debt for clearance, can highlight good investment opportunities that match their risk-return profile, can start to provide for their retirement and, in general, can increase their net worth in the most tax-efficient manner. Many individuals, particularly those with business qualifications or business experience, do follow good personal financial practices – other people are perhaps not as aware of the consequences of poor financial planning.

This text tries to shed some light on the financial planning process, by highlighting information that a typical financial adviser might gather before providing financial advice. It also considers possible influences on advice given. There are four key areas that have to be considered in light of the background information collected and influences identified. These include risk management, debt management, investment management and retirement planning. Having an understanding of the time value of money is also important for personal financial planning. An individual has to keep revisiting their plan as they progress along their financial lifecycle and should make changes to their plan when their circumstances change and as they get older. For example, it is recommended that younger people (who have the greatest capital rationing problems) should be frugal and should, even at this early stage, be thinking about their retirement needs. Responsibility for the encouragement of good financial practices should be championed by parents, educators and employers. A retired person will not be considering saving for retirement but will focus on how best to manage the release of funds from investments that already exist so as to maintain a good standard of living for the duration of their natural life. Retired persons will also be particularly concerned with ensuring that they have made a will and have considered the tax implications of this on their beneficiaries.

A brief explanation is provided in this text of the main types of investment product that an individual may invest in, either directly or through their pension. The most important issue to consider is the risk exposure of the various investments to external influences, such as the condition of the economy. It is highlighted that a diversified portfolio of negatively correlated investments is the best investment option, and individuals with higher net worth are in a stronger position to create this type of portfolio for themselves as they can afford property, equity, bonds and other investments such as wine, art or precious stones. However, opportunity is still there for those who are less well off but who have funds to invest to access these investments to an extent through, for example, unit trusts or mutual funds.

Pensions are reasonably complex: there are several types (public, private, occupational) and each has different rules and tax breaks. A brief synopsis of each type is given in this text, though readers should obtain more detailed information on the different types of pension from their financial adviser before investing in one.

Limiting a person's exposure to downside risk, such as loss of income, is also important for financial sustainability in the long term. Therefore, this textbook also discusses, in brief, the main types of insurance product that are typically used to reduce financial risk for an individual and/or their family.

PEDAGOGY

Learning Objectives: In each chapter the expected competencies to be gained by readers are outlined at the outset.

Chapter Clarity: Each chapter begins with an introduction which explains the flow and connection between topics included in the chapter. The body of each chapter provides detail and a conclusion sums up, by highlighting key points.

ROI and UK Sections: Government policy, tax laws and regulation is different in both jurisdictions. Where differences between jurisdictions occur then a separate section dealing with each is included with the heading highlighting whether that section relates to the ROI or the UK. Where there is no reference in the heading then the information in that section is applicable to both jurisdictions. A student from the ROI does not have to read any section that has UK in the heading, and vice versa.

Worked Examples: The worked examples increase in complexity as a chapter progresses.

Key Terms: When key terms are first defined in a chapter they are highlighted in bold and italicised. At the end of each chapter the key terms are summarised in a table. The reader should be aware of the key terms and should revisit the chapter when unable to define/explain the key term.

Websites: When relevant, lists of websites that can be visited by readers to obtain more information on the subject area being discussed in the chapter are provided.

Review Questions: These questions are designed to assist readers in identifying and revising the key issues within each chapter. It is a way for readers to provide themselves with feedback on their understanding of each topic. Some solutions are included in **Appendix 4**. The solutions to the challenging questions are provided to lecturers for use in tutorial classes. The questions range from short quick-fire questions, to examination standard questions. Successful completion of the more challenging questions demonstrates a thorough understanding of the issues covered in the chapter and indeed may refer to issues covered in preceding chapters.

Case Studies: **Appendix 1** contains three case studies. These integrate and examine topics that are covered in several chapters of the book. They aim to analyse an individual's personal circumstances, in terms of their current position, to provide guidance on risk, investment and to project the impact of the advice given on the individual's financial position in the future. Solutions to these case studies are available to lecturers.

Mathematics Made Simple: This text does not try to derive mathematical formula or to prove existing accepted models. In each instance the accepted approach is explained in simple terms using narrative. A formula is provided and an example of how to calculate the outcome of the formula using input variables is given.

Index Tables: Index tables have been provided in the appendices to save readers time when they are adjusting cash flows for the time value of money.

Abbreviations: A list of abbreviations used in the text has been provided, for quick reference for readers.

References and Bibliography: The readers of this text can deepen their understanding of areas of interest to them by sourcing the work of other authors. The bibliography contains text books, newspaper articles and academic literature that are considered relevant by the writer.

ABBREVIATIONS

AMRF	Approved Minimum Retirement Fund
APR	Annual Percentage Rate
ARF	Approved Retirement Fund
AVCs	Additional Voluntary Contributions
CARE	Career Averaged Re-Valued Earnings
CAT	Capital Acquisitions Tax
CBI	Central Bank of Ireland
CGT	Capital Gains Tax
Chng	Price change in the last 24 hours
CIS	Collective Investment Scheme
CPI	Consumer Price Index
CTF	Child Trust Fund
DBI	Death Benefit Insurance
DINKs	Double Income No Kids
DIRT	Deposit Interest Retention Tax
DMP	Debt Management Plan
DRC	Debt Relief Certificate
DRO	Debt Relief Order
DSA	Debt Settlement Agreement
DSFA	Department of Social and Family Affairs
EAR	Equivalent Annual Rate
ECB	European Central Bank
ESA	Employment and Support Allowance
FOS	Financial Ombudsman Service
FPC	Financial Policy Committee
FSA	Formal Scheme of Arrangement
FSA	Financial Services Authority
FSCS	Financial Services Compensation Scheme
FSO	Financial Services Ombudsman
GDP	Gross Domestic Product
IB	Incapacity Benefit
IFSRA	Irish Financial Services Regulatory Authority
IHT	Inheritance Tax

IPA	Income Payment Agreement
ISA	Individual Savings Account
IVA	Individual Voluntary Arrangement
JISA	Junior Individual Savings Account
KIPPERS	Kids in Parents' Pockets Eroding Retirement Savings
LIBOR	London Interbank Offer Rate
LTA%	Lifetime Allowance Percentage
MABS	Monetary Advice and Budgeting Service
NEST	National Employment Savings Trust
NI	Northern Ireland
NIC	National Insurance Contributions
NS&I	National Savings and Investments
NTMA	National Treasury Management Agency
OECD	The Organisation for Economic Co-operation and Development
PAYE	Pay As You Earn
PCLS	Pension Commencement Lump Sum
P/E	Price Earnings Ratio
PHI	Permanent Health Insurance
PIA	Personal Insolvency Arrangement
PMI	Private Medical Insurance
PPI	Payment Protection Insurance
PRA	Prudential Regulatory Authority
PRSA	Personal Retirement Savings Accounts
PRSI	Pay Related Social Insurance
ROI	Republic of Ireland
RPI	Retail Price Index
SDLT	Stamp Duty Land Tax
SERPS	State Earnings Related Pension Scheme
SIB	Securities and Investment Board
SSIA	Special Savings Incentive Accounts
SSP	Statutory Sick Pay
S2P	Second State Pension
TRS	Tax Relief at Source
UK	United Kingdom
USC	Universal Social Contribution
VAT	Value Added Tax
Vol.	Volume of transactions
xd	Share Price Ex-Dividend
Yld.	Dividend Yield

CHAPTER 1

INTRODUCTION

This textbook serves to cover the main issues of personal financial management at an introductory level. Personal financial planning can be considered to focus on six areas, as follows:

- current lifestyle;
- risk management;
- debt;
- savings;
- investments; and
- retirement planning (pensions).

Before the main personal finance decisions are discussed in detail, **Chapter 2**, 'Political and Economic Influences on Financial Planning', provides some background on the political and economic influences on an individual's financial situation. This chapter discusses the impact on an individual's financial position of changes in the Government's pension policy, stock market performance and changes in interest rates. This helps to highlight the growing importance of personal financial planning and provides an awareness of the growing risk to which individuals' finances are exposed. This chapter also provides a brief synopsis of the different types of tax that an individual may have to consider when making financial decisions.

In **Chapter 3**, the preparation of a financial plan for an individual is considered. This chapter is written from the perspective of the person preparing the financial plan, which is different to that of the individual being assessed. By assuming that the plan is being prepared for a different individual, the reader is made more aware of the process and the underlying factors that impact on a financial plan. In this text, the preparation of a financial plan has been broken into nine steps, including:

- determining the profile of the individual;
- identifying financial issues;
- assessing the individual's risk attitude;
- setting objectives for the individual;
- identifying the current financial position and earnings potential of the individual;
- preparing a financial plan for the individual; and
- reviewing the financial plan and updating it to take account of changes in the individual's situation.

Most financial advisers will prepare a variety of financial plans for an individual, reflecting different scenarios. A financial plan is only as good as the information it contains. This information is sourced from the individual, so the onus is on an individual to provide relevant, reliable and realistic estimates of cash flows expected, valuations for assets held and debts owed. The plan will only be of benefit to an individual if he/she provides relevant information, and if he/she heeds the advice given by the financial adviser and sticks to the projected plan.

Chapter 4, 'The Financial Lifecycle', considers factors that are deemed to be most important to an individual at different stages of their lifecycle. No two financial plans will be the same. Every individual is different. However, there are common issues that face most individuals as they progress through life. This chapter splits people's lives into periods, or stages, which are aligned with age, and highlights the main issues that affect individuals within these periods. The stages include children, students, young employed individuals, individuals who have dependants, established individuals and retired individuals.

Chapter 5, 'Insurance', introduces one of the first decision factors that an individual has to consider. Insurance reduces risk but costs money. An individual has to decide whether or not they are going to pay to reduce risk. It is generally advised that individuals, as a minimum, protect their homes, their income and take steps to cover the financial impact of a potentially critical illness. The amount of insurance taken depends on an individual's attitude to risk and on their personal circumstances. For example, a young, healthy individual with no partner or dependants is likely to opt for less insurance cover than a married individual who has children. If an individual is unable to build up savings and investments, then they are exposed to more risk and are more likely to opt for more insurance cover. This chapter describes the most common products used by individuals: family income benefit, permanent health insurance, critical illness cover, a variety of life assurance products, private medical insurance, motor insurance, house insurance and payment protection insurance.

Debt management requires particular attention in an individual's early years. If debt is not controlled from the outset, it can hinder an individual's ability to become financially self-sufficient. **Chapter 6**, 'Debt Management', considers the different types of debt, differentiates between what is regarded as 'good debt' and 'bad debt', details ratios that can be used to self-assess credit risk, highlights pitfalls that can cause an individual to end up in financial difficulty, and suggests steps to take to manage personal debt. The topic is of particular importance at the present time due to the economic environment in both the Republic of Ireland (ROI) and the United Kingdom (UK).

Two of the main decisions facing an individual throughout their life – determining the level of funds to invest and selecting the correct investment – are covered in **Chapter 7**, 'Savings' and **Chapter 8**, 'Investments'. **Chapter 7** considers the purpose of having savings, provides tips on good savings practices, and summarises briefly the main savings products that are available in the UK and the ROI differentiating between those with tax breaks and those without. **Chapter 8**, 'Investments', outlines the relationship between risk, inflation, debt and liquidity on individuals' investment policies and describes, in brief, the main investment products used in personal finance. This chapter provides more detail on investment in property relative to other investment products, as this type of investment is material, long-term and has become more popular with private individuals over the past three decades. Indeed, the recent financial crisis has had a major impact on this type of investment and, therefore, this is factored into the discussion on investing in property.

The different types of pension are discussed in **Chapter 9**, 'Pensions', for both the ROI and the UK and, finally, in **Chapter 10** the regulation of the financial services markets in both jurisdictions is explained.

CHAPTER 2

POLITICAL AND ECONOMIC INFLUENCES ON FINANCIAL PLANNING

Learning Objectives

Upon completion of this chapter, readers should be able to:

- explain the meaning of the key terms listed at the end of the chapter;
- outline the principles of personal financial management;
- explain the benefits of good financial planning;
- describe changes in policy that have resulted in more uncertainty for individuals' financial security; and
- explain the impact of economic changes on individuals' financial security.

Financial Planning

Good *financial planning* strives to provide individuals with the ability to meet their personal financial aspirations both now and in the future. Good financial planning should lead to social and economic benefits for an individual. It should increase the ability of an individual to be *financially self-sufficient*, to feel financially secure and to ensure that sufficient steps are taken so that this remains the case throughout the entire life of the individual (including when retired). The importance of having strong personal financial planning has increased over the past 30 years because of changes in government policy and an increase in the exposure of individuals' wealth to economic risk. This has been particularly evident over the past five years as the economic downturn has had a significant negative impact on many individuals' personal wealth. In particular, the value of many individuals' pension funds fell, as did property prices and income from interest rate products.

Personal Finance and Government Welfare

One source of income to individuals is government welfare. In the UK and in the ROI, government welfare is typically directed at providing support for people on low incomes (or with no income), providing a decent health service that is accessible to all, providing education for all, caring for the elderly and providing support for children. Policies in these areas will impact on the finances of most individuals, and knowledge of government welfare is important when an individual is planning for their future. Government policy in these areas is subject to change, particularly at the present time as the governments in both jurisdictions try to manage high national debt levels against the backdrop of poor economic performance. In other words, the national cash outflows have increased and the inflows (from taxation) have fallen. The result is unpopular cuts to public spending and to government welfare.

One area that is of concern to individuals is pensions. At one time, individuals could feel secure about their financial future if they were paying into a pension, both at work and with their 'stamp' (National Insurance Contributions (NIC) in the UK and Pay-Related Social Insurance (PRSI) in the ROI). This, they believed, was sufficient to take care of them when they retired. However, this may no longer be the case. The governments in the ROI and the UK currently operate a *'pay-as-you-go'* policy, paying current pensions out of current employee tax (there is no pension pot!). The Government in the ROI is taking some steps to put funds aside for future pension commitments; however, it has recently had to utilise some of these funds due to the country's financial difficulties (discussed later). The pension problem is exacerbated by the shift in the age demographics of both populations. People are living longer now than when the 'Welfare State' was first introduced, and the standard of living expected by pensioners has risen. The issues relating to government welfare and personal finance particular to each jurisdiction are now discussed.

United Kingdom

When Beveridge first proposed a Welfare State in the UK in 1942 the ideal was that the population would be looked after by the State from 'cradle to grave'. Over time, governments have progressively increased their financial commitments to the welfare system, and the expectations of the public have increased. The care expected from the National Health Service (NHS) has increased significantly; waiting lists are typically shorter and hospital facilities are better than ever before. The standard of education expected has also increased. Children now have to stay in school to 16 years of age (at one time this was 14), and this is mooted to increase to 18 in the coming years. In addition, the proportion of school-leavers attending university has increased significantly, with emphasis and support available for those students coming from lower income families. Governments also typically support training schemes for young people who are not interested in studying at university. The provision of public housing for those with no income/ low income has increased. In general, public spending has increased over the years to arguably unsustainable levels (given the current economic climate and the state of the country's finances). The recent Government cuts to public spending and welfare highlight that the Government is finding it difficult to service the welfare bill and to repay the country's debt.

The current cuts follow a trend that has been occurring to the welfare system since the late 1970s. *Private funding* has been creeping into the welfare system, with many individuals now having their own private health insurance, having to pay for university education (Northern Ireland (NI), England and Wales) and having to pay for dental treatment (these services were free in the UK in the past). Indeed, the Government is trying to shift the future responsibility for providing for individuals (when retired) back on to those same individuals, by introducing incentives to get people to cater for their own retirement. For example, Individual Savings Accounts (ISAs) are available. ISA products are afforded generous tax breaks and were established with the aim of encouraging individuals to save regularly and to lock funds away for a number of years. In addition to these savings products, tax breaks are also available for contributions to private pension schemes, though the tax benefit has been reduced in the 2012 budget. ISAs and pensions are discussed in detail in **Chapter 7**, 'Savings', and **Chapter 9**, 'Pensions'.

The UK Government also changed the way state pensions for employed individuals, who pay extra national insurance contributions (NICs), are calculated. At one time, when an individual paid NICs over a certain level, they were entitled to a second state pension. The level of this second pension was related to the level of additional NICs paid. This is no longer the case. The Government placed a floor (which benefits low-income individuals) and a cap on the pension that can be obtained from the second state pension (detrimental to high-earning individuals). Indeed, going forward, a flat rate pension is imminent.

The outlook for the future is that welfare payments are likely to contract. The Welfare Reform Act 2012 is going to bring in changes to welfare that aim to promote employment and to simplify welfare payments.

Most UK benefits are now means-tested. One of the last universal benefits (applicable to all regardless of income), child benefit, is now changing to a means-tested benefit. The 2010 budget froze the child benefit allowance until 2012. In the 2012 budget, after much controversy, it was announced that child benefit would be scrapped for any couple earning over £60,000 and would reduce on a tapering scale for couples earning between £50,000 and £60,000. Couples earning under £50,000 will continue to be entitled to the full benefit, though the amount of allowance per child was further frozen until 2014.

Another Government policy response to the recent economic crisis that impacts on the financial planning of a large number of individuals in the UK is public sector pay. In 2010, public sector pay was frozen for those earning over £18,000 (for two years). In the 2012 budget, this freeze was extended by a further year, and it was announced that a 1% cap would be placed on pay increases for those earning over £21,000 for two years thereafter. This reduces the disposable income of many individuals as inflation is positive. More cuts are likely in the future, unless the Government gets their debt level under control.

Republic of Ireland

The reduction in taxation revenue caused by the world financial crises, the resultant property crash and economic recession has meant that the ROI Government has insufficient funds to cover its outgoings, relying mostly on raising debt to meet its requirements. However, this cannot continue, as the country cannot continue to borrow indefinitely. As a result of this, each budget since 2009 has introduced a series of tax increases, new taxes, public sector cuts and cuts in welfare, and it is mooted that additional cuts will be required to stabilise the country's finances. This means that individuals should not rely on state welfare, as this will diminish, and it is difficult to foretell the extent of cuts in the coming years.

At present, welfare in the ROI can be categorised into three types. These are *social security benefits* (given to people who have contributed sufficient pay-related social insurance), *means-tested benefits* (payable to people who do not meet the social security benefits criteria and who meet the criteria for this instead) and *universal payments* (payable to all who meet the specific personal circumstances required regardless of income or social insurance record).

Most welfare benefits have either been frozen or received cuts in the budgets over the past few years; for example, child benefit was reduced by €16 per month per child in the 2010 budget. Child benefit has been frozen since 2010, and the 2012 budget continued the trend. The three €635 lump sum payments made on birth, on reaching four years of age and on reaching 12 years of age were scrapped. The uniforms and shoes grant has reduced by about 25% (for example, from €305 to €250 for children aged 12 or over) and the one parent family payment, which was eligible for individuals with children up to 14 years of age, has been reduced to 12 years of age in 2012 and will be further reduced to seven years of age by 2014. State pensions have been frozen since 2009, and this was also extended by the 2012 budget.

Under the Proposed National Pension Framework, the age at which people qualify for the state pension will increase from 66 years to 67 years in 2021, and to 68 years in 2028. The age at which public servants (people who are employed in the public sector) can qualify for the public service pension is now 66, and the maximum retirement age is being increased to 70 (from 65). Pensions to new entrants are reducing, and back payments on pensions, which were allowable for periods of up to five years, are now restricted to six months. The 2012 budget also shaved six weeks off the fuel allowance, a means-tested benefit that was payable to individuals on long-term welfare. It had been payable at the rate of €20 per week for 32 weeks; now it is payable for 26 weeks.

The future of the state pension is a concern for ROI governments, as the population are living for longer and the cost of living is increasing. To alleviate the potential financial burden, in 2001 the Government set up the National Pensions Reserve Fund under the National Pensions Reserve Fund Act 2000. It is expected that this reserve will start to fund part of the state pension from 2025. The Government plans to contribute 1% of GDP to this fund until 2055. However, the future of this fund can be called into question. Initially set up as an independent fund controlled and managed by the National Pension Reserve Fund Commission, this independence was eroded in 2009 by the National Pensions Reserve Fund and Miscellaneous Provisions Act 2009 and the Credit Institutions (stabilisation) Act 2010, which allows the funds to be used to purchase government and bank bonds. The portfolio of investments is now made up of two parts, a discretionary portfolio (the Commission's responsibility) and the directed investments portfolio (the Minister for Finance's responsibility). By June 2011 the fund had invested €7 billion in both Bank of Ireland and Allied Irish Banks preference shares.

Public servants also have had to suffer pay cuts, which ranged from 5% to 15% (beyond certain thresholds), and pay freezes, depending on salary level, and the associated public service pensions are now based on 'career average' earnings not final salary. The future cuts are unpredictable, and individuals should not assume that the Government will support certain activities such as third-level education. Individuals should start planning using the assumption that state support will be limited.

Concluding Comments on Welfare

The current budget deficit has caused a change in government policy in both jurisdictions. The impact of this is that there will be less benefits and more taxation. Public services are likely to reduce, and individuals will have to take more responsibility for their own futures and cannot rely on their respective government as a safety net. In particular, those who are high earners will have to suffer the greatest change in their wealth, as most of the current tax incentives and breaks are geared towards those on low incomes, with tax breaks to high earners being reduced or removed, and additional taxes being directed at high rate taxpayers. Individuals will have to make decisions as to whether they want to sustain their current level of disposable income for the rest of their lives; if they do, then serious steps need to be taken now to ensure that future spending power is maintained. In short, individuals have to take more responsibility for their own financial destiny and to place more emphasis on funding their own future.

Personal Finance and the Markets

Further complications to face individuals when they undertake financial planning are the risks associated with equity investments. Pension companies invest heavily in the equity stock markets, and the value of an individual's pension will be affected by movements in the value of shares quoted on stock markets. This impacts on every individual who pays into a pension scheme.

The impact of the global stock markets' decline on the value of company pension schemes in the 1990s meant that many individuals who retired in this period found that their private pension was not what they had anticipated. The same problem arose again in the last five years. Anyone who retired in the period after the latest world financial crisis started (2007) saw the value of their pension pots decline. Stock exchanges worldwide suffered serious downturns, and billions were knocked off the value of pension funds.

The pension problem has been compounded by the oil slick in the Atlantic Ocean. The value of BP's shares, which were £655.40 (stg) on 20 April 2010 had plummeted to £328.20 by 2 July 2010. In total, BP has lost almost £50 billion of its capitalised stock market value since the oil disaster began. Most UK and ROI pension funds have a considerable stake in this 'blue chip' company. BP's share price has recovered but not to the same extent. On 10 July 2012, BP's shares were trading at £429.10, 34.5% lower than their pre-disaster price of £655.40.

Many pension funds in both jurisdictions had also invested in banks, the share value of which has also deteriorated greatly over the past five years. Bank performance has been improving; however, many of the large banks have had to write-off their investment in Green Government Bonds – another exceptional loss that impacts negatively on their share price. Indeed, the Organisation for Economic Cooperation and Development (OECD), using data obtained from the UK's pension regulator, reported that returns on money invested by UK pension companies on behalf of savers fell every year between 2001 and 2010. They highlighted UK pension performance among the worst in the developed world – a concern for any individual with an occupational or private pension scheme (Hall, 2012).

United Kingdom Stock Market Performance in the Past 10 Years

The value of the FTSE 100 share price index as quoted by the London Stock Exchange fell by 38% from 6731 in 2007 to 3512 by March 2009 as market confidence declined due to the worsening global economic downturn and the financial crises. Thereafter, the market experienced steady growth until April 2010 when the index value was 5707. The index has stabilised since this time, though it seems to oscillate between 5000 and 6000. The peaks and troughs in the market typically occur due to political and economic uncertainties. Uncertainty arises as a result of there being a coalition government (conflict can arise within government due to the different parties having different policies), new government policies, crisis after crisis in the European Union, a return to recession, riots, bank scandals and downgrading of major institutions' (such as Barclays Bank) and countries' credit ratings by credit rating agencies, to name a few. All of these factors undermine market confidence. At the time of writing (July 2012), the market index had a value of 5674 (LSE website, 2012).

Republic of Ireland Stock Market Index

The value of the Irish Stock Exchange Overall Index fell by 80% from 9408 in December 2006 to 1880 by the end of October 2009. Prices then stabilised and started to increase again. At the time of writing (July 2012), the index had a benchmark value of 3192 (Bloomberg, 2012).

Concluding Comments on the Market

The volatility of stock markets and the collapse of some major companies and professional entities (such as UK Equitable Life, Enron, WorldCom, Arthur Andersen, Allied Irish Banks and Northern Rock) has reduced public confidence in private and occupational pension schemes. The consequence is that individuals cannot rely on their pension as the only form of investment to cater for their retirement, so they have to take responsibility for their own finances and to create a portfolio of investments, if they want to be financially self-sufficient.

Personal Finance and the 'Credit Crunch'

United Kingdom

The financial problems facing most individuals are exasperated by the current debt culture. The use of credit was promoted by the Thatcher Government in the 1980s when they deregulated the financial markets, opening up the

UK to foreign competition. This resulted in low-cost debt, which was easier to obtain. Having debt increases an individual's risk exposure to changes in interest rates, as debt has to be repaid and it has a fixed cost – interest – which must be paid periodically (typically monthly) regardless of a person's income. In 2006 and 2007 there were six 0.25% increases in interest rates in the UK, increasing the bank base rate from 4.5% in July 2006 to 5.75% in July 2007. Though the increasing interest rates, that occurred in 2006 and 2007 might be considered to have impacted greatly on individuals and the economy, the 1.5% increase over the nine-month period (bringing the base rate up to 5.75%) is minor relative to the rate increases that occurred on 16 September 1992. Then, the Conservative Government (under the leadership of Sir John Major) hiked base rates from an already high 10% to 15%, though they settled at 12% by the end of the day. The current world banking crises also contributed to financial uncertainty and nearly spelt disaster for one large financial institution based in London – Northern Rock Bank.

REAL WORLD EXAMPLE: NORTHERN ROCK

Northern Rock experienced a run on their accounts as customers withdrew their savings, worried about the level of mortgage arrears and bad debts being experienced by the bank. Northern Rock received assistance (about £55 billion) by way of an inter-bank loan from the central Bank of England and the UK Government and, in February 2008, the UK Government ended up nationalising the bank, after months of negotiations with a number of interested takeover parties, including Richard Branson and the internal management team. The UK Government felt that nationalisation was the only option open to them as so much of the public's funds had been invested in Northern Rock. Since its nationalisation in 2008, Northern Rock has been split in two, with the old mortgages and debts transferred to Northern Rock Asset Management, a state run company with the rest of the products, services and branches being sold to 'Virgin Money' on 1 January 2012. It is expected that Virgin Money will start to offer current accounts to the public in 2013.

To alleviate the problems facing the slowing economy in the UK, the Bank of England started to reduce interest rates in December 2007. At the start, the cuts were small, with a quarter of a per cent being the normal reduction. However, the cuts became more aggressive by the end of 2008, with a 1.5%

base rate cut on 6 November 2008 and a further 1% reduction in the next month. The cuts continued until March 2009 when the Bank of England base rate reached 0.5%. No changes had occurred to this rate by July 2012. The low interest rate has probably slowed the number and extent of repossessions that may have happened had the rate remained high. It will also have indirectly injected funds into businesses that now will have less interest to pay. On the negative side, it has reduced the returns that individuals can expect to obtain from savings products. This is of particular concern to retired individuals.

Republic of Ireland

The financial problems facing most individuals in the ROI are exasperated by the current debt culture. The use of credit was promoted in the 1980s when the financial markets were deregulated, opening up the ROI financial services industry to foreign competition, which resulted in low-cost debt that was easier to obtain. Having debt increases an individual's risk exposure to changes in interest rates.

The current credit crunch could be considered to have started at the end of 2007. The initial reaction of the European Central Bank (ECB) was to leave interest rates as they were at 4%. However, at this time inflation was also an issue, so the ECB raised its base rate from 4.00% to 4.25% on 9 July 2008 before starting a series of monthly decreases which ended up with the ECB base rate being at an all-time low of 1% by 13 May 2009. It has remained at this rate until 5 July 2012 when it was reduced by a further 0.25% to 0.75%. The low interest rate has probably slowed the number and extent of repossessions that may have happened had the rate remained high. It will also have indirectly injected funds into businesses that now will have less interest to pay. On the negative side, it has reduced the returns that individuals can expect to obtain from savings products. This is of particular concern to retired individuals.

The credit crunch has had a major negative impact on the Irish economy. GDP fell in every year from 2007 to 2010, resulting in an overall peak-to-trough decline of 12.4% before starting to increase again in 2011 due to strong export performance. A further increase is expected in 2012. Though manufacturing and exports are up, unemployment has increased from 4.8% in January 2008 to 14.4% by the end of 2011 – an additional 330,000 individuals are now out of work. The increase does not take into account the net outward migration that has been occurring over the past few years. However, the Department of Finance considers that unemployment is stabilising, as rates fell to 14.3% in March and April 2012. Annual government borrowing peaked in 2010 at €48,607 million, though this fell to €20,515 million in 2011. It is expected that the annual borrowing requirement will fall again to about €13,000 million in 2012 due to the austerity measures and tax increases implemented by the Government in the yearly budgets. The result of the yearly net borrowing requirements is an increase in overall Government debt to €169,264 million by the end of 2011. Part of the debt (€50,555 million) has been used to stabilise the Irish banks. Government interest expenditure as a percentage of general Government revenue has increased from just under 3% in 2007 to about 10% in 2011 and is expected to rise to 16% by 2015.

These summary statistics highlight the weak state of the economy. The Government has had to borrow at unprecedented levels to maintain current public sector spending, with the consequence that Ireland is now regarded as a risky international country in terms of its credit rating. This means that fewer investors are likely to purchase government bonds, or will require a much higher premium for loaning to the Government. This could restrict the Government's liquidity and make its debt very expensive.

The consequence of this is widespread for an individual's personal finance position. Government benefits cannot be relied on, as it is likely that the real value of these benefits will fall over time. A consequence of the economic downturn is weaker markets (discussed above). A weaker market impacts on pension schemes and individuals' investment values. In addition, debt will be more difficult to obtain and will be more expensive to service.

Concluding Comments on the Credit Crunch

In both jurisdictions, the interest rate increases in 2007/2008 (combined with the deterioration in the sub-prime lending market in the US) contributed to a slowdown in the economy, followed by a recession, a fall in consumer confidence and spending, a reduction in house prices and an increase in bankruptcy cases, mortgage arrears and house repossessions. Most people in today's society have debt and are exposed to risk from the impact of interest rate increases on their disposable income. Interest rates are currently at very low levels (Bank of England base rate 0.5%; European Central Bank base rate 0.75%). It is expected that the base rates will not increase whilst there is so much economic uncertainty; however, this may change if the UK and the ROI experience sustained economic growth, and individuals should always consider the impact of interest rate increases on their finances. Therefore, there is a greater need for individuals to manage personal finance appropriately. This process should involve considering, in advance, the impact of changes in interest rates on their disposable income before committing to debt.

Personal Finance and Inflation

Inflation impacts on individuals' spending power and on the value of their wealth.

United Kingdom

The past five years have shown that inflation within the UK can be quite volatile. Over the latter half of 2007 and in 2008, individuals experienced, at first hand, just how vulnerable their disposable income was to inflation. The soaring cost of energy (oil, electricity, coal and gas) had the knock-on effect of making virtually every product an individual purchases more expensive. In most instances, this reduced disposable income. This reduction is a particular problem for individuals who have high levels of debt, as governments usually use interest rate increases to curb spending which brings down inflation. Therefore, individuals with high debt levels may find themselves with liquidity issues as both the cost of living and the cost of debt increase.

This classic economist's approach to the control of increasing levels of inflation did not happen in 2008 and has not happened since, as inflation became a secondary problem, with the potential collapse of the banking system, soaring national debt levels and lack of economic growth being more pressing problems for the Government. In addition, the Government did not need to raise interest to dampen spending; individuals and companies were taking prudent steps to reduce their risk by increasing savings and reducing debt levels. The result: a reduction in demand, a shrinking of the economy, subsequent job losses and a general economic downturn.

Indeed, during 2009, the UK experienced negative inflation for a few months before it became positive again. The inflation rate as measured by the Retail Price Index (RPI) was 3.1% in May 2012. This rate is not comparable with other countries as the Consumer Price Index (CPI) is more commonly used to measure inflation. The CPI for the UK was 2.8% for May 2012, whereas the European Union annual inflation rate was estimated at 2.4%. The RPI inflation rate for the UK has ranged from –1.6% in June 2009 to 5.5% in February 2011. In the same period, the CPI fluctuated between 1.1% in September 2009 and 5.6% in September 2011. The fluctuating inflation rate has consequences for individuals' personal finances. Individuals find it more difficult to determine the level of surplus income that can be used for investment and debt management as expenditure is variable and typically increasing. It is also difficult to predict the future value of their portfolio of assets and, in addition, the periods of deflation highlight the fact that the value of individuals' investments can go down as well as up.

Republic of Ireland

The past five years have shown that inflation in the ROI can also be quite volatile. Over the latter half of 2007 and in 2008 individuals experienced, at first hand, just how vulnerable their disposable income was to inflation. The soaring cost of energy (oil, electricity, coal and gas) had the knock-on effect of making virtually every product an individual purchased more expensive. In most instances, this reduced disposable income. This is usually a particular problem for individuals that have high levels of debt, as governments usually use interest rate increases to curb inflation. Individuals with high debt levels may find themselves with liquidity issues, as the cost of living increases along with the cost of debt.

This classic economist's approach to the control of increasing levels of inflation did not happen in 2008 for two reasons. First, the Government cannot manipulate interest rates that are set centrally by the European Central Bank (ECB). Secondly, inflation became a secondary problem, with the potential collapse of the banking system and a deteriorating economy being more pressing problems for the Government. In addition, the Government did not need to raise interest to dampen spending; individuals and companies were taking prudent steps to reduce their risk by increasing savings and reducing debt levels. The result: a reduction in demand, a shrinking of the economy, subsequent job losses and a general economic downturn.

From 1 January 2009 to July 2010, the CPI inflation rates were negative, with the largest monthly decrease of 6.56% being recorded in October 2009. The rate was greater than 2% from February 2011 to March 2012 and has been below 2% since that time to the time of writing – June 2012 (1.7%). Inflation has consequences for an individual's personal finances, as income and expenditure levels change and the value of assets and investments either depreciate or appreciate. Therefore, it is important to consider the impact of inflation on personal finances.

Personal Finance and Taxation – In Brief

Individuals are subject to a variety of taxes, and careful consideration of these taxes needs to be made when making any financial decisions. This aspect of financial planning is complicated and is the main reason that many individuals elect to obtain the expertise of a registered financial adviser, who will be knowledgeable about current taxation and the impact of the various taxes on undertaking a particular course of action.

United Kingdom

Individuals need to be aware of the various types of taxes that they may have to pay. This section provides a brief outline of the main types of taxes that impact on financial decision-making for individuals in the UK. This section is not meant to be comprehensive, and the reader is advised to consult with Revenue and Customs and/or their financial adviser on the tax implications of each of their decisions. For example, this section does not consider council tax or property rates.

The main taxes to impact on financial decision-making for individuals in the UK are as follows:

Income Tax: The income tax year in the UK runs from 6 April to 5 April of the following year. Income tax is due on any income that is generated during the period from work, benefits or from investments. It is applicable to, for example, employment income ('Pay As You Earn' – PAYE), self-employed income, interest receivable, dividends receivable, rental income, etc. There is typically a tax-free allowance, currently £8,105 for 2012/13 (this is to rise to £9,205 in April 2013), for people below pension age. Thereafter, for 2012/13, income tax is payable at the rate of 20% on income levels up to £34,370, at 40% on income earned between £34,371 and £150,000 and at 50% on income earned over £150,000 (in April 2013 this will reduce to 45%). Where an individual has interest income, this is taxed first and is subject to 10% on the first £2,710 of interest earned in the period. The remaining interest is taxed at 20% until it reaches the £34,370 threshold, after which it is taxable at 40%, and so on. Dividends also have different tax treatments and rates depending on the overall income levels of the individual. In 2012/13 dividends are taxable at 10% on income levels up to £34,370 (lower rate taxpayers), 32.5% up to £150,000 (higher rate taxpayers) and at the rate of 42.5% thereafter.

National Insurance Contributions: Individuals have to pay *National Insurance Contributions* (NICs). There are different types of NIC depending on the activity that creates the earnings. For example, employment income is subject to NIC of 24.8% or 13.8%; 12.8% is paid by the employer, and the employee pays 12% on weekly earnings between £146 (annual amount £7,592) and £817 (annual amount £42,484), after which the employee pays contributions at 2% (for more information see the directgov.co.uk website).

Value Added Tax: Value Added Tax (VAT) is an important tax that also impacts on individuals, as it is included in the price of most goods and services purchased. Knowledge of VAT may be important if an individual decides to invest in commodities, which may be construed as a trading activity. The tax rate in 2012/13 is 20%.

Capital Gains Tax: Capital Gains Tax (CGT) is payable when capital items are sold. Like income tax, a certain amount of capital gain is allowed before tax becomes due. This annual exemption currently stands at £10,600 (2012/13 rates) and is payable at the rate of 10% for entrepreneurs (up to a £10 million limit), 18% for lower rate taxpayers (up to the £34,370 threshold) and 28% for higher rate taxpayers. There is no CGT on death, and certain exemptions are available for some transactions, such as a gain on the sale of an individual's sole principal private residence.

Inheritance Tax (IHT): Individuals generally become more interested in this taxation as they get older. IHT is a tax on the value of an individual's estate (net assets), which is payable on the death of the individual. There is an initial inheritance tax threshold, and tax is payable on the value of the estate above this threshold. In 2012/13 this was £325,000. All assets and monies in excess of £325,000 are subject to tax at 40% (from 2012/13 a lower rate of 36% will be applied when the deceased leaves 10% or more of their estate to a charity). IHT can also apply to any gifts of value that were made by the individual within seven years of death. There is a yearly exemption of £3,000 for these lifetime transfers, after which the recipient can become liable to 40% IHT on the excess. There are some other lifetime gifts that can be exempt from IHT, such as wedding gifts and small gifts (there are also limits on the size of these). Furthermore, there are exempted transactions, such as transfers between spouses, and these exemptions should be taken into account when deciding on investments and when writing a will.

Stamp Duty: Stamp duty is discussed under 'Investments' in **Chapter 8**.

Republic of Ireland

Individuals need to be aware of the various types of taxes that they may have to pay. This section provides a brief outline of the main types of taxes to impact on financial decision-making for individuals in the ROI. This section is not meant to be comprehensive, and the reader is advised to consult with the Revenue Commissioners and/or their financial adviser on the tax implications of each of their decisions.

Income Tax: Income tax is due on any income that is generated in a calendar year from work, benefits or from investments. It is applicable to, for example, employment income, self-employed income, interest receivable, dividends receivable, rental income, etc.

   The amount of tax paid depends on the status of the individual and the amount of tax credits that they are entitled to. Single or widowed individuals who do not have dependent children pay tax at the rate of 20% on the first

€32,800 of income with the balance being chargeable at 41% (2012/13 rates). The lower rate threshold is higher if the individual qualifies for the One Parent Family Tax Credit (€36,800). The individual's tax bill will then be reduced by the amount of tax credit that they are entitled to. For example, an individual is entitled to a personal tax credit of €1,650 and a PAYE tax credit of €1,650 if employed. The individual may also get a tax credit for several other expenses incurred such as health/medical expenses or tuition fees (see the Revenue Commissioners' website (www.revenue.ie) for a list of all the possible items).

Married couples[1] are taxed depending on whether they have one or two incomes. The lower rate threshold of 20% for married couples with one income is €41,800, with income in excess of this being taxable at 41%. The personal tax credit for a married couple with one income is €3,300, with a further PAYE tax credit of €1,650 if the income is from employment. Where the married couple have two incomes, the lower rate threshold varies depending on the size of the lower income. The lower rate threshold is €41,800, although it is extended by up to €23,800 (combined income of €65,000) depending on the size of the lower of the two incomes. If the second low income is only, for example, €20,000, then the extension is restricted to this. The balance is taxable at 41%. Married couples with two incomes have a personal tax credit of €3,300 and a PAYE tax credit of €1,650 each if their respective income is from employment.[2]

Universal Social Contribution (USC): The USC replaced the health and income levy in 2011. It is a tax payable on gross income. It applies to all employed and self-employed individuals with gross annual income in excess of €10,035. The USC rate is 2% on income up to €10,036, 4% on income from €10,037 to €16,016 and 7% on income above €16,017. There are some exemptions, however.

From 2012, the USC tax is exempt for individuals who earn less than €10,035. Income already subject to Deposit Interest Retention Tax (DIRT) is exempt, as are Department of Social Protection payments received (or similar Government payments). In addition, a maximum rate of 4% applies for elderly individuals (aged 70 and over) and for medical card holders regardless of age. Finally, a surcharge of 3% is payable by any individual (regardless of age or income type) on income that exceeds €100,000. Therefore, a person under 70 years of age will end up paying

---

[1] Civil partnerships are taxed in the same manner as married couples.
[2] 2012 rates taken from the Revenue Commissioners' website: www.revenue.ie

USC at the rate of 10% (7% plus the surcharge of 3%) on the excess, while a person over 70 years of age will end up paying USC at the rate of 7% (4% plus the surcharge of 3%).[3]

Pay-Related Social Insurance (PRSI): Individuals also have to pay PRSI on their income, and there are different types of PRSI depending on the activity that creates the earnings (for more information see the Revenue Commissioners' website). Most individuals are liable for Class A, which will entitle them to the full range of social insurance benefits. In 2012, PRSI is payable at the rate of 4% where the individual earns over €352 per week, though the first €127 is not taxable. Employers also have to pay PRSI of 4.25% on employee income where the salary is less than €365 per week and 10.75% on amounts in excess of the lower threshold of €365. The employer collects the employees' insurance and pays this and their portion of the liability over to the Department of Social Protection. Self-employed people also have to pay PRSI. They typically pay PRSI of 4%, subject to a minimum contribution of €253.

Value Added Tax: Value Added Tax (VAT) is also an important tax that is included in the price of most goods and services purchased by an individual. Knowledge of this may be important if an individual decides to invest in commodities, as this may be construed as a trading activity and, hence, may be subject to VAT. The standard VAT rate in 2012 is 23%, up from 21% in 2011.

Capital Gains Tax: Capital Gains Tax (CGT) is payable when capital items are sold. Like income tax, a certain amount of capital gain is allowed before tax becomes due. This annual exemption currently stands at €1,270 (2012 rate). Gains made beyond this are taxable at 30%. There is no CGT on death, and certain exemptions are available for some transactions, such as the gain on the sale of an individual's sole principal private residence or the transfer of a site with a market value of less than €500,000 from a parent to their child for the purpose of constructing the child's principal private residence.

Capital Acquisitions Tax: Capital Acquisitions Tax (CAT) is concerned with three taxes: gift tax, inheritance tax and discretionary trust tax. Individuals generally become more interested in these taxes as they get older, and a brief knowledge of them is useful when creating a personal

---

[3] 2012 rates taken from the Revenue Commissioners' website: www.revenue.ie

financial plan. Inheritance tax is a tax that is payable by a beneficiary on the value of assets (beyond a certain threshold) that have been donated to them in a will.

Inheritance tax (IHT) is payable at the rate of 30%. The exemption available to the beneficiary differs depending on the relationship that they had with the person who made the will. Where the beneficiary is a son or daughter, the exemption is €250,000. Where the beneficiary is a parent, brother, sister, niece, nephew or grandchild, the exemption is €33,500. Any other individual who is a beneficiary has an exemption of €16,750. These are the 2012 rates as disclosed on the Revenue Commissioners' website (accessed July 2012).

Lifetime gifts are also subject to taxation at the rate of 30% beyond the thresholds. There is an annual exemption of €3,000, and the excess may be included in the IHT computation. There are some other lifetime gifts that can be made exempt of IHT, such as gifts between spouses. Full details of these can be obtained from the Revenue Commissioners' website.

Stamp duty: Stamp duty is discussed under investments in **Chapter 8**.

Concluding Comment

Exact details of the impact of all these taxes should be obtained before making financial decisions. The information provided above is very brief and general in nature and should not be used as the basis for financial decision-making. For example, it only provides information on the main taxes; other taxes exist, such as the property tax (€100 per household). This is not included due to its immaterial value.

Financial Advice

Some people may want to prepare their own financial plan; others may feel that they require the help of a financial adviser. There are three types of financial adviser: those that offer products from one company (*tied advisers*), those that offer products from a selection of companies (*multi-tied advisers*) and those that offer financial products from the whole of the market (*independent financial adviser*). Tied and multi-tied advisers are typically paid for their advice from commissions received from the sale of financial products of the companies that they promote. Independent financial advisers must provide the option for the individual to pay for advice with a fee or commission.

United Kingdom

In the UK, individuals can access the website www.unbiased.co.uk and use it to find a list of independent financial advisers in any particular area, sorted by distance from the postcode entered. Alternatively, a list can be obtained from the Personal Finance Society website (www.thepfs.org), which will provide a list of registered financial advisers that reside within 5, 25, 50 or 100 miles of the postcode entered into the search engine. All financial advisers have to be registered with the Financial Services Authority (FSA), and they are tightly regulated. Even so, care should be exercised by individuals, as the FSA takes many successful cases against registered financial advisers who do not provide advice that is the most beneficial for the individual or within the spirit of the regulation.

Republic of Ireland

In the ROI, individuals can access the Central Bank of Ireland's registers to find out information about financial advisers. The Central Bank maintains two registers; the first enables the user to search by the name of the financial service provider or Collective Investment Scheme (CIS) and the second just provides a list by area (http://registers.financialregulator.ie). All financial advisers have to be registered with the Central Bank, however, there are some exemptions: solicitors (regulated by the Law Society) and tied insurance intermediaries that act under the full responsibility of an authorised insurance undertaking (on the Insurance Mediation Register). All financial advisers, whether authorised and regulated by the Central Bank or authorised and regulated by one of the two aforementioned bodies, are contained on the Central Bank's registers. Even so, care should be exercised by individuals as there have been many successful cases against registered financial advisers who do not provide advice that is the most beneficial for the individual or within the spirit of the regulation.

Conclusion

The extent of the economic changes that occurred over the past five years were not predicted, and most individuals, even those who had good financial planning, would have suffered some financial losses. Good financial planning is still vitally important and probably reduced the impact of the economic downturn for many individuals. Good financial planning always strives to ensure that individuals do not leave themselves exposed to such an extent that it causes financial difficulties.

KEY TERMS

Capital acquisitions tax (CAT)	National Insurance Contributions (NIC)
Capital gains tax (CGT)	Pay-as-you-go
Financial planning	Pay-Related Social Insurance (PRSI)
Financially self-sufficient	Private funding
Income tax	Social security benefits
Independent financial adviser	Tied advisers
Inheritance tax (IHT)	Universal payments
Lifetime gifts	Universal Social Contribution (USC)
Means-tested benefits	Value added tax (VAT)
Multi-tied advisers	

REVIEW QUESTIONS

(Suggested solutions to **Review Questions** are provided in **Appendix 4**.)

Question 2.1

What changes in government policy have occurred that have resulted in a greater need for individuals to take control of their own financial destiny?

Question 2.2

How do changes in interest rates impact on private individuals' personal wealth?

Question 2.3

How did the surge in oil prices in 2008 impact on private individuals' wealth?

Question 2.4

List two initiatives that the government in your jurisdiction has undertaken to encourage individuals to put funds away for their retirement.

Question 2.5

Explain how the banking and economic crises, which started in 2007, have impacted on personal wealth and subsequent financial planning.

Question 2.6

Outline the difference between a 'tied adviser', a 'multi-tied adviser' and an 'independent financial adviser'.

CHAPTER 3

THE FINANCIAL PLAN

Learning Objectives

Upon completion of this chapter, readers should be able to:

- explain the meaning of the key terms listed at the end of the chapter;
- list the nine stages to a financial plan;
- detail the background information required about an individual before preparing a financial plan;
- describe financial issues that individuals face that need to be considered before preparing a financial plan;
- prepare a schedule to determine an individual's risk attitude;
- determine the goals and objectives of an individual for the purpose of preparing a financial plan;
- calculate the net worth of an individual;
- prepare a personal cash budget based on an individual's current details;
- prepare projections, taking into account various scenarios; and
- detail how the plan should be monitored in the future.

Introduction: The Financial Plan

A *financial plan* consolidates information about an individual (and their partner) in one document. It summarises their financial aims and aspirations and formalises how these can be financed. When preparing a financial plan the same decision-making principles that are applied in business finance and management accounting in companies can be applied. Most decisions go through the process of planning, implementation and control. This is the same for decision-making in personal finance. Companies set their objectives and make decisions in light of these objectives. Individuals should do the same. There are also similarities between the major decisions that a company faces and those that individuals should consider. In companies the main decisions are categorised as the investment, finance and dividend decisions. In personal finance the decisions include the investment decision (savings, personal investments and pensions) and the finance decision (debt). These decisions are influenced by an individual's choice of lifestyle, attitude to risk, their income, expenditure, health, financial commitments and dependents. All of the decisions are interrelated. For example, if a person elects to have an extravagant lifestyle now, then the level of investment will be lower and debt may be higher. This may have long-term financial consequences. However, the individual may feel that it is worth it. An example here may be parents who give up work to look after young children. A conscious decision is made to forego income in return for quality of life. As long as individuals are aware of the future impact of their current decisions, this is not an issue.

The process of preparing a financial plan can be split into nine steps. The steps are outlined in the diagram in **Figure 3.1.** below:

Figure 3.1: Personal Financial Planning: the Stages

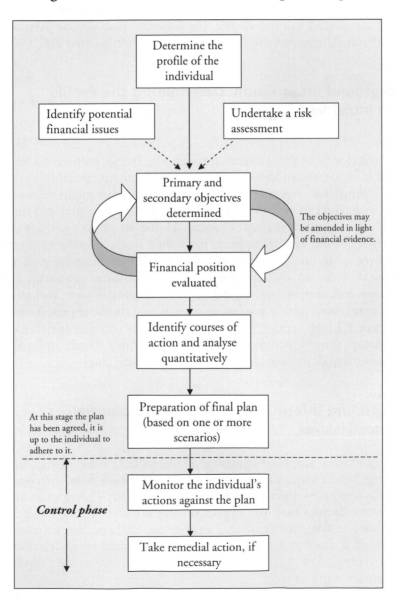

The first three stages identified in the diagram are concerned with obtaining background knowledge of the individual. Every individual is different and it is important to prepare a financial plan that is tailored to suit the individual. The next four stages (setting objectives, obtaining financial information, gathering information about and selecting a course of action, preparing the financial plan) are more concrete – they formalise a course of action to be taken by the individual to achieve their financial objectives. The final two steps are concerned with monitoring and control. Each stage is now considered in more depth. The financial plan can be prepared for the individual, or may include information on their partner also.

Background Information: Determining the Profile of an Individual

There are different financial stages to each individual's life and their financial goals will change as they progress through life. Before preparing a financial plan it is important to identify the stage within the financial lifecycle that the individual is at. Age is a proxy for determining what might be important to the individual for whom you are trying to plan (the personal financial lifecycle is covered in the next chapter). However, on its own, age cannot be fully relied on. For example, an individual in their forties may exit the workforce to retrain or to go to university. Their financial plan would be very different to an individual who is in full-time employment with a partner and dependents. Useful general information on an individual which is necessary before starting to prepare any financial plan is provided in **Figure 3.2** (see opposite). This example is not comprehensive. General information should include, at a minimum, contact details and sufficient information to determine the tax status of the individual.

Background Information: Identifying Potential Financial Issues

It is important at this stage to analyse an individual's risks. *Risk* in financial planning is the chance that an individual's actual cash flows turn out to be different to what was predicted in the financial plan. Therefore an analysis of common factors that may impact on an individual's ability to generate cash flows in the future, or that may create cash outflows, have to be considered at the outset. In particular, the plan should try to determine the expected lifespan of the individual. This will impact on savings, investment and pension requirements.

Figure 3.2: Proforma to Collect General Information on the Profile of the Individual/Family

	Individual	*Partner*
Title:	_____	_____
Surname:	_____	_____
Christian name:	_____	_____
Gender (*Circle*):	Male/Female	Male/Female
Date of birth:	_____	_____
Place of birth:	_____	_____
UK/ROI resident for tax purposes:	_____	_____
Domicile (if known):	_____	_____
National Insurance (PPS) No:	_____	_____
Occupation:	_____	_____
Telephone number (home):	_____	_____
Telephone number (work):	_____	_____
Mobile number:	_____	_____
Fax:	_____	_____
E-mail:	_____	_____
Home address:		
Postcode:	_____	_____
Year moved to home address:	_____	_____
Correspondence address (if different to home address):		
Postcode:	_____	_____
Married (*Circle*)	Yes/No	

Risk to Cash Inflows

Health is a ***critical risk factor*** which can have serious financial consequences. A person who does not smoke, take drugs or drink, has no family history of illnesses and who exercises regularly is likely to have a healthy, financially productive and long working life. Having this information strengthens the potential to make more accurate estimates of future earnings and life expectancy. This should be factored into the financial plan. If a person's health is not good and their life expectancy is short, a different financial plan will result and different advice will be given. An example of health assessments being undertaken to assess risk in practice is experienced by every individual when they obtain a quote for an insurance product. In addition, health checklists and medical examinations now form part of most entities' recruitment process. An example of some of the questions that might be asked by a financial adviser to assess health risk is included in **Figure 3.3**. Normally, the list of questions covers the history of major illnesses (including cancer, heart disease, etc.) in an individual's family, and the form can extend to several pages.

Figure 3.3: Proforma to Capture General Information on Potential Financial Issues

Health:	*Individual*	*Partner*
Current health *(Circle)*	Good/ok/poor	Good/ok/poor
Risk factors:		
Smoker *(Circle)*	Yes/No	Yes/No
Drink alcohol beyond recommended levels *(Circle)*	Yes/No	Yes/No
Other high risk factors *(Discuss)*	Yes/No	Yes/No
Education:		
Do you have any children *(Circle)*	Yes/No	Yes/No

If you have children who are dependent on you please provide the following details:

	Name	*Date of birth*	*Years to finance at education level*		*Expected yearly cost*
Child 1			(N)	(XX)	
			(P)	etc.	
			(S)		
			(U)		

Continued

Child 2			(N)		
			(P)		
			(S)		
			(U)		
Child 3			(N)		
			(P)		
			(S)		
			(U)		
Child 4			(N)		
			(P)		
			(S)		
			(U)		

Where (N) is Nursery school   *(P) is Primary school*
     (S) is Secondary school   *(U) is University*

Details of other dependants who are relying on you for financial help *(include an estimate of the yearly commitment and when this cash outflow is expected to start; this may include grandchildren or elderly parents)*

Influences on Cash Outflows

It is also important to identify potential *financial commitments*, such as having to finance dependants (children, or elderly parents). Most individuals are aware, from a young age, of their view on having children. Children are an expensive commitment and individuals who wish to raise children need to start thinking about 'nests' at an early stage. Children need to be financed for at least 18 years. If a child is disabled, the term of care extends to the child's lifetime and a responsible parent needs to ensure that the child is catered for financially for the period of the child's life (which may extend beyond the parent's life). From an early stage in the financial lifecycle, individuals can start to plan for the cost of providing for their children in the future.

Caring for elderly parents is another issue. Individuals should consider the possibility that they may need to take responsibility for the care of their parents in later years. The financial consequences of such care needs to be factored into the individual's financial plan. A proforma to capture this type of information is provided in **Figure 3.3**.

Background Information: Undertaking a Risk Assessment

Getting information on an individual's attitude to *investment risk* and *earnings risk* is also important. Some individuals are risk takers, others are risk averse. The financial plan should try to identify the risk profile of an individual at the outset. This will influence the financial plan and the financial advice given. An example of some questions that could be used to capture **investment risk** – the level of risk to which an individual wishes to expose their funds – is provided in **Figure 3.4(a)**:

Figure 3.4(a): Possible Questions to Assess Risk Exposure

Investment risk	*Individual*	*Partner*
How long are you willing to lock funds away for? *(This will depend on your future needs)*	_____Years	_____Years
How much are you willing to lock away?	€/£_____	€/£_____
Do you require it to be accessible *(circle)*?	Yes/No	Yes/No
If you answered yes, identify the proportion?	_____%	_____%
Do you have an emergency fund to provide for unexpected expenses?	Yes/No	Yes/No
What portion of your total assets (excluding your home) are you going to invest?	_____%	_____%
Would you be happy to risk part of your capital investment in the chance that you may get a higher return *(circle)*?	Yes/No	Yes/No
If yes, what proportion?	_____%	_____%

Continued

If you answered yes to the previous question, state the level of risk you are willing to accept *(circle)*.	High/Medium/Low	High/Medium/Low
What level of fall in the value of your capital investment would you be concerned with?	_____%	_____%
Do you need the remaining protected capital investment to accumulate growth/earn a return which is above inflation *(circle)*?	Yes/No	Yes/No

An example of some questions that could be used to capture **earnings risk** – the potential for changes in income and the impact of changes in income on the financial plan – are as follows in **Figure 3.4(b)**:

Figure 3.4b: Possible Questions to Assess Risk Exposure (*Continued*)

Earnings potential risk	*Individual*	*Partner*
Have you considered the impact on your finances of either of you passing away *(circle)*?	Yes/No	Yes/No
Circle importance	*Is this issue:* VeryImp/Imp/ NotImp	*Is this issue:* VeryImp/Imp/ NotImp
Have you considered the impact on your finances of either of you becoming incapacitated?	Yes/No	Yes/No
Circle importance	*Is this issue:* VeryImp/Imp/ NotImp	*Is this issue:* VeryImp/Imp/ NotImp
		Continued

Have you considered the options available when you are elderly and in need of care?	Yes/No	Yes/No
Circle importance	*Is this issue:* VeryImp/Imp/ NotImp	*Is this issue:* VeryImp/Imp/ NotImp
Have you considered estate planning?	Yes/No	Yes/No
Circle importance	*Is this issue:* VeryImp/Imp/ NotImp	*Is this issue:* VeryImp/Imp/ NotImp

Once this background information has been collected and reviewed, the individual's financial aspirations for the future should be recorded.

Determining the Goals of the Individual

As in any financial decision-making process an individual's *primary objective* has to be determined at the outset. This objective is a long-term strategic goal which will have a major impact on the individual's life. It is the ultimate goal and all actions should be taken with this objective in mind. An example might be the wish to build up sufficient funds to enable the individual's current lifestyle to be sustained when retired, or maybe to have a family and children, or to own a house. The objective does not have to be financial, but it usually has financial implications – for example, having children in itself is a personal decision but has major financial consequences.

Other *secondary objectives* should also be determined and ranked according to importance. Secondary objectives are not as important as the primary objective. These objectives might be short-term (buying a flash car, going on a skiing holiday, having laser hair removal), or long-term (obtaining a rental property, sending children to university, having a fund to pay for funeral expenses – personal planning involves being a little morbid!). It might be that there are conflicts between objectives. In these instances the secondary objectives which are more congruent with the primary objective should be selected. It may be that the individual has goals that are just not achievable given all the information provided.

Figure 3.5: Example of Information Collected on an Individual's Primary and Secondary Objectives (ranked in order of importance)

Objectives	Example responses	More information
Primary		
Short-term	Purchase own home	Mortgage-free when retired.
Long-term	Financial security for the family	Have net income of €/£50,000 when retired/ when partner dies/if disabled/if partner disabled, in today's terms.
Secondary		
Short-term	Finance children's education	Require a fund of approximately €/£80,000 for each child in today's terms.
	Be debt efficient/ intelligent	Reduce expensive bad debt. Reduce the financial pressure experienced each month.
Secondary		
Short-term	Start saving/ investing regularly	Analyse current income and expenditure and highlight potential savings to be made and investment opportunities.
Long-term	Start a financial fund for retirement	Linked to the primary objective.
	Purchase an investment property	Consider the local/overseas markets.
	Consider inheritance	Make a will/start a trust.

Identifying the Current Financial Position

This is where the financial plan starts to come together. It is the springboard of any financial plan. It has a significant bearing on a financial plan and the advice emanating from the plan. At the outset, a review of the current financial position of a person can provide an indication of whether the objectives discussed and formulated are realistic. The objectives may need to change when the current financial position of an individual becomes known. It also provides an insight as to the knowledge an individual has about money and can provide information on their attitude to risk, debt and savings. The current financial position has two separate parts. The first is to determine the *net worth of an individual* at the current time. This is simply the individual's value in terms of the difference between assets owned and debts owed. The second stage focuses on the individual's *personal earnings* – the earnings of the individual and their assets, relative to their expenditure on consumables, investments, pensions, savings and debt repayments. All cash flows should be included.

Personal Assets

Personal assets are items that the individual owns that have value. They typically include savings, investments, properties, company share schemes and tangible assets such as jewellery, artwork, wine and motor vehicles. When determining the net worth of an individual it is common practice to list the individual's personal assets, their partner/ spouse's personal assets, joint personal assets and the return being received on the personal assets in percentage terms (if known). These figures are likely to be estimates. In most instances, it would be a waste of an individual's funds to request proper valuations of assets for the purpose of financial planning only. The best approach to determining the personal assets of an individual is to provide them with a list of assets that are commonly held by individuals. The individual can then state whether, or not, they have that type of asset. The individual should be asked to place a value on the asset and to provide an estimate of the return being earned on it. Where they do not know the percentage return being earned, it might be worthwhile asking them for details of income earned and expenditure paid out on the asset yearly.

An example of a proforma asset sheet is provided in **Figure 3.6** (this list is not exhaustive):

Figure 3.6: Schedule to Calculate the Personal Assets of an Individual/Couple

Assets	Individual	Partner	Joint	Current return
Land and property				
Home			€/£500,000	
House contents			€/£40,000	
Other properties				
Rental 1	€/£200,000			
Contents	€/£5,000			
Rental 2		€/£180,000		
Contents		€/£1,500		
Commercial property	€/£100,000			8%
Agricultural land			€/£400,000	2%
Cattle stock			€/£8,000	
Forest			€/£25,000	
Other investments				
Savings account (term)			€/£52,000	3.5%
Deposit accounts	€/£5,000	€/£4,000		1.8%
Credit union share accounts	€/£500	€/£2,500		3.0%
Equity shares	€/£2,500			
Surrender value of life policies	€/£7,000	€/£25,000		
Other assets				
Inheritance expected		€/£200,000		
Jewellery	€/£500	€/£5,000		
Motor vehicles	€/£10,000	€/£6,000		
Total assets	*€/£330,500*	*€/£424,000*	*€/£1,025,000*	
Total joint assets			*€/£1,779,500*	

Personal Liabilities

After listing the assets according to their category, it is recommended that similar information is obtained for personal liabilities. *Personal liabilities* are commitments made to transfer economic benefits in the future. Examples of personal liabilities include mortgages, bank loans, credit union loans, hire-purchase agreements, leasing agreements, credit card balances, store cards balances and any other. A proforma list of potential liabilities can be used to make this task easier for an individual. A liabilities schedule might include the liabilities shown in **Figure 3.7** (this list is not exhaustive):

Figure 3.7: Schedule to Calculate the Personal Liabilities of an Individual

Liabilities	Individual	Partner	Joint	Current cost
Secured debt				
Home mortgage			€/£453,000	5.9%
Rental property 1	€/£150,000			7%
Rental property 2		€/£160,000		6.9%
Agricultural land			€/£150,000	7.2%
Forest			€/£10,000	6.5%
Other bank debt				
Loan account			€/£25,000	7.5%
Overdraft			€/£3,000	10.5%
Credit union account			€/£3,000	6.5%
Car loan 1	€/£8,000			8.2%
Car loan 2		€/£5,000		7.3%
Credit card debt				
Credit card A	€/£4,500			16.5%
Credit card B		€/£5,200		14.5%
Credit card gold	€/£2,000			12.5%
Total debt	**€/£164,500**	**€/£170,200**	**€/£644,000**	
Total joint liabilities			*€/£978,700*	

Therefore, this individual (combined with their partner) has a total net worth of €/£800,800 made up from their total assets less their total liabilities (€/£1,779,500−€/£978,700).

Personal Earnings/Cash Inflows

The second stage is to consider the earnings potential of the individual, including earnings from personal assets held. Income typically comes from employment (it is the after-tax figure that is important), self-employment, government benefits, rental properties, investments, savings and any other. One-off income should also be included, such as a legacy or a gift of funds. The income will highlight cash inflows that arise from normal activities and these one-off or exceptional items separately. A typical earnings schedule is provided in **Figure 3.8**:

Figure 3.8: Schedule to Calculate Income for an Individual (and their Partner) for One Year

Income	Individual	Partner
Employment – standard (net)	€/£50,000	€/£45,000
Overtime/bonus (net)	€/£6,000	
Pension		
Government benefits		€/£2,400
Income from self-employment (net)		
Consultancy	€/£5,000	
Farm income	€/£5,000	€/£5,000
Income from property		
Rental income	€/£3,000	€/£3,500
Investment income		
Interest on savings	€/£1,144	€/£1,144
Deposit account	€/£152	€/£122
Dividend on credit union account	€/£23	€/£112
Dividends	€/£300	
Total income	€/£70,619	€/£57,278
Total joint income		€/£127,897

This individual, and their spouse, have income from a variety of sources. They are employed, undertake some consultancy work, have rental properties, farm land and have investment income. In addition, they receive government benefits. Their total joint income amounts to €/£127,897.

Personal Expenditure/Cash Outflows

It is also important to get an indication of the current outgoings of the individual (and their partner) before advice can be provided. The same principle applies – ongoing expenditure such as the grocery bill and house bills should be highlighted and one-off cash outflows, such as paying for a holiday, should be separately identified. The full cash amount (capital and interest) for mortgage and debt repayments should be included, as personal financial planning is concerned with managing an individual's liquidity (cash position) whilst meeting their objectives. An example of a typical expenditure schedule is provided in **Figure 3.9**:

Figure 3.9: Schedule to Calculate Expenditure for an Individual (and their Partner) for One Year

Cash outflows	*Individual*	*Partner*
House running expenses	€/£12,000	€/£2,000
Repairs	€/£300	€/£500
Mortgage	€/£19,200	€/£19,200
Insurances	€/£2,000	€/£1,500
Rental property mortgages	€/£13,400	€/£14,500
Rental property expenses	€/£2,000	€/£2,000
Land expenses	€/£4,000	€/£4,000
Loan repayments	€/3,000	€/£3,000
Credit card	€/£2,600	€/£2,900
Credit union	€/£1,200	€/£1,200
Car loan	€/£4,800	€/£3,000
Car tax	€/£200	€/£180
Car insurance	€/£1,000	€/£800
Car fuel	€/£3,120	€/£2,200
Travel and leisure	€/£3,000	€/£1,800
Clothing and presents	€/£2,000	€/£4,000

Continued

Education	€/£1,500	€/£1,500
Charitable donations	€/£1,000	€/£800
Private pension	€/£1,300	€/£800
Additional taxation	€/£2,000	€/£1,800
Total expected expenditure	*€/£79,620*	*€/£67,680*
Total joint expenditure		*€/£147,300*

Note: a more detailed cash expenditure budget proforma is provided in the appendix to this chapter.

The total joint income per year for this couple is €/£127,897 and the total joint expenditure is €/£147,300. Therefore, this individual and his spouse have outgoings of €/£19,403 more than their cash inflows. This situation cannot continue. In addition, if the assets and liabilities are analysed, it is clear that they are operating with an overdraft; hence they do not have money in their current account. This situation will only worsen as time goes on. A key aim at this stage, regardless of the objectives set, would be to reverse the net cash outflow situation. The case study at the end of this chapter provides an example of the type of advice that might be provided to an individual after assessing their financial plan.

Identifying Various Courses of Action and Analysing Them Quantitatively

To assist an individual in deciding on their final financial plan, it is important to prepare a financial plan which projects the result of the current spending, debt and savings policy into the future, assuming the individual continues with this policy. This is called *cash flow planning* or creating *cash flow projections*. The outcome of this should be interpreted in light of the individual's primary and secondary objectives. When projecting cash flows the preparer has to adjust the data to take account of inflation, future earnings increases, expense increases and life expectancy. These adjustments are subjective.

Cash flow projections and budgeted statements of net worth should then be prepared to show the expected outcome, assuming the advice given is adopted. The plan should highlight the best ways to make use of existing resources and possibly take into account changes that the individual agrees to make which impact on their finances. This should be compared to the projected financial position calculated under the first paragraph and interpreted in light of the financial objectives set. It may be that the objectives require revising, or the financial plan is changed so that the individual achieves their objectives.

The plan might predict future cash flows and net worth under a variety of periods (one year, five years, 10 years, on retirement, etc.) and for a variety of options. One option may be to analyse the impact of pursuing some secondary objectives and dropping others. Steps may be identified that can help the individual achieve their objectives. For example, the consequences: of increasing/reducing mortgage repayments; of increasing/reducing the pension contributions; of reducing expenditure on non-essential items combined with the savings to be made by managing debt and the additional income that can be generated from suggested investments, can all be factored into the projections, either together or separately, as a series of 'what if' scenarios. In terms of major life changing events, the cost of having one, two, three, etc., children can be included, as can the impact of an individual retiring early. Some individuals may have early retirement as their objective, with a particular lifestyle in mind, so the financial requirement to allow early retirement can be highlighted.

Selecting and Implementing a Course of Action

The financial adviser should agree one course of action with the individual and prepare a final financial plan based on this agreement. The plan should include a summary of the profile of the individual, should detail their primary and secondary objectives, should highlight their current net worth, should outline the steps taken to improve their financial position, should list the assumptions made and provide a financial budget outlining the expected revenues and outflows and the expected net worth at the end of one year, possibly in five years, and may even project the expected net worth in the year the individual is expected to retire.

In general a financial plan should cover the following main themes:

- Background to the individual, including risk assessment
- Financial analysis of the individual's financial position
- Debt management
- Savings
- Investments
- Taxation
- Risk-management (insurances)
- Education planning (if dependants)
- Problems and issues (dependants/care)

- Retirement planning
- Succession planning
- Review process

The plan also needs to be written in a clear and concise manner which is understandable to the individual.

Monitoring the Situation in the Future

Discussing the impact of deviations from the financial plan at the preparation phase, when a variety of scenarios are considered, is beneficial for an individual as it makes them more aware of the impact of deviations from the plan. Even though this stage raises an individual's financial awareness, it is good practice to arrange a review of the position at some agreed date in the future. This may coincide with the planned achievement of a secondary objective, such as purchasing a property, or may simply be after an agreed timeframe, such as in one year's time.

Individuals should be encouraged to review their own position, on a monthly or quarterly basis, to identify if actual progress is according to plan. Many steps can be automated, for example, savings and pension contributions can be set up using direct debits, as can changes to debt repayments. Care is required when automating these functions as the cost of going into overdraft is punitive. Individuals should be encouraged to keep an emergency reserve to cover unforeseen costs. An individual may have liquidity problems if they overestimate their income, or underestimate their costs when preparing the financial plan. It is important to be realistic at this stage and not to prepare a wish list.

Individuals with business acumen should be encouraged to set up their own personal budget on a spreadsheet and to update this regularly. This will ensure that their finger is on the pulse of their own financial health.

Taking Remedial Action

If, at the review stage, it is clear that the initial financial plan is no longer valid (because the individual's situation has changed, or unforeseen circumstances have arisen, or the estimates were incorrect, or the individual did not make the suggested changes), then the plan needs to be re-prepared on the new basis and the individual should be made aware of the consequences of the changes made to their financial plan on their ability to achieve their specified objectives.

Conclusion

A financial plan consolidates information about an individual (and their partner) in one document. It summarises their financial aims and aspirations and formalises how these can be financed. The process of setting the aims and analysing the resources available can confirm whether the aims are achievable. The plan also sets out the steps that need to be undertaken to achieve these aims. Alternatively, at this stage it may become clear that the aims and aspirations are unrealistic. The individual then needs to change their financial objectives to achievable ones. The planning process should try to highlight inefficiencies in an individual's finances and suggest ways of becoming more financially efficient. The suggestions should be flexible and agreed by the individual. The plan should consider savings, investments, debt management, pensions, insurances and succession planning (wills and trusts). Taxation is a major issue which should be factored into each scenario. The process of preparing a financial plan should make the individual more aware of his personal finances and the consequences for his future of actions taken now.

Case Study – Preparing a Financial Plan

Kieran lives in his own home (worth €/£500,000). He has a €/£300,000 mortgage which he is repaying at €/£1,800 per month (€/£400 is capital). He has €/£2,500 in the bank, €/£3,000 in the local credit union, €/£15,000 in savings and a rental property valued at €/£180,000 (no debt). Kieran's net salary is €/£2,800 per month from his employment. He spends about €/£700 per month on general living expenses and about €/£300 per month on travelling, nights out and sundries. He also gets an income of €/£400 per month from the rent of the investment property. He receives a dividend of 3.8% on his credit union share account and he receives 4% interest (net) on his deposit account balance.

Required:

(a) Prepare a statement of Kieran's net worth.
(b) Prepare a statement of Kieran's projected cash flows for the coming year.
(c) Prepare a statement of Kieran's projected net worth at the end of the year (assume that there has been no increase in the capital value of the properties in the year).

Continued

(d) Identify any manipulation you would suggest in his assets and liabilities that might increase his personal net worth. Use estimates where appropriate.
   (Note: a variety of outcomes are possible.)
(e) Identify questions that you, as his financial adviser, would need answered before analysing the situation further.

Solution:

(a) *Statement of current net worth for Kieran*

Assets	Kieran	Current return
Home	€/£500,000	
Rental property	€/£180,000	
Current account	€/£2,500	
Deposit account	€/£15,000	4.0%
Credit union account	€/£3,000	3.8%
Total assets	*€/£700,500*	
Liabilities		
Mortgage	(€/£300,000)	
Total liabilities	*(€/£300,000)*	
Net worth	***€/£400,500***	

(b) *Cash budget for Kieran (yearly – year one)*

Income	Kieran
Wages (€/£2,800 × 12)	€/£33,600
Rent (€/£400 × 12)	€/£4,800
Credit union interest (€/£3,000 × 3.8%)	€/£114
Savings (€/£15,000 × 4% net)	€/£600
Total income	*€/£39,114*

Continued

Cash outflows	
Mortgage (€/£1,800 × 12)	(€/£21,600)
Tax on rental (€/£100 × 12 − estimate)	(€/£1,200)
Living expenses (€/£700 × 12 − estimate)	(€/£8,400)
Travel, leisure and other (€/£300 × 12 − estimate)	(€/£3,600)
Total outgoings	*(€/£34,800)*
Surplus expected in year 1	*€/£4,314*

(c) *Kieran's projected net worth at the end of the period*

Assets	*Kieran*
Home	€/£500,000
Rental property	€/£180,000
Current account[1]	€/£6,100
Deposit account	€/£15,600
Credit union account	€/£3,114
Total assets	*€/£704,814*
Liabilities	
Mortgage[2]	*(€/£295,200)*
Total liabilities	*(€/£295,200)*
Net worth	*€/£409,614*

Continued

---

[1] This represents the opening balance plus the surplus cash from the year (€/£2,500 + €/£4,314 − €/£600 − €/£114). The interest on the deposit account and the dividend on the credit union account will most likely be credited to the respective accounts.
[2] The mortgage balance will have decreased by the capital portion of the monthly repayment for the year to €/£295,200 (€/£300,000 − (€/£400 × 12)).

(d) *The suggested changes to Kieran's current financial position are pro-vided in the following net worth table:*

Assets	Kieran	Change	Amended current position
Home	€/£500,000		€/£500,000
Rental property	€/£180,000		€/£180,000
Current account	€/£2,500	(€/£2,000)	€/£500
Deposit account	€/£15,000	(€/£15,000)	
Credit union account	€/£3,000	(€/£2,000)	€/£1,000
Total assets	€/£700,500	(€/£19,000)	€/£681,500
Liabilities			
Mortgage – residential	(€/£300,000)	€/£109,000	(€/£191,000)
Mortgage – rental		(€/£90,000)	(€/£90,000)
Total liabilities	*(€/£300,000)*	*(€/£19,000)*	*(€/£281,000)*
Net worth	**€/£400,500**		**€/£400,500**

The changes are explained as follows (it is assumed that Kieran is single, is in his thirties, is averse to risk and is in good health).

At present the mortgage is costing Kieran 5.6% per annum (estimate the interest portion of the repayment for the year is €/£16,800 (€/£1,400 × 12)). When this is divided by the amount outstanding, €/£300,000, a rate of 5.6% results (€/£16,800/€/£300,000). This interest charge is higher than the interest being received on the deposit account, the credit union account and on the current account. It is also noted that there is no debt on the rental property and the consequence of this is that Kieran has to pay tax on the full rental amount (less relevant expenses).

The first suggestion might be to rearrange the mortgage and to reallocate some of the debt as a charge on the rental property.

Continued

€/£90,000 might be suggested. This could be obtained as an interest only mortgage (for now). As the capital value of the property is €/£180,000, obtaining this arrangement should not be difficult (50% secured mortgage). Assuming the interest on a mortgage on the rental property can be obtained for 6% (interest on rental properties is usually slightly higher than interest charged on loans on residential properties) then the total interest charge on the rental property would be €/£5,400 per year (€/£90,000 × 6%). This amounts to a monthly interest payment of €/£450. This will exceed the rent being received of €/£400 per month and leaves room for growth in rent from €/£400 to €/£450 per month in future years before tax becomes payable. The excess of the interest over the rent can be carried forward as a tax loss to be offset against future profits. This cushion of losses will ensure that this mortgage does not have to be renegotiated for a considerable period into the future[3].

The residential mortgage is currently sitting at €/£300,000 but this will fall to €/£210,000 because of the re-mortgaging of the rental property. In addition, it would make economic sense for Kieran to use most of the funds he has in his current account, his credit union account and in his savings to reduce the balance further. He should be encouraged to withdraw a total of €/£19,000 from his bank accounts (€/£2,000 from his current account, €/£2,000 from the credit union account and €/£15,000 from his savings account) and to use this to reduce the amount outstanding on his residential mortgage. This would mean that his new mortgage on the residential property would be on €/£191,000 (€/£210,000 − €/£19,000[4]). Before advising on withdrawing the maximum amount from the deposit accounts, the financial adviser is likely to interrogate Kieran about the likelihood of any other unusual or one-off expenditures that may become payable within the coming months and years. More will have to be retained within the deposit accounts if there is uncertainty about future outgoings. Also, if the terms of the mortgage are such that there are no penalties for making repayments, then Kieran could be more flexible and reduce the mortgage by less this year with the intention of reducing it by more in the coming years (assuming a cash

Continued

---

[3] ROI only: Interest relief on rental properties is restricted to 75% of interest paid (2012).

[4] ROI only: Kieran will qualify for yearly mortgage interest relief of €450 on his interest payments on his residential property (€3,000 × 15%) assuming he purchased his property four years ago (2010 rates) and is not a first time buyer. This relief will be given at source and amounts to €37.50 per month. This will be available until 31 December 2017.

build-up). If a penalty or costs are incurred on repayment, then Kieran should aim to repay the maximum amount off in one lump sum.

Assuming that Kieran retains the €/£400 capital repayment, this means that his overall repayment on the mortgage/mortgages would fall from €/£21,600 per year to €/£20,896.

Rental property interest	€/£90,000 × 6% =	€/£5,400
Residential property capital	€/£400 × 12 =	€/£4,800
Residential property interest	€/£191,000 × 5.6% =	€/£10,696
Total repayment		*€/£20,896*

The total residential mortgage repayment would be €/£15,496 (€/£4,800 + €/£10,696), or €/£1,291 per month (€/£15,496/12). This results in a saving in cash flows of €/£704 per annum (€/£21,600 − €/£20,896).

In addition, there will no longer be any tax due on the rental income resulting in a further cash saving of €/£1,200. However, Kieran will receive less interest income from his bank accounts[5].

A full summary of the impact of this change on income is shown below. Kieran can at this stage decide whether he wishes to keep the capital repayments as they are (€/£400 per month) and can reap a stronger increase in his yearly cash, savings and investment accounts or could start a pension. He will have less interest income in the earlier years, but this will increase over the years again as the current cash surplus continues to be invested.

Alternatively, he could elect to increase his capital repayments by approximately €/£158 each month ((€/£1,200 + €/£704)/12) without his current standard of living being affected. An increase in the capital repayments will reduce the length of the mortgage and leave Kieran in a stronger financial position when he is older.

Given the new restructured financial position, Kieran's net cash inflows will change to €/£5,542 per annum (assuming the surplus cash will not be used to increase the capital repayments on the mortgage).

Continued

---

[5] The tax saving will be different for ROI answers due to the tax treatment of interest on rental properties (see n.1 above).

Income	Adjusted	Before
Wages (€/£2,800 × 12)	€/£33,600	€/£33,600
Rent (€/£400 × 12)	€/£4,800	€/£4,800
Credit union dividend (€/£1,000 × 3.8%)	€/£38	€/£114
Savings interest		€/£600
Total income	€/£38,438	€/£39,114
Cash outflows		
Mortgage – residential	(€/£15,496)	(€/£21,600)
Mortgage – rental	(€/£5,400)	
Tax on rental (estimated)		(€/£1,200)
Living expenses (€/£700 × 12)	(€/£8,400)	(€/£8,400)
Travel, leisure and other (€/£300 × 12)	(€/£3,600)	(€/£3,600)
Total outgoings	(€/£32,896)	(€/£34,800)
Surplus expected in year 1	**€/£5,542**	**€/£4,314**

Therefore, Kieran will be better off by €/£1,228 per year (€/£5,542 − €/£4,314). *Note: there may be set-up fees in the first year to renegotiate the mortgage – this is not included above.* This review did not consider changes to Kieran's expenditure and it is likely that Kieran's salary and rental income will increase in the future; therefore, his cash savings should be utilised and a minimum balance left at this stage as these are likely to build up quite quickly over the coming months/years (assuming his job is secure).

Summary of Key Actions

The surplus from each month should be used to increase Kieran's savings in the first instance (until a suitable emergency reserve is re-established), to start higher return investments and a pension. As mentioned previously, Kieran might also opt to increase the capital repayments on his residential mortgage. This will reduce his cash flow risks in the future as his debt will be lower.

Continued

(e) The suggested changes outlined in (d) above assume that Kieran is a young, single man in his thirties. A financial adviser would be interested to build up more background information on Kieran than is given in the question. Questions he might ask include:

- What are your contact details?
- What age are you?
- Are you married/do you have a partner who cohabits with you or are you likely to get married/likely to have a partner who will cohabit with you?
- If married/cohabiting, is the relationship solid?
- Have you any dependants (children, elderly parents)?
- If you have dependants – have you taken any steps to ensure that the future financial commitments relating to the dependants are covered (provision for education expenses, provision for elderly care home expenses)?
- What are your work prospects (elaborate)?
- What are the details of your current employer?
- What is your attitude to risk (complete a risk assessment questionnaire)?
- What are your long-term financial objectives?
- Have you any immediate financial objectives (are you thinking of purchasing a motor vehicle, property, for example)?
- How much of an emergency fund do you wish to keep liquid?
- What are your views on succession – have you considered making a will/do you have a will?
- What are your views on securing an income in the event of becoming critically ill, etc. (discuss insurance cover)?
- Confirm the extent of his assets.
- Confirm the extent of his liabilities (ask about credit cards, etc.)
- Go through a checklist of common types of income and expenditures to ensure the figures in the cash flow projections are accurate estimates. Identify any cash savings that could be made.
- Do you have an occupational pension scheme (obtain details)?
- What pension income would you like to have; what are you willing to give up now to achieve this?
- Have you considered your own care when elderly (the importance of this question will depend on the age of the individual)?
- Do you expect to receive any legacies or other forms of income?
- Are you taxable under UK/ROI legislation only?
- Who are your professional advisers (obtain details)?

KEY TERMS

Cash flow planning	Net worth of an individual
Cash flow projections	Personal assets
Critical risk factor	Personal earnings
Earnings risk	Personal liabilities
Financial commitments	Primary objective
Financial plan	Risk
Investment risk	Secondary objectives

REVIEW QUESTIONS

(Suggested solutions to **Review Questions** are provided in **Appendix 4**.)

Question 3.1

Outline the key factors that should be considered in a financial plan.

Question 3.2

What financial strategies might an individual undertake to achieve financial independence?

Question 3.3

Explain risk in the context of a personal financial plan.

Question 3.4

A self-employed local businessman approaches you for advice on his personal finances. He supplies you with the following list of his investments, insurances and debt:

Investments

Credit union share account (4%)	€/£3,000
Deposit account at bank (2.5%)	€/£35,000
Cash ISA (5.5%) (tax-free term deposit account, assume a €/£5,100 deposit limit each year)	€/£15,000
Current account	€/£15,000
Personal pension (€/£500 per month)	€/£45,000
Investment property (cost)	€/£70,000
Share portfolio value	€/£18,000

Annual insurances – yearly premiums

Life assurance	€/£800
Permanent health insurance	€/£750
Voluntary health insurance	€/£500
Mortgage protection insurance	€/£450
Loan protection insurance	€/£300

Debt

Mortgage outstanding	€/£180,000
Loan on vehicle	€/£18,000

Other Information

- The small share portfolio has returned an average 10% per annum over the past five years.

- The businessman informs you that his private home has a market value of about €/£400,000 and the investment property is worth €/£150,000. The investment property has been increasing in value each year. The businessman is aware of the strong return it is making and has not rented the property as he would have to spend €/£10,000 now to make it attractive to tenants. The property could only be rented for €/£500 per month and the businessman considers that it would not be worthwhile undertaking the initial investment. The mortgage is secured on the private home.

- The general household costs are all purchased using the Visa card and amount to about €/£1,500 per month. The businessman pays €/£1,200 each month off the Visa bill. The outstanding balance has crept to €/£12,000. The Visa card company charges 1% per month on outstanding balances. The businessman regards this as not bad value.

Required: Prepare an opening statement of affairs for the businessman from the information provided above.

5 Marks

Question 3.5 (Challenging)

(Suggested Solutions to Challenging Questions are available to lecturers.)

Figure 3.6 provides a brief overview of the type of information to be included when calculating the personal assets of an individual/couple. One asset that many individuals are likely to have is a residential home, and a financial adviser is likely to require some detail about the financial aspects of the property.

Required: Design a proforma schedule to capture all the financial information that would be required when assessing an individual's personal financial position, risk and the impact of having the asset on the individual's net earnings.

Question 3.6

Discuss the advantages of using a detailed personal cash budget (as given in the appendix to this chapter) to record an individual's personal income and expenditure in yearly terms.

Question 3.7

Which of the following statements is most correct? Preparing a monthly budget can help an individual achieve financial security by:

(i) making the individual more aware of their cash inflows and outflows; thus helping them to make better cash allocation decisions.
(ii) reorganising debt limits and identifying where further debt can be sourced.
(iii) reducing the likelihood of having unexpected expenditures.
(iv) helping the individual to select the investments that are likeliest to be the most profitable.

APPENDIX: PROFORMA PERSONAL CASH BUDGET (YEARLY/WEEKLY)

	Now €/£	*If you died* €/£	*If partner died* €/£	*On retirement* €/£
Income				
Your salary				
Partner salary				
Bonuses				
Other				
Self-employed income				
Investment income				
Rental income				
Interest income				
State benefits				
Maintenance				
Pension income				
Tax-free income				
Other				
Other expected				
Total income				
Expenditure				
Home				
Mortgage/rent				
Second mortgage				
Furniture replacement				
Insurances				
Rates				
Repairs				
Garden				
Cleaning materials				
Total				

	Now €/£	*If you died* €/£	*If partner died* €/£	*On retirement* €/£
Utilities				
Electricity				
Oil/gas				
Wood/coal				
Water rates/cleaning septic tank				
Telephone				
Mobile				
Internet				
Cable/satellite				
Total				
Food and drink				
Groceries				
Drink				
Eating out				
Total				
Transport				
Car loan repayments 1				
Car loan repayments 2				
Petrol/diesel				
Insurance 1				
Insurance 2				
Car tax 1				
Car tax 2				
AA/RAC				
Repairs				
Tickets/parking				
Bus fares				

	Now €/£	*If you* *died* €/£	*If partner* *died* €/£	*On* *retirement* €/£
Train fares				
Taxi fares				
Allowance towards car				
Total				
Leisure				
Holidays				
Club subscriptions				
Cigarettes and alcohol				
Entertainment				
Sports				
Books				
Videos				
Coffee				
Total				
Family expenses				
Day care				
Child support				
School tuition				
Pocket money				
Clothes				
Uniforms				
Total				
Debt repayments				
Credit card 1				
Credit card 2				
Student loan				
Personal loan				
Total				

	Now €/£	If you died €/£	If partner died €/£	On retirement €/£
Personal care				
Haircuts				
Prescription medications				
Toiletries/makeup				
Clothing				
Total				
Pets				
Food				
Insurance				
Vet				
Grooming				
Total				
Donations				
Other one-off expenditures				
Total expenditure				
Surplus/(deficit)				

CHAPTER 4

THE FINANCIAL LIFECYCLE

OBJECTIVES

Upon completion of this chapter, readers should be able to:

- explain the meaning of the key terms listed at the end of the chapter;
- describe how personal financial management changes throughout an individual's life;
- list life-changing events that cause financial plans to have to be revisited;
- explain the primary focus of financial management for students;
- explain the main financial issues facing young employed individuals;
- explain the main financial issues facing individuals who have dependants;
- explain the focus of financial management for established individuals; and
- describe the financial issues facing retired individuals.

Introduction

No two financial plans are the same. Individuals may be at different stages in their financial lifecycle. They may have different financial hurdles to overcome and commitments to consider. They may have different objectives, incomes, expenses, expected lifestyles, different attitudes to the future and different attitudes to risk. Yet, some common issues are typical to most, depending on the stage a person is at within their *financial lifecycle*. This chapter assumes that individuals have a financial lifecycle – they go through six different phases during their lives – and that the financial issues facing individuals change as they progress between phases.

These phases lie along a continuum (which is more likely than not to be linked to age), and individuals progress along the continuum at different rates, depending on their initial net worth, their income, expenditure, circumstances, commitments and ability to manage their finances. The phases identified are the child phase, the student phase (teens to the early twenties), the young employed person phase (teens to the late twenties), the individuals who have dependants phase (late twenties to late thirties), established individuals (forties to retirement) and people who are retired.

As stated above, rates of progression along the financial continuum are likely to be different for different individuals. For example, a student with a child or dependent adult will face more constraints than a student who enters the workforce with no commitments. They will be constrained in the amount of work they can undertake (which may affect promotion and income), will have additional costs, hence are unlikely to be able to increase their net worth at the same rate as a student who has no commitments. They are also likely to take longer to raise the funds required to purchase their own home. As there are different financial stages to each person's life, the primary and secondary objectives will change as a person progresses through life. Because of this, a person's financial plan should be reviewed and amended as they get older, or as their situation changes.

The Child Phase

Children are totally dependent on their parents for all their financial needs. However, that does not mean that they are excluded from financial planning. Financial planning for children starts with their parents. In many instances, parents do provide their children with some education on the importance of money; however, many parents do the budgeting for their children by providing them with everything that they need. When this happens, children do not get a sense of how money works or its value. When children reach a certain age (and this varies per child), parents could provide opportunities for earning income to their children, such as washing the car, weeding the garden, ironing the clothes, unloading the dishwasher, walking the dogs, etc. These tasks should be separately identifiable and clearly defined from other chores that are normally undertaken (you do not want children to request payment for normal tasks, as this would have a detrimental impact on them also). By doing this, children can see the reward to be gained from working and can enjoy some financial independence from their parents by having their own money.

Though it is important to let children spend some of this money, parents should encourage their children to open a deposit account and to save on a regular basis. It is important to identify a goal to save for, such as a special toy, and at the same time to also stress the importance of saving for the future. This fosters a savings culture in children from an early age, which will lead to good financial practices in their future.

Credit unions are very active in promoting a savings culture in children, and many credit unions send staff/volunteers into schools to take deposits from children. Children are typically given a deposit account book, and they can see their money grow with each deposit. This will motivate children, particularly when they receive interest on their account balance. They will be able to see the relationship between the amount of interest received and the balance, and it should be stressed to them that the more you have the more you earn in interest. Many banks and building societies also have savings products for children and offer gifts to children when they open accounts. Again this is motivational for children.

The Student Phase

As previously mentioned, everyone starts off being financially dependent on their parents, or on the government. Very young people typically have little financial independence. This is usually the situation until a person reaches school-leaving age, whereupon they go to college/university, or get their first job. It is at this point that financial planning should start to take place in earnest. At this stage also each individual should be made aware of the benefits of financial planning, as bad habits can start early. In most instances, parents will have provided their children with some education on managing money in their school years. Now, the focus will be to try to get the child to start budgeting. Though it may be difficult to do, parents should provide periodic payments (effectively grants) to their children and should show them how to plan to make the funds last throughout the term (or month – whatever period the parent decides the child is mature enough to deal with). This should teach the child/ student how to budget and plan, something they will need to be able to do when they start earning. By providing funds to students on a drip feed basis, parents are doing the budgeting for the child, and while this reduces the risk of loss to the parent, it is not encouraging the student to take responsibility for their own financial destiny[1]. Many students work and/or receive a government grant in addition to receiving some funds from their parents. If a student has their own money, this allows them to have a higher standard of living and to have some financial independence from their parents. However, by working, a student may damage their future, as time spent working could be spent studying. Higher qualifications usually lead to higher earnings in later years.

---

[1] A word of warning! A colleague of mine paid his son's rent and gave him £800 to last him for the first term of college (October to Christmas). The son immediately purchased a television for his halls of residence room and, one month later, approached his parents for more funding. My colleague ended up buying the television off his son for a £50 discount. Both parties learned from the experience.

Cash Flows

Students are investing in their human capital. This is an important investment that has many costs. The largest cost is probably the opportunity cost of income foregone by not working in the years that they attend university. In addition, students usually have to move away from home and incur living costs for the first time in their lives. They have to purchase books, pay travel costs and purchase their own clothing and accessories (including phones, etc.) So students have plenty of cash outflows with limited cash inflows.

Most students are not independent of their parents, yet are at an age when they want to be. Their income is made up from parental 'hand-outs' (this does not have to be cash, but can take the form of parents paying tuition fees, purchasing clothes or a mobile phone, etc.), earnings from a part-time job, a student loan or a grant. Some students work during the summer period. The excess funds earned should be carefully managed so as to provide some financial independence during term time.

Financial Management

The issues facing students are very different to those facing a person who enters employment. Their financial planning is very limited as they do not have net income to plan with. The focus in this instance would be on minimising costs and debt. Debt can be accumulated very quickly and easily at high rates. Credit cards can be a major pitfall for students. Students should aim not to have a credit card (debt and credit cards are discussed under 'the young employed individual') and to only accumulate 'good debt' (discussed in **Chapter 6**). The main areas covered in a financial plan (outlined in **Chapter 3**) will also be considered, but prominence should be given to minimising costs and debt, whilst maximising educational attainment.

The Young Employed Person Phase (Typically Individuals in their Late Teens, or Early Twenties)

The young employed phase represents individuals who have started employment and typically covers the period from leaving school to one's late twenties. These people enter the workforce after school or after university. This category of person is usually living in rented accommodation, or at home. The primary objective at this stage is usually to try to get on the property ladder. Young employed individuals usually suffer from severe *capital rationing*. This means that the income they have available cannot cover the investments that they want to make.

Individuals who enter the workforce after university usually experience a large increase in their cash inflows. However, by this stage in their life, they often have a considerable amount of debt and no savings. Managing debt is vital at this early stage in their financial lifecycle.

In addition, most individuals of this age want to purchase a motor vehicle and a property. Many obtain credit to purchase a motor vehicle. This may end up as a 'Catch 22' situation – the additional debt increases the cash outflows each month, which means that the individual cannot build up savings. No savings means no deposit, which means no house! If possible, an individual should use public transport until they build up sufficient funds to purchase a vehicle in cash. It is vital at this stage to emphasise the need to be frugal. A budget should be used to plan the repayment of debt, to start saving for a deposit and to start investing for retirement – even if the latter is only a small amount.

Pitfalls: Debt

There are some key factors that both students and early-stage employed people should be aware of. The first is that 'there is no such thing as a free lunch'. Many electrical retailers, furniture retailers, clothes retailers, or motor vehicle dealerships use pretty effective marketing ploys to wrangle money from this section of the population. Advertising that emphasises the *affordability* of an item can cause individuals to take on too much debt (to become *overgeared*). This type of finance is easy to obtain and allows the buyer to get satisfaction from having a product immediately, without physically experiencing a cash outflow. The 'buy now, pay nothing until next year', 'zero financing', or 'this wide-screen TV can be yours for only €/£9 per week' is seen as attractive, but usually masks the true price of the product and the real cost of the finance on offer. In all instances, these items will have to be paid for in full. Purchasing goods in this manner from shops is obtaining debt, and young employed individuals should try to avoid debt if at all possible.

Credit cards are another huge pitfall for individuals who have just joined the workforce. Credit card debt is very accessible. Young employed individuals who are just learning the value of money should use them with care. Paying balances in full each month is the most efficient approach. Many young people get into the habit of paying the minimum payment each month. Credit cards are an expensive source of funds. A priority should be to clear high-interest credit cards. Getting into too much debt, strangles the ability of an individual to create personal wealth. However, that is not to say debt is always bad; it is not (discussed in **Chapter 6,** 'Debt Management'). An individual should always work out the total cost of each type of finance for each product and, in a separate calculation, should calculate the total payments being paid out each month. This is also covered in depth in **Chapter 6**.

Pitfalls: Consumable Expenditure

Individuals in this category should be made aware of the consequences of daily spending on consumable items, as highlighted by the maxim 'If you look after the pennies, the pounds will look after themselves'. A young person's long-term financial success is influenced by their day-to-day financial decision-making. For example, a student/young worker who purchases a coffee and a scone every morning in the local fancy café, would justify their action by saying, it's only a couple of euro/pounds (say €/£4–5 per day), then they may purchase a bottle of water for the office, or the lecture class (€/£1 per day), without realising the financial implications of their actions. The €/£5 per day, equates to €/£25 per week (assuming they do this five days per week) or €/£1,300 per year. If this money is invested to earn a return of 5% then one year's expenditure (€/£1,300) would grow in value to about €/£9,152 (€/£1,300 × 1.05^{40}), assuming forty years to retirement age.

Financial Management

The young employed should be encouraged to prepare simple cash budgets detailing expected cash inflows and cash outflows. They should set themselves financial goals; for example, to build up a deposit of €/£10,000 towards the purchase of a property, or to purchase a motor vehicle (preferably from savings). Car insurance at this age is expensive. Advice to the young employed individual will usually revolve around reducing expenditure, tackling debt, highlighting long-term issues such as the need to consider retirement, determining the type of lifestyle expected at retirement age, setting short-term goals, such as buying a house, purchasing a new vehicle, having children and vacations. It is very important for people who start taking charge of their own finances to prepare a statement of net worth and a personal cash flow budget to determine the sources of income, expenditures and surpluses. The cash flow budget can be utilised to identify potential cost efficiencies that could take place and this in turn will result in more surpluses which can be used for investment. The current debt and investment portfolio can be reviewed and advice given on whether an efficient balance of either is being maintained. At this stage of an individual's financial lifecycle, the retirement/pension decision is very important. Contributions to a pension scheme that are in the scheme longer will be worth more. Therefore, it is usually recommended that individuals join a scheme when they start their employment. Most employers offer a pension scheme as an employment benefit, with the employer contributing a proportion of the employee's salary each year. If this is not taken up by the employee, they lose the employer's contribution. Pensions are discussed in more depth in **Chapter 9**, 'Pensions'.

At this stage, financial advice is likely to extend beyond financial matters and to stress the importance of remaining healthy. With several years of life to go, the total financial requirement to service an individual in their twenties to thirties is greater. Maintaining good health increases the likelihood of working for longer at more efficient levels, hence building up more capital.

In terms of reducing risk, critical illness insurance and income protection insurance may be an option (discussed in **Chapter 5**). These insurances provide some form of income protection for the individual in the event of becoming seriously ill or providing income in the event of becoming unemployed. Typically, this type of insurance for young people is very affordable and tends to increase in price as people get older as the probability of claims occurring increases.

The need to retain important documentation and to organise this documentation in a systematic fashion should be stressed. Important documentation will include items such as a person's employment contract, their loan agreements, mortgage agreements, house deeds, warranty agreements, will, etc. It is important to get a systematic organised approach to the retention of these important documents, as part of an overall financial plan for the individual.

The other areas covered in a financial plan (outlined in **Chapter 3**, 'The Financial Plan') will also be considered, but prominence should be given to the aforementioned areas.

The Individuals with Dependants Phase (Typically Individuals in their Late Twenties to their Late Thirties)

Individuals in their late twenties to late thirties will have been in employment for over 10 years and should have experienced pay increases, have more secure employment, have reduced debt levels (perhaps paid off their student loan in full), own a motor vehicle and a property and should have amassed savings. The largest influence on this category of individual is likely to be having responsibility for dependants.

Financial plans are not static; they change every time there is a change in an individual's circumstances. When an individual forms a relationship with another, such that their assets and incomes become intertwined (for example, moving in with a partner/spouse, having children) or decide to take responsibility for the care of parents in their old age, then their long-term financial objectives change. The financial plan should not just focus on one individual but should take into account the assets and liabilities of the partner/spouse and should factor in the financial consequences of having children. The proforma documentation suggested in **Chapter 3**, 'The Financial Plan', has been prepared to allow the individual completing the schedules to include information on their partner.

Joining a Partnership

When entering into any relationship that involves a merger of assets and incomes, it is vital to consider the financial consequences of the relationship ending in the future. In the UK, there are 3.08 divorces per 1,000 people. (In NI, the rate is lower; there were 2,600 divorces in 2010, representing about 1 per 1,000 people.) (www.nisra.gov.uk.) In the ROI, about 0.7 divorces occurred per 1,000 people in 2011 (this equates to an average number of divorces of about 5,000 in that year (www.cso.ie). As regards financial settlement in the case of divorce, the court can make a variety of orders, including lump sum payments, periodic payments, property adjustment orders and pension adjustment orders. High-profile divorce cases (for example, Sir Paul McCartney and Heather Mills or Madonna and Guy Ritchie) highlight the financial problems that can arise when a relationship ends. If there is a clear imbalance in the assets of each party in the relationship, then it might not be unreasonable to consider some form of premarital agreement.

After considering the impact of a separation and possibly forming an agreement to cover that eventuality, it is important to start planning with two people (or more where children are expected) in mind.

Financial Planning with your Partner: Two Incomes, No Children

When both parties in a relationship are employed, there are many *economies of scale* gained. There are two incomes, yet only one expense for many items, such as the mortgage, or the expenses of running a home. Where the couple have no children they are referred to as *DINKs* (*double income, no kids*) and typically have an enviable lifestyle. It is more likely than not that this couple will have surplus income and savings. They are likely to own their own property as they will have been able to accumulate a deposit quite quickly and will be categorised as low risk by the bank, so they will have little problem in obtaining a mortgage. The financial crisis has made it more difficult for individuals to purchase properties. Many financial institutions now require a 10%–15% deposit, which means accumulating about €/£20,000 towards a property costing €/£140,000. Other costs, such as solicitors' fees, surveyors' fees and stamp duty also have to be covered. However, poor financial management could see this category of individual remain in a financial rut if their current expenditure increases to such an extent that it negates the impact of the surplus income they have at their disposal. This category of individual should not have any bad debt.

Financial Management: Like all financial plans, the efficient use of resources will be recommended. Although this category can afford to spend more on consumables, this is only recommended if they are on target to achieve the goals that they set. These goals might include purchasing a property or purchasing/replacing a car, putting aside funds for retirement (savings, investments and pensions) and may include debt management (reducing their mortgage). The other areas covered in a financial plan (outlined in **Chapter 3**, 'The Financial Plan') will also be considered, however, prominence should be given to the aforementioned areas.

Children: the Work versus Life Dilemma

When the additional costs associated with having children, coupled with the cost of working (for example, childcare, tax, National Insurance/PRSI, commuting, clothes, etc.) are taken into account, an individual could find themselves working for a salary that is actually lower than the minimum wage rate. In addition, on a psychological level, most working parents suffer stress and guilt because they elect to work. This combined with expensive childcare costs raises the question 'is it worth working?'

In some instances, the lower-earning partner leaves work to look after the children. However, this decision should never be taken lightly. Leaving the workforce might damage an individual's future career. In most careers, the role evolves over time, with new rules, regulations, products, contacts, etc., making it difficult to re-enter the workforce in the same role or at the same position. Then there is the future to think of. If an individual leaves the workforce, they stop paying into their pension, as do their employers, and this will impact on the final pension they receive when they retire. The non-financial issues also influence this decision. Some individuals find it difficult to stay at home, needing adult company; whereas other individuals are happy to do so and enjoy the role (reaping psychological rewards). Some individuals believe that day-care is institutionalising children at too young an age; others feel that day-care provides social and interpersonal skills that a child would not get at home. The choice of whether to continue working or to take a career break and look after children is a personal choice, so the financial plan should consider both options as an aid to the decision on whether to work or not.

Financial Planning with your Partner: Two Incomes, Children

When a couple indicate that they wish to have children, this should be factored into the financial plan. Children are a real financial cost.

A pro rata increase in consumable expenditure can be expected. A major outflow that will have to be taken into account is childcare costs, which are typically €200/£140 per week per child (in some instances this amount can be more or less, depending on location and type of childcare sought). Discounts of up to 20% are usually available when there is more than one child.

Financial Management: The financial plan will consider the resources available, the surplus cash available, savings levels, debt levels, investments made, retirement planning and will consider these in light of the individual's aspirations. This category of individual is likely to have surplus funds, though they will also have more demands on these funds. With so many dependants, insurance becomes quite important, particularly life assurance, critical illness insurance and income protection insurance (discussed in **Chapter 5**). In addition, the decision has to be made as to whether to pay for the education of the children, or not. Investments need to be started where the couple decide to pay for their children's education. Normally a termed investment is recommended, which is organised to mature when the children start third-level education.

The other areas covered in a financial plan (outlined in **Chapter 3**, 'The Financial Plan') should also be considered, though prominence should be given to the aforementioned areas.

Financial Planning with your Partner: One Income, Children

Where one partner is not earning, then the financial plan will have to take this into consideration as one source of income will have to cater for the future needs of both individuals and any children. The relevant risk-reducing insurance policies (see **Chapter 5**, 'Insurance') will have to be updated and the pension company informed of the existence of the dependent spouse (pension companies normally provide a pension to widows). Unless the single income is very high, the financial plan will be constrained by income and the individuals concerned will have to accept a lower standard of living (though will consider this worthwhile as they may feel that they have a better quality of life), whilst still ensuring that a portion of their income is invested to provide them with an income in their pension years.

Financial Management: Financial advice is likely to focus on analysing current money management, including identifying potential efficiencies/savings in costs. Non-essential expenses should be listed, ranked, and reduced in order of least needed. These expenses might include satellite television, holidays, telephones (where there is a landline plus mobile phones), entertaining (this will be even more costly now as babysitters will also require payment), travel costs (if situated within a town it may be possible to operate with one car). If after this the budget still does not return a surplus, it might be possible to extend the length of the mortgage to bring down the monthly repayments. Another option might be to relocate to a cheaper property with a lower mortgage. The advice given will depend on a variety of factors, including the potential deficit in income, the skills of the person leaving the workforce, the likely ease of their re-entry to the workforce, the period of time that person is leaving the workforce and the investments already in place.

Having appropriate insurance is very important due to the reliance on one parent for the family income. In particular, life assurance, critical illness insurance, mortgage protection insurance and income protection insurance should be considered (discussed in **Chapter 5**), though the cost of four insurances may limit choice.

The financial plan will also have to consider debt management – in particular it should ensure that a sufficient level of emergency funds is kept available. It will be more difficult to build up savings from one salary. This increases the liquidity risk for the couple, so a larger buffer balance of cash is required. The plan should also try to encourage some savings and should highlight the appropriateness of the retirement fund provision. Education planning should also be discussed, though it may not be possible to fund this at this stage.

The single income period may only be for a short time (in many instances a parent stops work to look after the children when they are very young, returning to work when the children go to school). This will be factored into the financial plan and, for example, building savings for retirement may be put on hold until the future. Depending on the level of the salary being earned by the working partner, it may be that the couple are entitled to government assistance such as medical or accommodation assistance. This should also be discussed. All the other areas covered in a financial plan will also be considered but are not as prominent as those discussed above.

The Established Individuals Phase
(Individuals in their Forties to Retirement Age)

This category typically includes people in their forties who are already on the property ladder, who are paying into a pension scheme, who have investments and whose children (if any) are post-primary school level. The financial comfort of this category of individual depends on how they conducted their financial planning in their twenties and thirties. If they followed a tight financial plan, minimising costs, investing wisely and putting away for their retirement, then they are likely to be in a very comfortable financial position. These individuals probably have their own property, which they purchased at least 10 years earlier and may even have upgraded in the 10-year period. Where the economy has grown in the period since the individual purchased the property, it is likely that the property will have risen in value, yet the initial mortgage will be lower (after 10 years of repayments). Moreover, the individual's salary will have increased, yet the mortgage repayments will be similar to those being paid 10 years earlier. This rule is not likely to hold when there is a recession. Given the recent economic climate and the state of the housing market, it is likely that many individuals have negative equity in relation to their property and are unable to move. However, so long as the individuals are not under pressure to sell their property, they should not suffer financially as, historically, property prices have always rebounded after a slump in the market. The question is 'how long will it take?'

At this stage, many individuals start to consider 'winding down', going part-time, reducing working hours or planning to retire abroad. All these goals would need to be factored into the financial plan. However, it is becoming more and more difficult for this age group to take a step back from generating income when dependants are involved.

An issue that is becoming more common for this category of individual is *KIPPERS (Kids in Parents' Pockets Eroding Retirement Savings)*. A survey by the Money Programme (the BBC) found that one in four sets of parents have to fund their children well into adulthood. Children remain at home rent free, and many do not contribute to household expenses. A major contributor to this problem is the state of the economy which affects employment opportunities and salaries and the prohibitive cost of getting on to the property ladder. In the UK, the average age for first-time buyers is now 34, and many of these individuals relied on their parents for financial assistance with the deposit. Indeed, there have been cases in Italy and Spain of parents taking legal action to force their children to leave home. In Italy the phenomena is called 'bamboccione' or 'big baby'!

As one of the main causes of children becoming KIPPERS is the high cost of getting on the property ladder, many financial institutions have created a number of mortgage products based on parental guarantees. In these types of mortgage, the deposit can be lower (10% to 15%). The terms of these mortgages are that parents (or close family relatives) provide a guarantee over the mortgage repayments. This is typically only available where the parents (or close family relative) are less than 60 years of age. This is a long-term risk exposure for the parents but is becoming more and more common in the current mortgage market place and, hence, individuals should consider it when preparing their financial plans (additional emergency funds are likely to be required).

Personal Financial Management

The issues facing this category of individual will include deciding on the type of investments and the level of pension required. In addition, at this stage in an individual's life, serious consideration needs to be given to the financial consequences on the family unit of the death of one or both parents. A will, detailing the wishes of the individual, should be advised with the individual being made aware of the impact of inheritance tax and the rights of their surviving family members under succession law on their wishes (taxation advice is likely to influence the contents of the will). Individuals should be advised to discuss their wishes with future heirs as this can uncover issues and reduce bitter feelings in the future.

The *investment decision* will include looking at the current portfolio of investments, discussing the objective of each, considering the risk of the investments and advising on future action. At this stage most individuals will have moved to their target residence or plan to move to a target residence in the near future; therefore financing this will be an important issue. Some investments may be encashed to reduce the level of debt if necessary. At this stage another financial issue becomes imminent – the funding of third-level education. Where the individuals have decided to fund their children's education expenses, then it is likely that they will be advised to pay into a termed investment, which will mature in time to pay for third-level education costs. It is important to determine periodically if this investment is on track to cover the estimated costs. If not, corrective action is required.

So long as an individual is on target to meet their objectives, and has a pension and/or a sufficient portfolio of investments that is sufficient and on-track to cover the individual's retirement needs, then they should have sufficient surplus funds to be able to enjoy a more luxurious lifestyle.

If they have not been contributing to a pension scheme or building up investments and/or savings, then this becomes a priority. Depending on age, the type of investment becomes important. A general rule of thumb is that individuals who are close to retirement should not invest in risky investments. The potential cost of care in old age should also be considered. If the individual is in good health, this may still be a long way off; however, if the individual is not in good health, this becomes an urgent issue to plan for.

Individuals Who Are Retired

When an individual retires their objectives will change again. The focus will no longer be on building up a pot of funds for the future. Individuals who have retired and who have taken financial advice in their earlier years, will now own their home outright and should have limited or no debt.

Though income has fallen, outgoings should also have fallen. The main source of income will be a private and/or work pension, the state pension, income from investments and cash from selling investments (if necessary).

The individual should also ensure that they are getting all the retirement benefits to which they are entitled. This can be quite complicated as there are several benefits available for retired individuals, many of which are means-tested (see **Chapter 9**, 'Pensions'). Funds should not be invested in risky type investments, such as shares. More appropriate types of investment include bonds and high interest savings accounts (financial advice should be sought).

At this stage, an individual might wish to downsize their property in an attempt to reduce their costs and their household management issues. This will also release equity for their disposal. Some individuals will remain working as this is what they want to do (at retirement age, working for income should not be necessary), or the individual may travel. It is important to point out to an individual that travelling and working is more likely to be feasible in the earlier part of their retirement.

Key issues facing a retired person include the cost of care when infirm, funeral costs and how their estate should be distributed to heirs. At this stage, banks, building societies, credit unions, investment companies and pension companies should be informed of the name and details of the person to whom the cash or assets should pass to, in the event of death. Having a formalised financial plan throughout an individual's life will mean that they have their documents in an organised manner. If this is not the case, then now is the time to put it right, so that heirs are aware of all the assets owned. It is useful to make heirs aware of the individual's updated wishes. This makes it less likely that heirs will contest the individual's wishes on death.

As with the other stages, a retired person should review their financial plan periodically as they may have to finance themselves for over 30 years!

Conclusion

When considering the focus of a financial plan, it is important to determine the stage that a person is at in the financial lifecycle. Though all the main areas covered in a financial plan are relevant, some are more important than others, depending on an individual's personal circumstances. In general:

- Parents should try to foster a savings culture and should try to give some financial responsibility to their children. A good start is to open a deposit account for the child and to encourage the child to save regularly.

- Students are advised to focus more on being frugal and on minimising their exposure to debt.
- Young employed people should also be frugal and should focus on debt management. In addition to this, saving becomes important.
- Individuals with dependants have to extend their financial plan to take account of others. Their financial plan will depend on the resources available to them and the demands on these resources. Balancing the need to fund the future of dependants and putting away for retirement is important. It is likely that investment levels will be low. Having appropriate insurance is more important at this stage.
- Established individuals are likely to be focused on providing for their retirement. This will include eliminating debt before retirement. Succession planning also becomes more important than the other key areas of a financial plan.
- The whole process changes when an individual retires. It is no longer about saving, but about achieving a comfortable lifestyle from the investments and pension built up. Succession planning is very important at this stage.

KEY TERMS

Affordability

Capital rationing

Double income no kids (DINKs)

Economies of scale

Financial lifecycle

Investment decision

Kids in Parents' Pockets
  Eroding Retirement Savings
  (KIPPERS)

Over-geared

REVIEW QUESTIONS

(Suggested solutions to **Review Questions** are provided in **Appendix 4.**)

Question 4.1

Outline the key financial factors that should be focused on in a financial plan for a:
(a) Student, and
(b) Retired individual.

Question 4.2

Outline the key factors that should be considered in a financial plan by someone who is 30 years of age and who has just got married.

Question 4.3

Percy is 48. He has just been made redundant. He worked for a company for 20 years and paid into its pension scheme. It is a large reputable company and, even though Percy has been made redundant, the company has several other factories and branches that are successful. Percy owns his private home and €/£70,000 is still outstanding on the mortgage.

Required: Detail the type of information that you would now include in Percy's financial plan.

Question 4.4

Mary is 40. She has two children and does not work. Her husband has just passed away. He was earning €/£60,000 per year.

Required: You have never met Mary before. Provide a list of information that you will require before you start to prepare her financial plan.

Question 4.5

Outline the benefits of being frugal in the earlier years of an individual's lifecycle.

Question 4.6

You are a personal financial advisor. You are preparing to meet a client Mr Mark Murphy and his son Peter. Mark is 52 years of age and Peter is 22 years of age and about to graduate from college.

Required: Compare and contrast the likely financial goals and positions of Mark and his son.

8 Marks

(Source: Chartered Accountants Ireland, CAP 1, Summer 2008, Q6(a))

Question 4.7

Outline briefly the main financial considerations and implications associated with any two of the following circumstances:
  (i) Death
 (ii) Disability
(iii) Retirement

9 Marks

(Source: Chartered Accountants Ireland, CAP 1, Summer 2009 (Extract from Q7))

Question 4.8 (Challenging)

(Suggested Solutions to **Challenging Questions** are available to lecturers.)

You are working as a personal financial adviser. You have been asked to meet a new client, J. Smith, who has recently inherited €/£150,000 and is seeking advice as to the best use of this cash.

Required: List three key pieces of information needed by you and outline the financial requirements and their impact on your advice where J. Smith is aged:

  (i) 25 years
 (ii) 45 years
(iii) 65 years

10 Marks

(Source: Chartered Accountants Ireland, CAP 1, Summer 2012 (Q6b))

CHAPTER 5

INSURANCE

> Upon completion of this chapter, readers should be able to:
>
> - explain the meaning of the key terms listed at the end of the chapter;
> - define income protection and explain how it works;
> - describe some insurance products that offer income protection;
> - describe the different types of common life assurance products;
> - explain how critical illness cover works;
> - describe the extent and limits of private medical insurance;
> - describe payment protection insurance and explain the controversy surrounding this form of insurance; and
> - describe other insurances that an individual may consider.

Introduction

There are insurances available to cover virtually any risk an individual is exposed to, so long as the individual is willing to pay for them. It is down to personal choice. However, there are a number of products that are usually recommended. These are focused on in this chapter.

As individuals progress through their lives, their financial commitments and risks change. A young individual with no partner or dependants can be selfish. They only have to look after themselves. Their focus would be on maintaining their income (income protection), ensuring that they were cared for in the event of a major health problem (critical illness) and ensuring that they have any acute health problems dealt with quickly (private medical insurance). Rather than opting for private medical insurance an individual may rely on the public health service. An individual who is risk averse is likely to opt for all the above products and possibly some more.

When an individual gets married, the situation changes again. At this stage the aforementioned insurances are relevant but an additional insurance, 'life assurance', becomes important, as individuals do not wish to leave their partner with debt to cover on their own. Again it depends on the individual's circumstances. Where the individual has life assurance through their work pension which has a lump sum payment that will cover their debt, or has a wide range of capital assets that could be sold to cover their debt, then they are at less risk and may opt not to take out additional private life assurance. Income protection may not be as important now, as two salaries are coming into the house and the loss of one salary may not affect the couple's lifestyle. Again it is a matter of choice. It may be worthwhile looking at some of the investment insurance products that provide a lump sum on death. For example, where the individual feels that their estate will be subject to a large inheritance tax bill, an insurance can be taken out which will pay out a lump sum on death. The amount assured can be estimated to cover the inheritance tax bill, leaving the individual's assets free to be transferred to the beneficiaries.

When an individual has children they usually become quite risk averse. One income may not cover the current lifestyle expense, income protection becomes more important, as does life assurance and critical illness cover.

Finally, when a person gets close to retirement age, they may find that they have to pay large premiums for health insurances and most of the income protection policies only operate for the working life of the individual. Retired people are usually less able to insure themselves against risks. Finally, regardless of age, most individuals require motor insurance and home insurance, and many elect to take out loan protection insurance and death benefit insurance.

The main insurances are now considered in turn.

Protecting Income Levels

Income protection is where an individual takes out an insurance policy to protect their (or their family's) income level falling below a certain level. This is likely to happen when an individual dies (family income benefit insurance) or becomes too ill to work (permanent health insurance (PHI). The level of premium required for each insurance will typically depend on the extent of cover required (duration and amount), an individual's age, gender, health, whether or not the individual smokes or drinks alcohol and occupation (is it dangerous?). The two main types of income protection insurance policy are now considered in turn.

Family Income Benefit

Family income benefit is predominately a UK policy which aims to replace the shortfall in annual income when one or both of the income providers in a family dies (depending on how it is set up). The premiums paid into it are not accumulated to pay a lump sum. The payout is typically a monthly payment, which may be a flat rate payment or pegged to an index such as the Retail Price Index (RPI). The insurance covers a period of time and, if the income provider survives to the end of the policy, it just lapses with no payout. The premiums on this type of income protection policy are typically less than a PHI policy and, hence, are more attractive for younger people (who experience capital rationing) who have children and are concerned about being able to cover the expenses associated with children. It is not treated as taxable income on the recipient but as a capital gain and is, thus, subject to capital gains tax.

The following worked example highlights how this type of insurance typically works:

WORKED EXAMPLE: FAMILY INCOME BENEFIT

Jane and her husband, Frank, are 26 years old and have two children, aged 5 and 2. Both parents are keen to obtain financial security for the family until their children are 18 years of age. Jane is not employed but Frank is. He takes home €/£40,000 per year, and this covers their mortgage and general living expenses, with a small amount left over for savings, etc. Jane and Frank would like to secure an annual income of about €/£30,000 until their children are 18 years of age.

Required:

(a) Outline which income protection insurance would be most appropriate for Jane and Frank given their specific requirements.
(b) Calculate the payments that would be receivable on the insurance policy, assuming Frank was to die in:
  (i) Three years' time
  (ii) 10 years' time
  (iii) 20 years' time
(c) What caveats should be stressed to Jane and Frank when taking out the policy?

Solution:

(a) A family income benefit policy is suited to their requirements. The family want a set annual income to be paid out on the death of Frank (the earner), which has low premiums. Family income benefit policies typically have lower premiums than other income protection policies that also pay out on illness or injury. A family income benefit policy can also be tailored to cover the period that the family are most concerned about – the childrearing period. A family income benefit policy will ensure that Jane has an income when the children are young, though the requirement and risk diminishes as the children get older. Therefore, a family income benefit policy that pays €/£30,000 per year for 16 years is required. Most insurance providers limit the amount of cover to 75% of the earner's salary. As €/£30,000 is 75% of Frank's salary it is likely that they will have no bother getting insurance cover.

Continued

(b) The payments that Jane will receive from a family income benefit policy are as follows:
   (i) If Frank dies in three years' time, then Jane will receive 13 yearly payments of €/£30,000 (€/£390,000 in total).
   (ii) If Frank dies in 10 years' time, then Jane will receive six yearly payments of €/£30,000 (€/£180,000 in total).
   (iii) If Frank dies in 20 years' time, then Jane will not receive any payout under the policy, as the term of the policy has ended.
(c) It should be stressed to Jane and Frank that they have not covered every eventuality. Were Frank to become ill or incapacitated by an accident, then the family income benefit policy would not pay out, yet Frank may not be able to work. In these instances, it would be difficult to maintain payment of the mortgage, and mortgage protection insurance should be discussed, as well as critical illness and PHI. However, all insurances have a cost, and this should also be discussed.

Permanent Health Insurance (PHI)

Another form of income protection is *permanent health insurance*. PHI guarantees a replacement income when someone is unable to work for medical reasons. It does not apply if someone just loses their job. It does not pay out a lump sum when the individual becomes critically ill or dies, nor does it cover medical expenses. It just provides income to an individual. The income level to be insured is typically the income requirement plus debt repayments, minus any income being received from other sources. PHIs typically pay between half and 70% of an individual's salary, less state benefits. This is so that the individual is always better off working, and it encourages the individual to return to employment. However, the amount varies depending on the policy taken. There may be limits on the payout term, which means individuals have to be careful to read the small print when setting up their policy. Terms can range from two years, five years or until the individual turns 65 years of age.

When taking out the policy, some individuals may elect to defer the income from the policy for a period of time after the loss of income from employment. This will reduce the premiums to pay. The deferment period can range from four weeks to one year. The longer the deferral period, the greater the reduction in the premium to pay. Women usually have to pay higher premiums than men because they have a history of making more claims. The policy usually has to be renewed if the individual changes job as the risk associated with employment may change. The insurance company cannot cancel the policy so long as the premiums continue to be paid. The payments from this type of policy usually continue until the person is employed again, retires, dies or until the end of the contract. In the UK income received from these policies is tax exempt and the premium paid is not tax deductible. In the ROI the income is taxable and the premium is tax deductible. If this is a benefit that is provided by an employer the premiums are treated as a taxable benefit on the individual and are tax deductible by the company (UK and ROI).

When an individual does not have valid insurance cover they are entitled to some income either from their employer, or the government, or both. The amount and rates of benefits available when ill are now outlined for the UK and the ROI.

UK: Sickness Benefits

In the UK, most employed individuals have access to work-related sickness schemes. These differ from company to company. Some can be very generous, providing full pay for a period of time, while others only provide the statutory minimum, which is statutory sick pay. As this is common to all employed individuals, it is now discussed.

When an employee, who earns over £107 per week, is unable to work because they are sick, they are entitled to *statutory sick pay (SSP)* from day four to 28 weeks at the rate of £85.85 per week.[1] This is paid by the employer, is included as part of normal pay and is subject to tax and NIC. The employer gets some relief, by getting a reduction in their national insurance contributions bill (there are some restrictions). Some employers will pay more, maybe even the whole salary. It depends on the contract of employment agreed with their employees. When the 28-week period is over, the employer is no longer obliged to provide any finance to the employee. At this stage the employee has to claim an *Employment and Support Allowance (ESA)*.

The ESA was introduced on 27 October 2008 to replace incapacity benefit, severe disablement allowance (both discussed below) and income support paid on incapacity grounds for new customers. Anyone who was claiming incapacity benefit is still treated under that system. The ESA aims to help people who are incapacitated to move into work and is available from day four of the incapacity to individuals who are:

- off work/out of work;
- self-employed;

---

[1] 2012/13 rates.

- employed but cannot get SSP, or who were getting SSP but it has now stopped;
- who are under state pension age; or
- who had been getting Statutory Maternity Pay (SMP) and have not gone back to work for the employer because of illness or disability that affects their ability to work.

(Source: direct.gov.uk website)

The ESA is either contribution-based (were the individual has paid sufficient NICs) or income-related (where an inappropriate level of NICs have been paid and/or savings are less than £16,000 and the individual's partner (if relevant) works for less than 24 hours each week on average). Individuals who are state pension age (60 for women and 65 for men) are not entitled to ESA. Men who are aged between 60 and 65 are entitled to the pension credit (discussed in **Chapter 9**, 'Pensions') and may receive the ESA, though the claim is restricted to those who are entitled under the contribution based version of the benefit.

When an individual makes a claim for ESA and they have not received SSP they are entitled to the basic rate of ESA for a period of 13 weeks. This is the assessment period. During this period the benefit paid is £56.25 for individuals who are under 25 and £71.00 if over 25.[2] Thereafter, the individual is entitled to the 'main phase' allowance, a higher allowance of £99.15 for a single person in the work-related activity group and £105.05 for a single person in the support group.[3]

When the individual has qualified for SSP then they are entitled to the ESA after the 28-week period so long as they qualify.

Where an individual became incapacitated before 27 October 2008 they are still entitled to *incapacity benefit (IB)*. This entitles them to £74.80 per week for the first 28 weeks (£95.15 if over state pension age), £88.55 for weeks 29 to 52 (£99.15 if over state pension age) and £99.15 per week thereafter.[4] If an individual's gross pension exceeds £85 per week, then their IB is reduced by half of the excess over the £85.

Individuals who qualify for ESA and IB can undertake 'permitted work' so long as a doctor and the benefit office's personal adviser approves. Permitted work is work that:

- earns the individual less than £20 per week;
- is for less than 16 hours per week where earnings do not exceed £97.50 per week; or

---

[2] 2012/13 rates.
[3] 2012/13 rates.
[4] 2012/13 rates.

- is for less than 16 hours per week where earnings do not exceed £97.50 per week and the work is supported permitted work (supervised by someone who is employed by a public, or local authority or a voluntary organisation and whose job it is to arrange work for disabled people).[5]

(Source: direct.gov.uk website)

ROI: Sickness Benefits

In the ROI, employers do not have a legal obligation to pay their employees sick pay, though many opt to do so as a perk of employment. Individuals who become ill in the ROI are entitled to illness benefit, disability allowance or invalidity pension. If the illness is short-term then the relevant benefit is *illness benefit*. This is a contributions-based payment that is open to individuals who have paid certain levels of social security and who are now unable to work. The number of weeks PRSI has been paid alters the length of time that individuals are entitled to illness benefit. However, in the 2009 budget an overall limit of two years was introduced for claims that start after 1 January 2009 and other time limits were introduced.

Individuals who are eligible to claim illness benefit are entitled to receive amounts of up to €188.00 per week plus up to €124.80 for a qualifying adult and €29.80 for each qualifying child. The personal benefit payable ranges from €84.50 to €188.00 per week, depending on the weekly income of the individual. The rates for each qualifying earning band from 2 January 2012 are as follows:

Table 5.1: Illness Benefit Rates for Income Levels 2012

Average weekly earnings	Personal rate (per week)	Qualified adult rate (per week)
€300 or more	€188.00	€124.80
€220–€299.99	€147.30	€80.90
€150–€219.99	€121.40	€80.90
Less than €150	€84.50	€80.90

---

[5] 2012/13 rates.

Illness benefit (excluding increases for child dependants) is considered as income for tax purposes and is taxed accordingly. An employee must take illness benefit into account for PAYE/PRSI purposes.

Disability allowance is a long-term, means-tested benefit which is available to individuals who are deemed unable to work for periods of more than one year. This benefit tops the individual's weekly income to €188.00 per week. Hence, an individual assessed to have a weekly means of €180.00 will be entitled to a disability allowance of €8.00 per week. An individual can also claim €124.80 per week for a qualifying adult and €29.80 for each qualifying child. Individuals living alone are entitled to a weekly supplement of €7.70, and individuals living on certain offshore islands can claim a supplement of €12.70 per week.

Invalidity pensions are for individuals who have paid PRSI and are classed as having a long-term illness (permanently unable to work). This benefit amounts to €193.50 per week for the afflicted individual with a further €138.10 available if there is a qualified adult (both under 66) and €29.80 for each qualifying child in the house. If the individual is 65 years of age or over, the benefit increases to €230.30, and if the qualifying adult is 66 years or over, the benefit for that individual is €206.30. Individuals are also entitled to the living alone allowance and the offshore island allowance if they qualify.

The information included in this section is not comprehensive and is subject to change in each budget. What is of note is that the sickness benefits are becoming less generous and the qualifying criteria are becoming stricter. Therefore, it is more important that individuals start to consider other options that may secure income, or provide funding in the event of becoming ill. The insurances discussed in this chapter may be an option.

Protection from Financial Distress in the Event of Serious Illness

The rates of benefits available from the government for an individual who has a long-term illness are outlined in the previous section. The benefits available may not be deemed to be sufficient, particularly where the individual has debt that has to be paid periodically (for example a mortgage). An individual can take steps to reduce the risk of having to rely on benefits, or having to run down their savings to cover their current living expenses when a serious illness occurs, by taking out critical illness cover.

Critical illness pays out a tax-free lump sum on the diagnosis of a range of illnesses or accidents that may occur during the policy term. It may also pay out a regular income after the illness is diagnosed or after an operation. Typical illnesses include cancer, heart attack, coronary artery bypass surgery, major organ transplant, strokes and kidney failure. To qualify for this insurance an individual has to be over 18 to take out a policy, and under 65 to start a policy. The policy usually only pays out if the policyholder lives for a month after the illness is diagnosed. The policy sold is usually for a minimum term of five years but will usually not cover an individual when they are over 70 years of age. The sum that can be insured typically ranges from about £25,000 to £500,000 (euro equivalents). The policy will pay out on diagnosis of one of the specified critical illnesses. If your illness is not on the list you will not be covered.

Critical illness cover can be attached to another product. Two common examples are fixed-term cover (with critical illness) and mortgage protection insurance (with critical illness). *Fixed-term cover* combines critical illness with life insurance and will pay out on the diagnosis of a critical illness or on the death of the policyholder within the policy term, to the beneficiaries/estate. When the individual wants to pass the lump sum on death to their children, it is good practice to set the policy up in trust for the children. This may avoid inheritance tax.

Mortgage life cover (with critical illness), otherwise known as *mortgage protection insurance*, is a *decreasing protection policy*. The level of cover provided each year reduces roughly in line with the outstanding balance on a repayment-type mortgage. A lump sum is paid on the death or diagnosis of a critical illness. This lump sum is then used to pay off some or all of the mortgage depending on the terms of the insurance.

Providing for Dependants on Death

An individual who has a partner or dependants will be interested in ensuring that their dependants are not financially burdened as a result of the individual's death. In the prior paragraphs an option was introduced – critical illness cover combined with life insurance. This provides a lump sum to the beneficiary if the policyholder dies during the term of the policy.

Another more commonly used product, *life assurance*, is taken out by individuals to pay a lump sum on death, or at the end of a specified period. The policy can be with-profits, or non-profit. In a with-profits policy, the value of the underlying fund increases in line with the value of the underlying portfolio held by the insurance company. In a *basic life assurance policy*, an individual can pay one lump sum at the start, or can pay an annuity over a fixed period of time, or until death. The amount receivable under the terms of the policy may be a fixed lump sum which is guaranteed by the insurance company, or it may be linked to the performance of an index or portfolio of assets. Policies also have the option of being based on a single or joint life basis. The insurance company usually pays out when just one dies (the first one) or it can be set up to pay out on the death of both. Each policy is different.

For some life assurance policies, death does not have to occur during the term of the policy – *whole-of-life policies* pay out on the death of the policyholder. These policies are more expensive than term assurance policies as the insurance company is definitely paying out. A policy which only pays out on death within the policy term is called a *term policy*. There are two types of whole-of-life policies. One involves the policyholder paying premiums for a set term after which the policy is treated as being paid-up. The lump sum will be paid on death afterwards. The other option involves paying contributions for the rest of the policyholder's natural life. Whole-of-life policies might be used to cover expected inheritance tax liabilities on the individual's estate.

Some policies pay out on death or on a specified date, whichever occurs first. These are known as *investment policies*. Many individuals take these policies out with the sole intention of building up a lump sum for the future. Their intention is not life cover. These policies can be cashed earlier than their maturity date, however, the insurance company will charge a surrender fee, which makes this unattractive. These types of policies can be taken out to fund college education.

Real Life Cover

Real life cover is made up of two pots. One covers life insurance and pays out if death occurs during the term of the policy; the other is called the Living Fund and pays out on all income protection, critical illness or child and partner carer's cover during the term of the plan up to the amount of the Living Fund assured. The individual decides on the sum to be assured, and premiums are set to provide the required cover. An individual can make multiple claims so long as the overall cumulative claim amount does not exceed the Living Fund amount assured. Life cover is not affected by these claims, as this is a separate fund.

Pensions and Life Assurance

Most private and company pension schemes have an element of life cover. This is called the *personal pension term assurance*. The premiums are paid by the pension company.

If the pension is a company pension scheme, the life cover is usually linked to salary level in the year of death. If the pension is a personal pension (see **Chapter 9**, 'Pensions' for a discussion of the different types of pension), then the lump sum will be linked to fund value. When an individual has a pension with life cover, it is recommended that they top up the life cover to the amount they require. This may not be necessary – it depends on the circumstances of the individual and the level of the pension scheme fund.

Other Life Insurance/Assurance Products

There are several versions of life assurance, however, only two more are briefly mentioned in this text. *Convertible renewable term assurance* gives the insured person the right to extend the insurance period without further medical underwriting, or convert to an investment plan (this is useful for older people) and *increasing term assurance* increases the level of cover in line with inflation or annually by a fixed amount. The annual cost of the premiums paid to an increasing term assurance policy usually also increases.

Finally, many companies may provide a *company life assurance scheme* for their employees. This scheme is usually administered by the employer on behalf of an insurance company. Except for time spent administering the policy, the company does not usually contribute to the scheme. Employees should shop around to determine if the life assurance is good value and decide whether they need it before electing to take it. Some companies pay life assurance for their employees as a perk. In these instances the annual premiums are treated as a benefit-in-kind and the employee is taxed on their value.

Other Commonly Insured Risks

Health

In the UK the National Health Service provides the full range of health care free for all residents regardless of their income. However, in many instances the waiting lists are long and individuals opt to take out private medical insurance to have their (or their family's) medical complaint dealt with more quickly. In recognition of this, tax relief at 20% of the premium amount is available. In the ROI the health service is not totally free to all, and private medical insurance is a necessary expense. In the ROI all residents are entitled to public health service but some have to pay a small contribution.

Private Medical Insurance (PMI): Each medical insurance contract is different and the medical service on offer varies from contract to contract and depends on the individual's circumstances. For example, people with pre-existing conditions are typically not covered for these conditions in the future. PMI typically pays for treatment for acute curable conditions. The treatment might be an operation or a short-term course of treatment. PMI does not cover long-term illness, or chronic illness. So PMI is likely to cover the diagnosis stage, but not treatment, where the diagnosis is long term.

Different PMI policies offer different levels and ranges of treatment. Usually the more you pay for, the more you get. In most instances the policyholder has to get authorisation from the PMI provider before getting treatment and may be restricted to a set number of medical care providers that the insurance company uses.

PMI can be provided by an employer as a perk, and as such PMI is treated as a benefit-in-kind and its value is taxable on the individual.

Debt Repayments

Payment Protection Insurance (PPI): Payment protection insurance is a form of income protection which aims to cover debt repayments when an individual is unable to repay their debt because of sickness, an accident, unemployment or death. It is usually sold by debt providers to an individual when they are obtaining a loan. The insurance usually covers the loan repayment for a set period of time, typically 12 months. After this time the individual has to start repaying the loan from other means. This insurance has received bad press over the past decade as several debt providers were found guilty of mis-selling this product to individuals, many of whom could not claim on the insurance because they did not meet the conditions for the insurance in the first place. In several instances policies were sold to self-employed individuals who were exempt from being able to claim against the policy. In addition, it was not explained that the policy would not pay out for six months, or only paid six-month repayments.

Many debt providers informed the individuals that the debt was only available if this insurance was taken up, or at least that is what the consumers were led to believe. Indeed, several used to quote the monthly repayment on a loan gross (including this insurance premium) and some still do, though cover themselves by showing the repayment without the insurance! PPI is considered to be an expensive form of protection with the cost ranging up to a quarter of the amount borrowed. Some credit unions provide this insurance cover for free.

Two other insurances commonly provided by credit unions are now discussed.

Death Benefit Insurance

Death Benefit Insurance (DBI) is provided by many credit unions for their members. This insurance provides basic life cover at an affordable price. The aim of the insurance is to relieve the burden of bereavement costs. The available cover varies from credit union to credit union, but the minimum cover offered by credit unions in the ROI is €1,300, while the maximum is €3,250. The minimum cover offered by credit unions in NI is £1,000 and the maximum is £2,500. For example, Ballyhackamore Credit Union Limited (a credit union located in NI) assures a £2,000 lump sum to be payable on the death of the member to the person nominated by the member on payment of a £12.68 annual premium. To qualify for this insurance, the member typically must be over 16 years of age and to have joined before reaching 70 years of age (conditions may vary across credit unions).

Life Savings Insurance

Life Savings Insurance (LSI) is provided by many credit unions free of charge for their eligible members as an incentive to save regularly. The benefit is paid out on the death of the member to a person nominated by the member. The amount of benefit typically depends on the amount and length of time savings (shares) have been lodged/invested in the credit union (without withdrawal).

Car Insurance

Many adults own a car and, by law, must obtain car insurance to drive on public roads. Car insurance can provide financial protection for the driver against physical damage to the car and personal injury resulting from a car crash, and it also protects the driver against claims by other persons involved in a collision. Some car insurance may also pay out when the vehicle is stolen or damaged in other situations (accidental damage). There are several different levels of insurance, but the two most commonly used in the UK and in the ROI are 'third party, fire and theft' and 'fully comprehensive' insurances. These are now discussed briefly.

Third party, fire and theft insurance covers all third party liabilities and also pays out the value of the vehicle to the insurer (less an *excess* – an amount of money that the driver agrees to pay in the event of an insurance claim) in the event of the vehicle being destroyed by fire, either maliciously or due to a vehicle fault, and theft itself.

Fully *comprehensive insurance* covers all third party, fire and theft risks and, in addition, covers damage to the vehicle, injury and vandalism. It is the most expensive type of vehicle insurance cover.

Car insurance is particularly expensive for young people, and the premiums are also impacted on by the driver's occupation type, location, agreed excess level, driving offences received by the driver and previous claims made on any car insurance policy. A no-claims bonus is generally accumulated by the driver, and this provides a discount of the full premium price. The discount generally increases for each year that the driver does not make a claim. Most car insurance companies allow this no-claims discount bonus to be protected in the event of a claim.

House Insurance

Any individual who owns a property should have house insurance. This typically has two parts (house and contents) which can be purchased separately or as a combined product. Mortgage providers typically require that the rebuild value of the property be insured. The cover can be general or can include accidental damage (more expensive). Each policy is different with the premium amount being affected by a number of factors, such as location (crime rate in area), risk of flooding, prior claims, age of building, construction type, number of bedrooms, rebuild value, excess level agreed, etc. Individuals should read their policies carefully before agreeing to them to make sure that they have the cover that they require. Whether the individual owns a property or rents a property they should consider contents insurance to cover the replacement cost of their property (furniture, carpets, jewellery, computers, electrical goods, etc.) in the event of theft or damage (flood, fire, etc.) Payouts on accidental damage are also possible, though these policies are more expensive.

Conclusion

Insurance is a difficult topic on which to advise. Most people have several demands on their funds, and liquidity can be an issue. Even so, it is generally regarded as prudent for individuals to take out car insurance, home and contents insurance, some form of income protection and critical health cover. Premiums to insurance companies for insurance/assurance products range in price and in quality. It is always advisable to shop around and to read policy documents carefully. When a policy document says premiums may rise in the future, or premiums may be reviewed, then assume it is likely that they will rise. When a death or illness cover policy is started it is important not to let it lapse, as it is more expensive to initiate these products as individuals get older.

Finally, insurance/assurance products differ in price as they are tailored to take into account the risks associated with the individual being insured. Premiums are affected by age, gender, general state of health and risk factors. Risk indicators include medical history of family, being a smoker, a drinker, taking drugs and participating in extreme sports. All insurance/assurance companies will ask questions about these types of activities. The answers will impact on the price of the premiums. When an individual provides incorrect details, the insurance/assurance is invalid.

KEY TERMS

Basic life assurance policy
Company life assurance
   schemes
Comprehensive insurance
Convertible renewable
   term assurance
Critical illness
Death Benefit Insurance (DBI)
Decreasing protection policy
Disability benefit
Employment and Support
   Allowance (ESA)
Excess (insurance)
Family income benefit
Fixed-term cover
Illness benefit (IB)
Incapacity benefit
Income protection
Increasing term assurance

Invalidity pensions
Investment policies
Life assurance
Life savings insurance
Mortgage life cover
Mortgage protection
   insurance
Payment Protection Insurance
   (PPI)
Permanent Health Insurance
   (PHI)
Personal pension term assurance
Private Medical Insurance (PMI)
Real life cover
Statutory Sick Pay (SSP)
Term policy
Third party, fire and theft
   insurance
Whole-of-life policies

Review Questions

(Suggested solutions to **Review Questions** are provided in **Appendix 4**.)

Question 5.1

Explain the difference between insurance and assurance.

Question 5.2

Explain the difference between a term policy and a whole-of-life policy.

Question 5.3

What is the most important insurance for a family man with three children?

Question 5.4

A young married couple with limited income and one incapacitated child are in the process of buying their first home. They are considering which of two 25-year mortgage loan offers to accept: Offer A or Offer B. The interest rates are identical, but one offer (Offer 'A') does not insist on mortgage protection life insurance, while Offer 'B' is conditional on taking out life assurance with a range of options including a term policy and a 'whole-of-life' policy. The couple are unsure of the differences between Offer A and B and think it would be easier to accept Offer 'A' and take out some life assurance in a few years' time when their income increases.

Required:

(i) Explain the difference between a term policy and a whole-of-life policy.
(ii) In the context of the young married couple advise them on the suggested choice of policy, giving the reasons for your choice.

6 Marks

(Source: Chartered Accountants Ireland, CAP 1, Summer 2009 (Extract from Q7))

CHAPTER 6

DEBT MANAGEMENT

LEARNING OBJECTIVES

Upon completion of this chapter, readers should be able to:

- explain the meaning of the key terms listed at the end of the chapter;
- differentiate between good debt and bad debt;
- list five pitfalls that can lead to high debt levels;
- prepare a debt schedule;
- calculate the cost of debt using the time value of money;
- measure an individual's debt exposure;
- calculate the quickest way to eliminate expensive debt, given an individual's financial position and current earnings; and
- explain the different routes to manage debts when repayment in full is unlikely.

Introduction: Debt Management

Not all debt is considered bad. Credit referencing companies rank different types of debt, with some types of debt such as mortgages or student loans being considered investing activities that add value to individuals. Mortgages are discussed in detail in **Chapter 8**, 'Investments'. In short, any debt which is used to acquire an appreciating asset or which improves overall financial health, is generally regarded as '*good debt*'. Whereas any debt which is used to finance items that depreciate in value or are consumed, is considered to be '*bad debt*'. This type of debt, while sometimes necessary, may lead to an unhealthy financial position and may cause financial distress.

Credit card debt, holiday loans and car loans are regarded as examples of bad debt, even if the debt is affordable. In this day and age, obtaining debt for consumables is easy. It is more difficult to obtain debt to purchase a property. A person can creep into financial difficulty without noticing the extent of the problem until it is too late. This chapter starts by providing information on one of the most common forms of personal credit – credit cards – including their advantages and disadvantages. Financial distress, including actions that can lead to financial distress, is then explained. The latter part of the chapter focuses on debt management, including the debt management schedule, ratios to monitor debt, crisis planning and insolvency options.

Credit Cards

Credit cards are cards that are used to pay for goods or services or even to withdraw cash. They provide instant credit to the cardholder up to a limit and are accepted by most traders as a means of payment. When a purchase is made by the cardholder, the credit card company pays the trader the amount due less commission (typically 1%–3%). The credit facility is revolving with compulsory monthly minimum payments, interest charges and further credit being available (up to the credit limit). The credit card company sends a monthly statement to the cardholder identifying transactions in the month, interest charged, repayments made, the balance outstanding and the credit facility available. Most credit card companies do not charge interest on transactions when the balance is paid off each month (the credit cardholder gets up to one month of free credit); however, if the full balance is not paid, interest starts to accrue from the date of purchase even if the minimum repayment is made. If the minimum repayment is not made, then a late fee/penalty applies.

Many credit card companies provide offers to individuals to attract them to transfer their business to them. These offers are typically at a low Annual Percentage Rate (APR – discussed later) or at zero interest for a period of time. This means that a credit card account can actually be subject to different rates, a low rate for balance transfers and the normal rate for purchases made using the credit card since that date. When repayments are made by the credit cardholder, they are typically allocated against the zero interest/low interest balances first until they are repaid in full before being allocated against the higher rate balances. Interest rates vary between credit card companies and can increase dramatically if the credit cardholder misses a payment.

Credit Cards: Advantages

Credit card debt is quick, flexible and convenient. It allows the credit card holder access to a short credit period for small purchases. When the balance is repaid in full monthly, this credit is free to the credit cardholder. Credit cards usually provide fraud protection, and some also provide warranties on products purchased using the credit card, car rental insurance and travel insurance at no cost. Some credit cards provide rewards to the credit card holders based on usage. This is particularly common with retail store credit cards such as Sainsbury or Tesco.

Credit Cards: Disadvantages

If a payment is missed, the penalties can be high. The interest rate is likely to increase dramatically and/or penalty charges apply. Credit card companies can also increase the interest rate just to increase their own revenue without the credit cardholder making a default on payment. Most traders/companies who accept credit cards as a form of payment inflate their prices for all customers to cover the cost of the commission that they have to pay to the credit card company. Finally, it is argued that individuals with credit cards are likely to spend more in general and, in particular, to spend more on consumables, which is not good for the overall financial position of the individual.

Financial Distress

Financial distress is a reduction in *financial efficiency* as a result of having insufficient levels of cash. When an individual is being efficient with their resources, they are taking steps to acquire goods at a low rate. For example, by purchasing in bulk, an individual is able to obtain goods at a lower cost. If the individual does not have sufficient funds to purchase the items in bulk, then they will have to buy the goods individually at a higher price. Overall, the individual is worse off.

In the UK, many individuals on low income purchase their electricity or gas using card meters. These cards can be purchased for amounts starting at £5 upwards. The electricity/gas sold through meters is more expensive than that which is purchased when an individual has a credit account with the utility company and pays their energy in one bill. This practice has received much attention from the UK Government and pressure groups, who argue that the utility companies are causing financial distress. The result is that energy prices for this method of paying for supply have fallen. However, the utility companies still differentiate between individuals who can afford to pay and those who have difficulty by allowing a discount for payment received by direct debit. Again, not getting this discount is deemed to be an example of a financial distress cost.

When it is clear that an individual is experiencing financial distress, it is likely that the focus of a financial plan will be on *crisis management*, whereupon steps will be suggested that reduce the debt burden and reduce the financial distress being experienced.

Common pitfalls that lead to a person ending up with too much debt are now outlined.

PITFALLS THAT LEAD TO HIGH DEBT LEVELS

Using credit for daily consumables: Unless the credit card bill is cleared each month, it is bad practice to use credit cards for consumable purchases such as groceries, fuel, or clothing. The temptation is always to buy more than is affordable as credit card users are typically not as aware of the total amount being spent in a period. When using cash to purchase daily consumables, an individual is more aware of the amount available and is more likely to make decisions to remain within their budgeted monthly amount.

Using credit when cash is available: This is a bad habit. Some people want to hold onto cash and to use credit because the credit is available

Continued

and psychologically they do not want to pay for the good just yet. However, if there is a reluctance to pay for a good now, it is likely that this reluctance will only increase after the good has been consumed.

Using debt to repay debt: Discussed below. Using credit cards to repay credit cards is not good practice. It is not dealing with the debt problem. It is just rearranging it, usually at a cost each time! In most instances, a person ends up worse off than when they began.

Spending more than is earned: If a person takes home €/£1,000 each month and spends €/£1,400, then this will ruin their financial position. The monthly deficit might come from savings accumulated from a windfall gain made (inheritance or a gain on the sale of a property) or might come from debt sources, such as a credit card or a loan.

Spending money you do not have: Taking out a loan to purchase something (such as a car) when there is insufficient income to cover the repayments will result in financial distress.

Efficiency in Debt Management

Debt management forms part of most financial plans. To help make decisions in respect of debt, it is good practice to prepare a *'debt schedule'*. This schedule details all the types of debt held (including loans from family members), the balance outstanding on the schedule preparation date, the interest rate charged, the minimum payment agreed and the date that the payment has to be made. A debt schedule might look like the one shown below in **Figure 6.1**:

Figure 6.1: Debt Schedule

Debt schedule on: xx/xx/xxxx				
Debt source	Interest rate	Balance	Minimum repayment	Date due
TOTAL				

The schedule should rank the debts. Bad debt usually has higher interest rates and should be paid off first. Where bad debt has the same rate of interest as good debt, it should also be targeted for additional repayments before good debt is cleared. The *minimum repayment* is required to be disclosed, not the actual repayment, as this information can be used for debt planning. The interest rates included should be comparable. They should reflect the *Annual Percentage Rate (APR)*. The APR, otherwise known as the *Effective Annual Rate (EAR)*, expresses the interest rate on debt for a whole year (annualised). The APR can be expressed in two ways: the nominal APR and the effective APR. The *nominal APR* is the annualised interest rate excluding set-up fees and charges, whereas the *effective APR* includes the set-up fees and charges as part of the annualised interest cost of the loan.

Calculating the APR

In some instances, credit cards are advertised with monthly rates (the yearly APR is also provided, though may not be as prominently positioned). Advertising that the rate charged on a credit card is 1% per month seems better than advertising it as 12.68% per year. The APR takes into account the fact that lenders always charge interest on the full balance that is outstanding, which includes the interest that they have already charged. So interest is charged on interest. For example, if you borrowed €/£1,000 at 1% per month, then in month one you would get charged €/£10 interest (€/£1,000 × 1%); in month two, however, you would get charged €/£10.10 interest (€/£1,010 × 1%) and so on. In yearly terms, the amount of interest charged would be €/£126.83 not €/£120.00 as you might have expected. This problem is more accentuated the higher the interest rate.

The monthly rate can be converted to the yearly rate using the following formula:

$$\text{Yearly rate} = (1 + r)^n - 1$$

Where **r** is the interest rate being charged for the period and **n** is the number of periods.

WORKED EXAMPLE 6.1: MONTHLY AND YEARLY RATES

A credit card advertises a rate of 1.6% per month.

Required: Calculate the yearly interest rate equivalent.

Solution: The yearly rate of interest is:

$$((1 + 0.016)^{12} - 1) = 20.98\%$$

Calculating the APR when the Repayments are Fixed Amounts

An *annuity* describes a certain pattern of cash flows, wherein a set amount of cash flow is received, or paid, over a set period of time. For example, if you borrowed €/£4,000 now from a bank (this is commonly referred to as the *present value* of the debt), and the terms of the loan require you to repay €/£1,000 every year for five years starting at the end of the year, then this would be described as a five-year annuity of €/£1,000. The total repayments amount to €/£5,000, and you might think that this repayment schedule is costing you 4% per year or €/£1,000 in total (€/£5,000 – €/£4,000). This is calculated at 20% (€/£1,000/€/£5,000) over five years which equates to 4% per year (20%/5). However, the cost is actually higher because the €/£4,000 is not outstanding for the whole five years. In fact, €/£1,000 is being paid off each year. So what you need to determine is the interest rate that is charged which equates five yearly €/£1,000 payments to a present value of €/£4,000.

The relationship between the loan received and the repayment amounts is expressed in the following equation:

Present Value = Annuity × Annuity Factor

The present value is the amount being borrowed now. The annuity is the yearly amount being repaid and the *annuity factor* is a statistic which represents the present value of the interest rate that is being charged for the periods involved. This text is not concerned with teaching mathematics, so the annuity factors are provided in tables in **Appendix 3** for rates ranging from 1% to 30% for annual periods of up to 15 periods. To read the tables, select the number which represents the number of periods involved and go along the row that corresponds to this number of periods, until you come to the amount that equates to, or is close to, the annuity factor value worked out from the above equation. When the periods extend beyond 15 periods, the formula provided in **Appendix 2** can be used.

To return to the previous example:

> Present Value = Annuity × Annuity Factor
> €/£4,000 = €/£1,000 × annuity factor
> Annuity factor = €/£4,000/€/£1,000
> Annuity factor = 4 (five periods at X%)

By reading the tables this equates to 8% (the annuity factor for five periods at 8% is 3.993, which is just below the target amount of 4).

Therefore, when the cash flows and the amount that is being borrowed are known, the annuity tables can be used to decipher the actual APR that is being charged.

WORKED EXAMPLE 6.2: NOMINAL APR

Amanda's car insurance premium is now due. The new premium is €/£1,200 for the year. The company offers two payment alternatives. The first is to pay the full €/£1,200 immediately. The second allows Amanda to repay the premium monthly at the rate of €/£106.62 per month. Amanda considers this to be very competitive.

She explains that she is only paying €/£6.62 per month for the financing and this equates to 6.62%.

Required:

Advise Amanda of the real annual percentage interest rate being applied to this finance deal.

Solution:

The yearly rate of interest is:

€/£106.62 annuity for 12 periods at X% = €/£1,200
Annuity for 12 periods at X% = €/£1,200/€/£106.62
Annuity for 12 periods at X% = 11.255

Using the annuity tables this equates to 1% per month.
Which is the equivalent of 12.68% ($(1+0.01)^{12}-1$) per year.

As mentioned earlier, the effective APR includes all the charges associated with obtaining debt, including set-up fees to provide an overall annual cost of debt. This is now further examined in **Worked Example 6.3**:

WORKED EXAMPLE 6.3: EFFECTIVE APR

Sean is going to receive a legacy in four to five months' time and has just obtained a €/£15,000 loan from the bank at a rate of 1.2% per month for six months to purchase a vehicle. The full €/£15,000 plus interest and charges is to be paid off in full at the end of the six-month period. The bank charges an up-front fee of €/£450 for setting up the loan.

Continued

Required:

(a) Calculate the lump sum that will have to be repaid to the bank in six months' time.
(b) Calculate the nominal APR for the six-month loan.
(c) Calculate the effective APR for the six-month loan.

Solution:

(a) The repayment will be:

	€/£
Capital	15,000
Fee	450
Interest*	1,113
Total repayment expected	16,563

	€/£
*Interest:	
Month 1: €/£15,000 × 1.2% =	180.00
Month 2: €/£15,180 × 1.2% =	182.16
Month 3: €/£15,362.16 × 1.2% =	184.35
Month 4: €/£15,546.50 × 1.2% =	186.56
Month 5: €/£15,733.06 × 1.2% =	188.80
Month 6: £15,921.86 × 1.2% =	191.06
Total interest	1,112.93

(b) The nominal APR on the loan is:

$$(1.012)^{12} - 1 = 15.4\%$$

(c) The effective APR on the loan is:

€/£450/€/£15,000 = 0.03 (3%) for 6 months
which annualised comes to $(1.03)^2 - 1 = 6.09\%$

Overall interest rate = 21.49% (15.4% + 6.09%)

In many instances, companies stress the *affordability* of the product they are selling, by focusing on the small size of the monthly/weekly repayment. The annual interest rate being charged is clearly disclosed in the agreement, but is typically not highlighted as part of the marketing strategy.

Measuring an Individual's Debt Exposure

One method of assessing a person's *debt exposure* is to calculate their *personal debt ratio*. This ratio is also known as the *debt-to-income ratio* and is expressed as follows:

$$\frac{\text{Monthly spend on debt}}{\text{Net income}} \times 100 = \%$$

Where '*monthly spend on debt*' is either the total amount paid on debt in the month, or the amount paid on bad debt.

WORKED EXAMPLE 6.4: DEBT-TO-INCOME RATIO

R. Kyle takes home €/£2,500 each month from his regular employment and gets €/£500 per month in rent. He pays €/£400 per month to cover the minimum repayment on credit card A and €/£200 to cover the minimum repayment required on credit card B. His mortgage amounts to €/£1,000 per month, he pays €/£500 per month to the bank for his car loan and €/£100 per month to the credit union for his holiday loan.

Required:

(a) Calculate the debt-to-income ratio for R. Kyle for a typical month from the information provided above (calculate both versions – total debt ratio and the bad debt-to-income ratio).
(b) Advise Mr Kyle as to the appropriateness of his current debt position.

Solution:

(a) Mr Kyle's debt-to-income ratio is as follows:

$$\frac{\text{Monthly spend on debt}}{\text{Net income}} \times 100 = \%$$

Where the total monthly spend on debt is €/£2,200 (€/£400 + €/£200 + €/£1,000 + €/£500 + €/£100).

Total income is €/£3,000 (€/£2,500 + €/£500).

$$\frac{€/£2,200}{€/£3,000} \times 100 = 73.3\%$$

Continued

The total monthly spend on bad debt is €/£1,200 (€/£400 + €/£200 + €/£500 + €/£100).

$$\frac{€/£1,200}{€/£3,000} \times 100 = 40\%$$

(b) Mr Kyle is over-geared. He has too much debt. This is a risky situation to be in, as there is little left over after servicing debt to pay for living expenses, for making savings and for contributing to investments for his retirement. Mr Kyle's disposable income will be seriously affected by changes in interest rates.

As a priority Mr Kyle should be advised to focus his attention on reducing the extent of his bad debt. As a benchmark, an individual should aim to have a total debt-to-income ratio of about 36% and Mr Kyle has a ratio of twice this. If Mr Kyle pays off all his bad debts, it will still take 33% of his disposable income to service his mortgage. Though this is acceptable, he should be advised to aim to reduce this further in the future.

Regardless of whether debt is good or bad, a lower debt-to-income ratio is considered favourable. As mentioned in the above example, a total debt-to-income ratio of 36% or lower is considered to be acceptable, with a total ratio of below 30% considered to be excellent. A ratio of over 40% is considered to be too high. When the ratio focuses on bad debt only, a ratio of over 10% is considered to be too high.

Debt Management: Crisis Planning

A variety of options are available to an individual for managing their debt exposure when they cannot service their current debt repayments from current income. These are now explained in brief.

Debt Restructuring

There are a variety of loan companies which strive to help individuals manage their debt, by bundling it all into one product, or by encouraging individuals to increase their good debt (mortgage) to repay their bad debt (credit cards). This is called *debt restructuring*.

Repaying debt using debt is never the best solution, but repaying debt with cash is. If an individual increases their mortgage, they end up paying it off over a longer period, which will increase their outgoings over a longer period of time and reduce their ability to build up equity value in their home. This problem is more pronounced when house prices are stagnant or increasing very slowly and inflation is low, as the value of an individual's equity does not rise with general price increases. However, when an individual is facing cash flow problems and experiencing financial distress, then a short-term option may be to renegotiate debts, or to consolidate debts to improve liquidity so that the individual is left with some flexibility and less financial distress.

Care always has to be taken when obtaining debt, even good debt. It is vital to ensure that sufficient liquidity is maintained to fund an individual's lifestyle (assuming the lifestyle is affordable, realistic and is within the individual's overall aim), to accumulate an emergency reserve and to invest for retirement.

Managing Debt (UK)

Administration Order

An individual with debt problems can apply for an administration order. An *administration order* is where an individual can apply to the county court to have all non-priority debts restructured into one consolidated monthly affordable payment. This is possible if the total debt is less than £5,000 and; there is a County Court or High Court judgement against the individual, who cannot pay it in full; money is owed to at least two creditors and the individual can prove that he can afford regular payments. The court will decide on the size of the monthly repayment and can stipulate a lower overall debt level to repay. If the individual can only afford to repay a percentage of his debts, the court will issue a *compensation order* instead. When passed, the individual makes payment to the court and creditors have no further action against the individual so long as the repayments are made (Citizens Advice Bureau, 2010).

Debt Management Plan

The *Debt Management Plan (DMP)* is a Government-supported scheme in which individuals who have personal unsecured debts that are causing financial distress, can get financial advice on debt management (crisis management). An adviser takes details of all the debts owed by the individual, notes the amounts to be repaid, the interest rates, the income of the individual, etc., and makes an assessment of whether the individual can repay. If they can, then the lenders are approached to agree to a more realistic repayment schedule. It is up to the lender to agree to the new repayment schedule. At this stage, they are encouraged to freeze the interest and charges that are being added to the debt. The individual agrees to pay the debt management company a lump sum each month (they charge a fee for the service), and the debt management company apportions this between all the creditors. The debt management company takes their fee off first before distributing the balance between the creditors. The Consumer Credit Counselling Service provides this facility for free. If the individual cannot pay, this option is not open to them and they will have to go into Individual Voluntary Arrangement.

Individual Voluntary Arrangement

Individual Voluntary Arrangements (IVAs) are available to individuals in the UK when they cannot repay their debts and they do not want to be made bankrupt. This arrangement is regulated under the Insolvency Act 1986. It involves setting up a formal contractual repayment agreement between the individual and their lenders, usually for unsecured debts, and is organised by an insolvency practitioner.

The insolvency practitioner assesses the individual's finances and prepares a plan for presentation to the creditors based on the amount of disposable income available and the overall debt outstanding. The repayment schedule is typically set up for a period of about five years, and the repayments are affordable to the individual. A lump sum can also be paid off. After the five-year period, the remaining debt is written off. The creditors are called to a meeting to vote on the proposed repayment plan; if over 75% agree, then the IVA proceeds. As this point, the creditors lose the right to take legal action to recover their balance, provided the individual does not break the terms of the IVA plan. A fee typically has to be paid to the insolvency practitioner, and this comes out in full from the repayments made by the individual.

Debt Relief Order

Debt Relief Orders (DROs) are substitutes for formal bankruptcy. They are available to people who have relatively low levels of debt (less than £15,000), little surplus income (less than £50 per month), few assets (less than £300, excluding one car to the value of £1,000) and who cannot get access to debt relief elsewhere. Individuals can obtain DROs through registered financial advisers, who can complete the application to the Official Receiver online. There is a standard application fee of £90, which is non-refundable if the application is unsuccessful. If approved, the Official Receiver will make the DRO without having to involve the court. This means that the individual's debt will be written off after 12 months, so long as the individual keeps to the terms of the order. In this 12-month period, creditors will not be able to request payment from the individual and cannot charge interest/penalties to the debt. An individual will not be awarded a DRO if they have an existing bankruptcy order, bankruptcy restrictions order, an IVA, or have had a DRO in the last six years.

Bankruptcy

Bankruptcy occurs when an individual legally declares that they are unable to pay their debts. To be eligible, an individual's unsecured debt must outweigh the value of their assets. Lenders/creditors may file a bankruptcy petition with the High Court against the individual in an attempt to recoup some of the funds that are owed to them, or the individual may declare themself bankrupt. This is the worst case scenario for the individual and, indeed, for the lender. A fee of £700 (£175 to the court and £525 to the Official Receiver) is payable to file for bankruptcy. If the Official Receiver approves the bankruptcy, then creditors must stop charging interest on the debt and cannot contact the individual or take legal action to recoup the debt. In some instances, where an individual has disposable income, the Official Receiver may ask the individual to make monthly repayments towards the debts. This is known as an *Income Payment Agreement* (IPA). If the individual has assets, these will also have to be sold with the proceeds going to cover the creditor debts. The balance outstanding to creditors at the end of the process will have to be written off.

Managing Debt (ROI)

Money Advice and Budgeting Service

The *Money Advice and Budgeting Service (MABS)* is a Government-supported scheme in which individuals who have personal unsecured debts that are causing financial distress, can get financial advice on debt management (crisis management). An adviser takes details of all the debts owed by the individual, notes the amounts to be repaid, the interest rates, the income of the individual, etc., and makes an assessment of whether and how much the individual can repay. If they can, then the lenders are approached to agree to a more realistic repayment schedule. It is up to the lender to agree to the new repayment schedule. At this stage, they are encouraged to freeze the interest and charges that are being added to the debt. The individual agrees to pay the debt management company (they charge a fee for the service) a lump sum each month, and the debt management company apportions this between all the creditors. The debt management company takes their fee off first before distributing the balance between the creditors. A number of government backed charities provide this facility for free. If the individual cannot pay, this option is not open to them, and they will have to enter into a Formal Scheme of Arrangement. From 2012, a number of other options are expected to be available and these are discussed below.

Formal Scheme of Arrangement

The *Formal Scheme of Arrangement (FSA)* is otherwise known as an 'Arrangement under the control of the court'. It is an arrangement between the individual and their creditors. At least 60% of the individual's creditors need to agree to the arrangement before it becomes binding on them all. It involves setting up a formal contractual repayment agreement between the individual and their lenders, usually for unsecured debts, and is organised by an insolvency or legal practitioner. When this agreement does not work bankruptcy may need to be considered.

Bankruptcy

Bankruptcy occurs when an individual legally declares that they are unable to pay their debts. To be eligible, an individual's unsecured debt must outweigh the value of their assets. Lenders/creditors may file a bankruptcy petition with the High court against the individual in an attempt to recoup some of the funds that are owed to them or the individual may declare themselves bankrupt. This is the worst case scenario for the individual and, indeed, for the lender. The cost of bankruptcy can be as much as €6,000 (www.nationaldebtrelief.ie). The bankrupt is released from their debts after five years (reduced from 12 years in 2011).

Forthcoming Insolvency Options for Individuals

The European bailout had a number of conditions, one of which was to revise the legislation on personal insolvency. As a result of this, new legislation is expected in 2012. Draft copies of the legislation were available at the time of writing, and this section provides a general introduction to the proposed system going forward, but may be subject to change when the legislation is finally agreed on. Three types of debt settlement options for individuals are proposed that do not involve going to court: a Debt Relief Certificate; a Debt Settlement Agreement and a Personal Insolvency Arrangement. These are now discussed in turn.

Debt Relief Certificate: It is proposed that a ***Debt Relief Certificate (DRC)*** will allow for the full write-off of small, unsecured debts of up to €20,000 after a one-year period. To be eligible to apply, applicants need to prove that they have disposable income of less than €60 per month and assets and savings of less than €400 (assets do not include a car with a value of less than €1,200, household equipment and equipment used by the individual for their employment). The application for a DRC will be made to the Insolvency Service through an approved intermediary and will cost €90 (non-refundable). When a DRC is granted, creditors who are listed on the DRC cannot start action, legal or otherwise, to reclaim their debt. At the time of writing, there was no clause forbidding creditors from continuing to accrue interest/penalties on the debt over the one-year period. An individual obtaining a DRC cannot apply for another within six years and can only obtain two DRCs in their lifetime.

Debt Settlement Agreement: The ***Debt Settlement Agreement (DSA)*** option is open to individuals with unsecured debts in excess of €20,000 (not mortgages). In this instance, the individual agrees to pay some or all of the debt outstanding. To obtain a DSA, an individual has to appoint a personal insolvency trustee who applies to the Insolvency Service for a protective certificate. This will provide 30 days of grace during which creditors are unable to take action against the individual to reclaim funds. The personal insolvency trustee will then prepare and send a DSA to the creditors for their agreement. The DSA will set out the repayment plan over a five-year period and will detail any conditions. If over 65% agree, then the DSA proceeds, and the DSA is formally registered by the Insolvency Service. Assuming all the debt repayments agreed to in the DSA have been made by the end of the five-year period, then all the remaining outstanding debts identified in the DSA would be written off. Individuals cannot apply for another DSA within a ten-year period.

Personal Insolvency Arrangement: The ***Personal Insolvency Arrangement (PIA)*** is an option for individuals with secured and unsecured debts of between €20,001 and €3,000,000. It has to be applied for by a personal insolvency trustee. The personal insolvency trustee applies to the Insolvency Service for a protective certificate, which protects the individual for a period of between 40 and 60 days from action by their creditors. The personal insolvency trustee prepares the PIA, which typically includes a restructuring of mortgage debt (writing down an element of this and extending the duration of the mortgage, suggesting a lower interest rate) and a payment plan for unsecured debt covering a period of up to six years. The individual cannot be forced to sell their principal private property (their home) as part of the arrangement. The creditors are invited to a creditors' meeting and, if over 65% agree to the PIA, then it is registered by the Insolvency Service in the Personal Insolvency Register. The individual must notify the personal insolvency trustee if their financial circumstances improve within the term of the PIA so the arranged repayments can be adjusted upwards. If the individual does not fulfil the terms of the PIA, then the creditors can file for bankruptcy. Where the PIA is successfully completed, all the remaining unsecured debts covered by the PIA are discharged. The individual will still be liable for their mortgage but on restructured terms.

Conclusion

Debt should never be taken lightly; it is usually easy to obtain, is costly and results in cash outflows and financial risk. Financial risk usually leads to liquidity problems and financial distress. It may even impact on an individual's personal welfare due to stress. If debt gets out of control, an individual may end up bankrupt. There are serious legal consequences to becoming bankrupt, and it will result in a black mark being placed on the individual's credit record, which will impact on their ability to access credit in the future.

Not all debt is regarded as bad. Debt that is used to increase an individual's worth is regarded as good debt, while debt that does not is considered to be bad debt. Even when the debt being sourced is good debt, an individual should not accept debt unless they can afford it. Good financial planning using projected cash flow budgeting and projected net worth statements should highlight the affordability of debt or may identify when the item can be purchased in cash, if a savings option is taken. A rule of thumb is that cash flows spent on debt should not exceed 36% of an individual's disposable monthly income and about a quarter of this should be on bad debt.

KEY TERMS

Administration order
Affordability
Annuity
Annuity factor
Annual Percentage Rate (APR)
Bad debt
Bankruptcy
Credit cards
Compensation Order
Crisis management
Debt exposure
Debt management
Debt management plan (DMP)
Debt relief certificate (DRC)
Debt relief order (DRO)
Debt restructuring
Debt schedule
Debt settlement agreement (DSA)
Debt-to-income ratio
Effective APR

Effective annual rate (EAR)
Financial distress
Financial efficiency
Formal scheme of arrangement (FSA)
Good debt
Income payment agreement (IPA)
Individual voluntary
    arrangement (IVA)
Minimum repayment
Money Advice and Budgeting
    Service (MABS)
Monthly spend on debt
Nominal APR
Personal debt ratio
Personal insolvency arrangement
    (PIA)
Present value

WEBSITES THAT MAY BE OF USE

There are many sites that are geared towards giving advice on debt management. A number have been highlighted here, though a Google search would provide you with a wealth of information.

- For information on how to manage debt in the UK, visit: *www.debtfreedirect.co.uk*
- For information on insolvency in the UK, visit: *www.insolvency.gov.uk*
- For information on how to manage debt in the ROI, visit: *www.nationaldebtrelief.ie*
- For more information on insolvency in the ROI, visit: *www.moneyguideireland.com*

REVIEW QUESTIONS

(Suggested solutions to **Review Questions** are provided in **Appendix 4**.)

Question 6.1

Seamus has taken out a car loan which attracts an interest rate of 10% per year. The loan is for a one-year period, with the repayments being made monthly.

Required:

Calculate the APR applicable for this loan.

Question 6.2

What is the difference between good debt and bad debt?

Question 6.3

Fernando has just received a pay increase that will result in him having €/£500 additional cash from his employment each month. Fernando has approached you to get some advice on the quickest and best way to pay off his credit card bill of €/£5,000. He informs you that he is paying interest on the card at the rate of 24.8% APR. At present he is paying the minimum repayment amount of €/£300 per month to the credit card company, but his repayment just about covers the current month's expenditure and the interest. The debt on the card has not fallen over the past number of months and this is worrying Fernando as he is considering purchasing a property and thinks that the bank manager will look poorly on his inability to clear the credit card and to raise a deposit. He currently has €/£2,000 in his current account, which he has earmarked for a deposit on a property.

Required:

(a) Calculate the monthly interest rate being charged by the credit card company.
(b) Calculate the current monthly spend on the credit card on consumables by Fernando.
(c) In light of your answer to (b) advise Fernando on a repayment schedule to undertake, to repay the credit card debt. The debt should be repaid quickly, though should not leave Fernando having liquidity problems each month.

Question 6.4

What are the advantages of an individual entering into an IVA (NI) or an FSA (ROI) when they are experiencing financial distress?

Question 6.5

Which of the following debts should an individual who has just inherited €/£15,000 pay off/reduce first?

(i) A loan received from the individual's parents for €/£10,000.
(ii) A student loan of €/£50,000 which charges interest at 1% above inflation rates (currently 2.5%).
(iii) The credit card debt of €/£8,000 which has an effective annual percentage rate of 21%.
(iv) The mortgage on their home of €/£120,000 which has an effective annual percentage rate of 7%.

Question 6.6

Which of the following individuals is likely to have to pay the highest interest and finance charges?

(i) A person with a mortgage, who has never missed a repayment and who pays their bills on time.
(ii) A person who pays the minimum repayment on their credit card each month.
(iii) A person who pays off their full credit card balance each month.
(iv) A person with quite a bit of debt who missed one repayment two years ago.

Question 6.7

Which of the following is the best way to manage your credit card expenditure?

(i) Spend right up to the credit card's limit as they only charge 2% interest per month.
(ii) Pay the interest off each month.
(iii) Pay the balance off in full each month.
(iv) Pay the minimum repayment as suggested by them each month.

Question 6.8

What is the monthly payment on a five-year car loan for €/£16,000 at an annual interest rate of 12%?

Question 6.9

Barbara Scratchett receives a net salary after tax of €/£2,600 each month from her regular employment. She normally receives rental income of €/£600 per month but has to make mortgage loan payments of €/£800 (interest element €/£450) on this property. She owns her own residence and pays €/£900 per month on this mortgage, which she borrowed more than 10 years ago and now receives no tax relief on the interest.

Barbara has €/£6,000 'emergency' savings, earning 1% per annum deposit interest. Over the years, she has experienced occasional rental tenant problems requiring expensive repairs and unpaid rent and electricity bills exceeding tenants' deposits. In some years she had no tenants for several months between lettings. However, given the recent poor performance of her defined contribution pension plan, she regards the rental property as essential for her retirement.

She pays €/£300 per month to cover the minimum repayment on her credit card and, although the credit card company states the APR is 20.98%, the monthly interest charge is only 1.6%, which she regards as reasonable 'given the safety of not carrying large amounts of cash on the street'.

Barbara pays €/£380 per month to the bank for her car loan which, will be paid off in two years' time, and she puts €/£100 per month into a credit union savings account for Christmas expenses and her annual holiday.

Finally, Barbara's car insurance premium is now due. The premium is €/£2,400 for the year – due to a recent accident and claim resulting in penalty points on her driving licence and the consequent loss of her insurance no-claims bonus.

The insurance company can be paid €/£2,400 in full immediately or by monthly payments of €/£213.24, which seems reasonable to her as it only costs €/£13.24 a month on top of €/£200 which looks like only 6.62%.

Required:

(a) Calculate the debt-to-income ratio for Barbara Scratchett for a typical month.

5 Marks

(b) Advise Barbara as to the appropriateness of her current debt position.

6 Marks

(c) Calculate the interest rate equivalent for the monthly car insurance payment.

4 Marks

Total 15 Marks

(Source: Chartered Accountants Ireland. CAP 1. Summer 2009, Q7)

Question 6.10 (Challenging)

(Suggested Solutions to Challenging Questions are available to lecturers.)

The time value of money is 6%. You owe €/£15,000, which has to be paid in three years' time. What is the maximum sum you would be prepared to pay now to settle this liability?

Question 6.11 (Challenging)

Mary has a credit card that she likes to use on a regular basis. She admits that she does not always manage to clear her credit card when she gets paid at the end of month. When she does try to clear the balance she ends up going into her overdraft and she finds in those months she cannot put anything into savings. Advise Mary as to how she should manage her finances each month.

7 Marks

(Source: Chartered Accountants Ireland, CAP1, Autumn 2011, Q7a)

CHAPTER 7

SAVINGS

Learning Objectives

Upon completion of this chapter, readers should be able to:

- explain the meaning of the key terms listed at the end of the chapter;
- outline some practical steps that can be taken to establish a good savings policy;
- explain what an emergency fund is and provide some guidance on the level of funds to hold for emergencies;
- explain the difference between a current account and a deposit account;
- calculate the return earned on a range of investment products; and
- describe a number of savings products that are available with and without tax breaks.

Introduction: Savings – The Principles

Debt management, savings management and investment management are the three key elements underlying an individual's financial success. If an individual has savings, they do not need to get into debt to obtain perishable goods. They can invest from their savings pot whilst ensuring that they have sufficient emergency funds at hand to cover unforeseen financial requirements. Therefore, the management of savings is very important. It is good practice to get into the habit of saving from an early age. Many individuals do not save, they tend to purchase items using debt and to treat this as a form of saving. However, this ends up being very costly to the individual. Without saving it is impossible to achieve financial security. This chapter starts by explaining a variety of factors that influence household saving. It outlines some practical tips for saving before providing a description of the most commonly used savings products by individuals. Particular attention is afforded to savings products that have tax breaks.

Savings Indicator

The *household savings ratio* provides an indication of the extent of saving activity within a household. It is calculated as household saving divided by household disposable income, where *household saving* is disposable income minus household consumption (Harvey, 2004). There are many reasons cited for explaining the change that occurs in the saving behaviour of households. Berry, Williams and Waldron (2009) suggest a number of influences.

Permanent Income: Consumption theory suggests that households base their current spending decisions on their expected lifetime incomes. Therefore, if income is high now but they expect it to be lower in the future, they are more likely to save for the future. Conversely, if income is low now but expected to increase in the future, individuals are more likely to spend more now (even obtaining debt to spend). Therefore, when there is an economic downturn that reduces wages, individuals are more likely to run down savings in the anticipation of income levels increasing after the economic downturn (they will do this if they anticipate an upturn).

Interest Rates: When the real risk-free after-tax return on savings is positive (greater than inflation), then individuals are more likely to save as the capital value of their funds increases and the return is positive. They will be more willing to curb consumption in this situation. If, however, interest rates are below inflation rates, then the real return is negative, and individuals are more likely to spend their disposable income as they can purchase more from it today than they might be able to do in the future, due to capital depreciation.

Credit Conditions: When the cost of credit increases and the availability of credit reduces, individuals are more likely to save to obtain goods in the future at less costly rates. They will also have less debt to repay as credit has been rationed.

Uncertainty: When there is economic uncertainty, individuals become more uncertain about the future of their main source of income, typically their employment income. In these situations, they are likely to save more.

Wealth: The relationship between wealth and saving is complicated and depends on the nature of the wealth and a variety of factors. In brief, when an individual's wealth increases (equity share portfolio value) they are likely to save less, as the opportunity cost of holding funds in savings is higher and their risk perception is lower. However, many people do not invest in equities or do so indirectly (through pension companies) and are unaware of the state of the stock market.

A reduction in house prices can improve the saving behaviour of first-time buyers (who wish to accumulate a deposit). A rise in house prices may make more credit available, which needs to be paid back. This will reduce disposable income and, consequently, savings.

Government and Corporate Saving: Savings by companies and the Government should result in lower priced products, higher dividends and lower taxation. In principle then, the saving potential of individuals should increase, as their costs (product costs and taxation) have fallen and their income has risen (dividends).

Inflation: When inflation rates are high, the value of financial assets is eroded. Therefore, to maintain wealth, individuals will have to save more (or invest more). So, higher inflation may lead to higher savings (so long as interest rates exceed inflation rates and consumption levels fall).

Demographics: In terms of a country's overall household savings ratio, the lifecycle/permanent-income model (already discussed) suggests that individuals' saving behaviour will change over their lifetimes. Typically, individuals will borrow when they are young and their income is low, save for retirement in middle age when their income is higher, and then run down their savings and investments when retired. This pattern should achieve a certain constant lifestyle. Therefore, when the age structure of the population of a country changes, the country's reported household savings ratio will change accordingly.

The UK yearly household savings ratio has increased from 1.5% of gross income in 2008 to 5.4% in 2011. In the first quarter of 2012 it was 6.4%. The household savings ratio for the ROI reached 8.6% in 2011, up from 1.7% in 2007 (Global Finance, 2012).

In both the UK and the ROI the savings ratio declined in the 10-year period in the run up to the financial crisis in 2007. Some reasons to explain the decline in the savings ratio over this period were provided by the Bank of England in their Quarterly Bulletin (2009) and include:

- The availability of credit in the period to the start of the credit crunch in 2007 encouraged individuals to take out loans; this increased their recurrent expenditure, which reduced their resultant savings amount.
- Rising house prices encouraged people to borrow because of the positive wealth effect of obtaining a property. The additional mortgage repayments reduced the amount of spare cash available for savings.
- Cultural and social trends encouraged an attitude of borrowing and consumer spending.
- Low interest rates meant that, not only was debt cheap, but the return on savings products was low, in many instances lower than inflation which means that the capital value of the savings diminishes over time.
- Greater macroeconomic stability reduced the incentive/perceived need to save.

Many individuals are still suffering because of their lack of thrift in this period. Many households had low savings levels and high debt. This means that financial planning is very important for these households, as it can help to alleviate the problem by highlighting savings that can be made and correctly allocating resources. When individuals cut back on expenditure on consumption, and when they borrow (good debt only), they can accumulate financial assets such as shares, bonds, savings and property. This increases their long-term financial position and security. The relationship between funds raised and assets accumulated can be expressed as follows:

$$S + D = A + H$$

where S is saving, D is the acquisition of debt (good debt), A is the net acquisition of financial assets and H is the net acquisition of housing assets.

So long as liquidity is maintained, an individual should try to maximise their assets accumulated (A + H) from their funds raised (S + D).

PRACTICAL TIPS FOR SAVING

- It is always good to set a *savings goal*. This provides more motivation for the act of saving. A savings goal might include accumulating sufficient funds to have a deposit for purchasing a house (the larger the deposit, the cheaper the finance) or paying a lump sum off your mortgage the next time the mortgage comes up for renegotiation, or accumulating sufficient funds to pay for a family holiday (avoiding interest costs) or a car (avoiding interest costs).
- It is important to establish a separate savings account and to budget to transfer a certain minimum amount of cash to this account each month. If this is treated as a necessary cost, then it will be easier to achieve each month. If the transfer is automated, then this makes it harder to skip or reverse in a month when the individual wishes to spend more.
- Saving should never involve an individual going into debt or obtaining an overdraft (even if short term) in order to save, it should involve budgeting and cutting back on unnecessary expenditure or generating more income in order to meet savings targets.
- It is good practice to decide on a fixed percentage of your earnings to save and to try to stick to this each month. A benchmark of 10% of earnings is suggested, though this should be regarded as a

Continued

minimum and would increase in line with an individual's future financial aims. Indeed, people who are approaching retirement age tend to save between 20% and 30% of their income each year.

- When it is known that expenditure will rise in a month (e.g. in December), then additional amounts should be reserved within the current account to deal with this – it should not be a case of reducing savings.
- When one-off income is received, this should not be used to 'treat' the individual (as can happen!), but should immediately be put into savings; this can speed up the aim of the savings, resulting in increased financial wealth and stability. This is particularly the case if the savings are going to be used to purchase an appreciating asset.
- Where an individual has to utilise their savings to cover an unexpected expenditure, this reduction in savings should be treated as a loan in the mind of the individual that must be repaid to the savings account in the future.

Emergency Funds

A minimum level of savings should be set aside to cover emergencies. This is holding cash for *precautionary motives*. The greatest financial impact on an individual is likely to be the loss of their income due to unexpectedly becoming unemployed. In this instance, income will fall dramatically; however, most individuals have a fixed level of costs that do not fall. The largest of these is probably their mortgage. Insurance can be obtained to cover mortgage repayments in the event of unemployment; however, this will only cover a set number of months, and it takes time to get the claim processed. It is advised that individuals accumulate a minimum level of savings (an *emergency fund*) that is equal to between three and six times their monthly costs. Therefore, when an individual's monthly costs are estimated at €/£2,000 per month, they should keep a minimum level of savings of between €/£6,000 and €/£12,000. Other large unexpected costs can include house or car repairs, and these should be factored into the savings plan. Where a recession is expected, the individual should extend their emergency fund, as the likelihood of losing income is greater. Emergency funds should be kept in an instant-access, high-interest deposit account.

As well as covering emergencies, individuals should save for their retirement. The governments in both the ROI and the UK have established tax-efficient saving schemes to encourage individuals to save for retirement. These schemes earn a strong rate of interest and are not subject to income tax, making them attractive (discussed later).

Savings Types

Like businesses, individuals need to hold cash for transaction motives, precautionary motives and speculative motives. Cash for transaction motives is usually held within a current account with funds for speculative and precautionary motives being held in a deposit account. Both types of account are now considered.

Current Accounts

Current accounts typically offer a very low return (below inflation), and an individual's wealth will be damaged if they retain excess funds in a current account. Current accounts are working accounts that deal with the majority of an individual's transactions. As such, they typically have cheque books attached, debit cards and are used to pay bills and to receive income electronically. Individuals have to keep sufficient funds in their current accounts to deal with these daily transactions (*transactions motive*).

Cash required for *precautionary motives* (to cover cash emergencies as discussed earlier in the chapter) and to allow speculative investment opportunities to be taken when they arise (speculative motives) should be held in a high-interest bearing but flexible deposit account (*instant access*). In addition, cash can be invested in savings products as part of an individual's investment portfolio. Various types of savings products are explained in brief later in this chapter.

Deposit Accounts

The most commonly used taxable savings product is a *'deposit account'*. In the past, these accounts were less flexible, with individuals having to leave monies untouched to receive bonus rates. Now with the advent of Internet banking, competition has turned these into quite flexible products, many of which are instant access. Large supermarket and Internet banking companies usually offer high rates of interest. This has caused high street banks and building societies to become more competitive and to offer rates that are not too far below the bank's lending base rate. It is worthwhile shopping around before a deposit account is selected.

Assessing the Return on Savings

When an individual decides that savings should form part of their overall investment portfolio, it is advisable to consider products that have been earmarked by the Government for tax breaks and products that involve locking the funds away for long periods of time. It is important to consider the overall return on a variety of savings products before selecting one for investment and to compare them on a consistent basis. That involves working out the after-tax cost of taxable savings products and comparing this figure with the tax-free products. This is now considered in **Worked Example 7.1**:

WORKED EXAMPLE 7.1: COMPARISON OF SAVINGS PRODUCTS

George has €/£100,000 to invest, and he wants to invest it in a deposit account. He has identified two deposit accounts: a one-year term deposit on offer from the local bank that provides a guaranteed interest rate of 4% per annum (so long as the funds remain within the account for the year) and a five-year, Government-backed, tax-free savings product with a return of 3.5% per annum so long as the funds remain within the account for the full five years. The tax rate on deposit interest income is 30%.

Required:

(a) Advise George as to the best option to maximise his interest income. Your answer should show the interest differential rate and the benefit in Euros/Sterling.
(b) Would your answer differ if the tax rate on deposit interest fell to 10%?
(c) What other factors might George take into account when making his decision?

Solution:

(a) The net rate payable to George on both products is as follows:

Bank one-year deposit account (4%(1 − 0.30)) =	2.8%
Government backed deposit account =	3.5%
Interest rate differential =	0.7%

Therefore, the overall benefit from investing in the tax-free account is €/£700 (€/£100,000 × 0.7%).

(b) In this instance, the net interest rates would change to:

Bank one-year deposit account (4%(1 − 0.10)) =	3.6%
Government backed deposit account =	3.5%
Interest rate differential =	0.1%

Therefore, the overall benefit from investing in the bank deposit account is €/£100 (€/£100,000 × 0.1%).

Continued

(c) The tax break on interest is subject to change in Government budgets, so the position needs to be reviewed year on year to determine if it is still beneficial to invest in the tax-free product. However, there may be penalties for withdrawing the funds before maturity.

The bank's one-year term account is more liquid, as the funds only have to be locked away for one year, relative to the Government deposit account that requires that the capital remains locked away for five years.

The Government guarantees the investment in the Government deposit account. This is part of the national debt and, hence, is subject to the insolvency risk facing the Government.

When assessing the interest to be earned on a savings product, it is important that you have an understanding of the different types of interest – simple and compound.

Compound Interest: When interest is compounded, it is added to the principal and earns interest in the next period; therefore, the interest will earn interest. The cumulative impact of this process is called compounding.

Simple Interest is the name given to interest that is earned on the principal amount that is not added to the principal when future interest payments are calculated; hence, the interest received does not qualify for interest.

Compound interest relating to one year is known as the Annual Percentage Rate (covered earlier in Chapter 6, 'Debt Management'). The compound interest rate is calculated using the following formula:

$$(1+r)^n - 1 = \text{Compound interest rate}$$

where r is the interest rate for one period and n is the number of periods.

Worked Example 7.2: Compound Interest Rate

Required:

If the bank offers a monthly interest rate of 0.8%, what is the APR?

Solution:

$$\text{The APR is } (1.008)^{12} - 1 = 10\%$$

A formula to calculate the maturity value of an investment is as follows:

$$FV = PV (1 + r)^{nt}$$

where FV is the future value (maturity value of the savings), PV is the present value (the amount deposited, the current amount), r is the notional interest rate earned per period, n is the number of periods compounded per year, and t is the number of periods.

This basically calculates the future value of a present amount invested over a period of time for a set interest rate. **Worked Example 7.3** provides a typical example of this type of calculation:

WORKED EXAMPLE 7.3: IMPACT OF COMPOUND INTEREST ON SAVING

Roger invests €/£50,000 in a five-year term account that pays 2% every six months.

Required:

(a) Calculate the APR.
(b) Calculate the expected maturity value of the term account assuming Roger does not withdraw any funds between now and its maturity.

Solution:

(a) The APR is:

$$(1.02)^2 - 1 = 4.04\%$$

(b) The closing balance on the term deposit account after five years will be:

$$FV = PV (1 + r)^{nt}$$

$$PV = €/£50,000$$

$$r = 2$$

$$n = 2$$

$$t = 5$$

$$FV = €/£50,000 (1.02)^{10}$$

$$= €/£60,950 \text{ (rounded)}$$

There are many savings products on offer from financial institutions, and these change regularly and require investigation each time an individual reviews their savings position and the returns received on their savings products. This review should take place yearly.

This chapter continues by outlining the main savings products that are or have been earmarked for some form of Government tax break in the ROI and in NI.

Saving in the ROI

In normal deposit savings accounts, banks in the ROI take 30% (33% for interest payments made less frequently than in a one-year period) of the gross interest payable to customers from the interest payment and pay this over to the Revenue Commissioners. This is called the *Deposit Interest Retention Tax (DIRT)*. The security of deposits in the ROI is guaranteed by the *Deposit Protection Scheme*, which covers €100,000 in savings per individual per financial institution. The deposit guarantee scheme does not extend to accounts offered by An Post. Funds invested in An Post are 100% Government backed, and their security relies on the solvency of the Government. Individuals who are over 65 years of age and have income of less than €18,000 (€36,000 for a couple), or who are permanently incapacitated, are exempt from having to pay DIRT on any savings product. Since 2007, these individuals can apply to have their interest paid gross. If the individual has not made this claim, they can reclaim the DIRT deducted by the bank by completing Form 54D, 'Claim for Repayment of Deposit Interest Retention Tax for the year 2012', which can be obtained from any local tax office.

Quite a large proportion (over 76%) of adults in the ROI use credit unions; therefore, a brief synopsis of the tax treatment of the returns to be earned on credit union accounts is now provided.

Credit Union Accounts: Credit unions offer share accounts and deposit accounts. There are two types of share account, both of which are entitled to a dividend at the discretion of the credit union. The dividends are subject to taxation. The two accounts are the regular share account and the special share account. DIRT is not deducted at source by the credit union, and the full amount of the dividend is subject to taxation at the individual's marginal rate of tax (which may be as much as 41%, or zero if the individual is not subject to taxation). Special share accounts are subject to DIRT, which is deducted by the credit union at the rate of 30% and paid over by the credit union to the Government. Credit unions also offer special term accounts that have a set term and limits on the amounts that can be deposited in them (the specific details of special term accounts are covered later).

In response to uncertainties arising due to the euro crisis, several individuals from the ROI moved their savings from ROI banks to banks located in other countries in the early part of the financial crisis. Some points that may be relevant when deciding on this course of action are now covered.

Saving Abroad: The treatment of interest on foreign-held savings should be examined in detail, as the treatment may differ from country to country. In general, all EU deposit interest received by Irish persons is liable to taxation at 30% where the tax return is filed on time. If not, the taxpayer's marginal rate applies. Other factors to consider are currency risk and inheritance tax. When funds are placed in a different currency, the value of that currency may change relative to the Euro, and the capital value may fall (or rise). Finally, inheritance tax rates in other countries may differ to that of the ROI, which may be advantageous or disadvantageous depending on the country.

The main savings with tax breaks available for savings in the ROI are now covered.

Savings with Tax Breaks (ROI)

The most publicised Government-targeted saving programme available in the ROI was the *Special Saving Incentive Account (SSIA)*, an interest bearing five-year account that was available for investment by the public between the period from 1 May 2001 to 30 April 2002. These accounts matured between 31 May 2006 and 30 April 2007. Under this scheme, the Government provided €1 for every €4 saved by an individual up to a deposit limit of €254 per month. On maturity, the interest earned on the account was subject to tax at the rate of 23% (this was deducted by the administrating financial institution and sent to the Revenue Commissioners). The contribution to the account by the Government over the life of the account was not taxed (so long as the funds were held intact for the full five years).

A current tax-efficient deposit account on offer by financial institutions is the *Special Term Account*. These are available from financial institutions such as Allied Irish Banks (AIB), Bank of Ireland and credit unions. At the time of writing, AIB was offering a special term account for balances of between €6,000 and €25,000 for periods of between three and five years. The interest rate on offer is 1.5% per year for the three-year account and 2% per year for the five-year account. The tax break is in two parts. For accounts that have a five-year term, tax is not payable on the first €635 of yearly interest. Interest received over €635 is subject to tax at the individual's marginal rate of taxation. A similar rule is applied for accounts that are being held for three years, except the exemption threshold level is €480 per annum.

Certain Government-guaranteed savings accounts are DIRT free. The savings schemes currently available are typically administered by the National Treasury Management Agency.

The *National Treasury Management Agency (NTMA)* is a Government agency that was set up in 1990 to borrow funds for the Exchequer and manage the national debt. Part of that borrowing includes borrowing from the general public, which the NTMA calls its retail customers. A suite of state-backed savings products called *'State savings'* are provided by NTMA and are made available to the general public through the commercial company 'An Post'. An Post has 1,200 branches throughout the ROI that are open six days of the week and offer the 'State savings' products as part of their services. All the 'State savings' products are 100% guaranteed by the Government, many are repayable on demand or within seven days' notice and are free from fees, commission and transaction costs. The range of products available with tax breaks are now discussed in brief:

National Solidarity Bond: Individuals can invest from €500 to €250,000 in National Solidarity Bonds. There are two options: a 10-year bond and a four-year bond. In July 2012, the 10-year bond offered a fixed gross return of 50% over a 10-year period. The return is of two types: an annual interest of 1% (amounting to 10% overall) and a 40% capital gain which is payable on the maturity of the bond. The interest is subject to DIRT (current applicable rate is 30%), but the capital gain is tax-free. Therefore, the net gain is 47%. This equates to an annualised APR of 3.93%. Individuals can access their funds at any time, so long as they give seven days' notice. This would not be advisable, as the individual will no longer be entitled to the capital gain. The four-year bond has the same terms, except the capital gain is 11% gross. This means that the overall gross return is 15% (1% each year for four years and the capital bonus of 11%) or 13.8% after DIRT of 30% on the yearly interest ((4% × 0.7) + 11%). This net APR is 3.29%.

State Guaranteed Savings Certificates (Savings Certificates): Individuals can invest between €50 and €120,000 (or have a joint account of up to €240,000) in Savings Certificates. This savings product provides a fixed return of 21% after 5½ years, so long as the amount invested is not withdrawn. If it is, the return will be lower. The interest paid on the certificates is not taxable on the individual. The return, if held to maturity, equates to an APR of 3.53%.

State Guaranteed Savings Bonds (Savings Bonds): Individuals can invest between €100 and €120,000 (or have a joint account of up to €240,000) in Savings Bonds. This product provides a fixed return of 10% after three years. The return is tax free and equates to an APR of 3.23%. The annual return is lower if the funds are withdrawn before maturity.

Instalment Savings Scheme: This savings product provides a tax-free return of 20% if held for five years. The scheme takes six years in total to mature from when it begins. The first 12 months are spent building up the capital amount by monthly instalments of between €25 and €1,000. No interest is paid in this period. After this, the total capital collated starts to earn interest, and no further instalments take place. The APR of this product is 3.37%, taking the full six-year period into account.

Prize Bonds: Prize bonds do not offer interest or capital growth. The bonds are entered into a prize draw which takes place weekly. The Government pays out 3% of the fund value in prizes yearly. At the time of writing, each draw has a monthly €1 million main prize, a weekly €20,000 prize, and approximately 7,800 other smaller prizes, which start at €75 (www. prizebonds.ie, 2012). The prize winnings are tax free. Each bond has a purchase value of €6.25, though individuals must purchase a minimum of four bonds (€25). There is no upper limit on the amount that can be invested. It is highlighted that the capital portion of this investment will decrease over time, and winnings are not guaranteed.

There is also a range of savings products available from the Irish State/ the National Treasury Management Agency, **without tax breaks**. These include:

- *Deposit Account Plus:* At the time of writing, this product offered a variable return of 3% per annum and is subject to DIRT. The account is statement based, and an individual has to give 30 days' notice when they wish to withdraw their funds.
- *Post Office Savings Bank Deposit Account:* At the time of writing, this account offered a variable rate return of 1% per annum and is subject to DIRT. The account has a pass book, and the funds can be withdrawn on demand.
- *Pension Save Account:* This account is available to pensioners. Their pension payments can be paid into this account and therein can earn interest at the variable rate of 1%. The interest on this account is subject to DIRT, though individuals who are over 65 years of age no longer have to pay DIRT (discussed previously). The funds in this account are accessible on demand.

- *Childcare Save Account:* This account provides a convenient way to save child benefit payments. It provides a variable return of 1% per annum, and the funds are accessible on demand. The interest is subject to DIRT.

Savings in the UK

In the UK, the Financial Services Compensation Scheme (FSCS) administered by the Financial Services Authority (FSA) provides protection for deposit accounts of up to £85,000 per individual per licensed financial institution. In addition, since 1 January 2011, the European Economic Area (EEA) deposit protection plan provides protection for deposit accounts of up to €100,000 per individual per bank.

In the UK, interest income is subject to different tax rules relative to other forms of income. Unlike other income, the first £2,710 of taxable savings income received in excess of the personal allowance is taxed at 10%. However, all other income must be taxed first. Therefore, where an individual has income of £17,000, including interest income of £3,000, they will not be eligible for the 10% band, as the interest is treated as the last income to be taxed. The interest income is treated as being in the income band from £14,000 to £17,000. The £14,000 starts at a level that is above the personal allowance (£8,105) and the 10% band (£2,710). If the individual had income of £12,000 including interest of £3,000, they would be eligible for tax at 10% on £1,815, calculated as follows:

The taxable income is £3,895 (£12,000 – £8,105 personal allowance). The other forms of income must be taxed first; therefore, £895 (£3,895 – £3,000) represents other income which must be taxed at 20%. This means that of the interest income of £3,000, £1,815 (£2,710 – £895) should be taxed at 10%, and the remaining £1,185 (£3,000 – £1,815) should be taxed at 20%. The 10% band only applies to interest (not to other income). Taxable saving income beyond the £2,710 income level and up to £34,370 is taxed at 20%; taxable saving income between £34,370 and £150,000 is taxed at 40%; and taxable saving interest received in excess of a £150,000 income level is taxed at 50%.[1]

As mentioned earlier, when making the decision to invest in a savings product, the gross interest rate of the product with the tax break should be compared to the net rate available on other products. For example, it is not worthwhile going for a tax-free product that provides an interest return of 2.5% if a taxed alternative offers 5%, as the after-tax return on the taxed

---

[1] 2012/13 rates.

alternative is higher at 3% (5% × (1 – 40%)), assuming the individual is a 40% taxpayer.

Most savings products in the UK are subject to a 20% tax deduction at source. This is taken off the gross amount of interest, the investor being credited with the *net* amount (after-tax amount). Higher-rate taxpayers will have to pay additional tax on the gross interest in their tax returns. In many instances, non-taxpayers can complete a Form R85, 'Getting your interest without tax taken off', which is sent by the bank to Revenue and Customs and allows the bank to pay the interest gross. Alternatively, the individual can claim the tax paid back using their self-assessment form, or Form R40, 'Tax Repayment Form'. This includes children who also are eligible for the personal allowance (£8,105 for the year 2012/13).

As mentioned earlier, there are many savings products on offer from financial institutions, and these change regularly. Individuals need to consider all the options that are available and to review their savings products at least yearly as the rates of interest change regularly. All banks will deduct tax at source unless the R85 has been submitted. Credit unions pay dividends to their members. These are treated as interest by the Revenue and are subject to the same rules for tax purposes as interest. However, credit unions do not deduct tax at source. The dividends need to be declared in the individual's tax return each year and the relevant tax paid.

Most of the savings products provided by financial institutions are taxable. However, two common tax efficient accounts are widely available: Individual Savings Accounts (ISAs) and Child Trust Funds (CTFs). These are now discussed in turn.

Individual Savings Accounts (ISAs) – ISAs can be used to save cash or to invest in stocks and shares. Cash ISAs are available to individuals who are over 16 years of age, and stocks and shares ISAs are available to individuals who are over 18 years of age. ISAs have a yearly investment limit of £11,280, of which a maximum of £5,640 can be in the form of a cash ISA, with the balance allowable in the stocks and shares ISA. Interest earned on the cash portion is tax-free to the individual. Income earned on the stocks and shares ISA is partially tax-free. Any capital gain is tax-free, and any additional taxation on dividends is not payable. However, the 10% tax that is deducted from dividends at source is not reclaimable. This still provides a 22.5% (32.5% – 10%) tax benefit for higher-rate taxpayers when compared to owning stocks and shares outside the ISA vehicle. A downside to this product is that the value of the capital invested can go up or down and, where capital losses are made, they are not eligible to be used to offset capital gains from other chargeable asset sales in the period.

On 1 November 2011, *junior ISAs (JISAs)* were introduced with a limit of £3,600 per year for each eligible child. The JISA could be cash and/or shares, but the overall contribution limit is restricted to the £3,600 per annum.

Child Trust Funds (CTFs) – CTFs are long-term, tax-free savings accounts that were set up for children born between 1 September 2002 and 2 January 2011. They were a Government initiative to promote a savings culture in children. It involved the Government issuing a £250 (from 2010 this was £50) voucher to parents to open an account in the child's name. To further incentivise parents to save for their children's futures, the Government allow a further £3,600 to be lodged yearly to this account (this was restricted to £1,200 until 1 November 2011). Interest on these accounts is tax-free.

JISAs and CTFs will be index linked from April 2013.

Government Savings Products in the UK

Some UK Government savings products are tax-free. Interest is paid without the deduction of tax (paid gross). Most tax-free products are issued by the *National Savings and Investments (NS&I) department* – a Government department which offers savings and investment schemes to the general public, some of which are tax-free. It is simply the Government loaning funds from the public and paying a return for being able to do this. The investments are secure, as they are guaranteed by the UK Government. The **tax exempt products** available from the NS&I department are summarised briefly as follows:

- *Direct Individual Savings Accounts (ISAs)* – These are offered by the NS&I department to those who are over 18 years of age. ISAs have a yearly investment limit of £11,280, of which a maximum of £5,640 can be in the form of a cash ISA, with the balance allowable in the stocks and shares ISA.[2] Interest earned on the cash portion is tax-free to the individual. Income earned on the stocks and shares ISA is partially tax-free. Any capital gain is tax-free. This is an online/telephone banking cash ISA account that offers 2.5% interest, though this rate may change as it is variable.[3]
- *Index linked savings certificates* – These are inflation-beating saving certificates (bonds) with tax-free returns that are issued by the NS&I

---

[2] 2012/13 rates.
[3] Rate applicable in July 2012.

department. The April 2010 issue offered an interest rate of 1.00% above the Retail Price Index (RPI). The capital is guaranteed, as is the 1% interest premium which is paid even if deflation occurs. The interest is added yearly and, once added, cannot be reduced in future if deflation occurs. An investor can invest between £100 and £15,000 in these products for terms of two, three and five years. They are free from income tax and capital gains tax (so long as the investor holds the product for a period of more than one year). At the time of writing (July 2012), no issues were on general sale.

- *Fixed Interest Savings Certificates* – These allow individuals to invest lump sums at pre-determined guaranteed rates of interest that are set by the NS&I department. An investor can invest between £100 and £15,000 in these products for terms of two to five years. They are free from income tax and capital gains tax. In the April 2010 issue, the NS&I department was offering annual interest rates of circa 1.25% for the two-year certificate and 2.25% for the five-year certificate. As the interest is tax-free, the five-year rate of 2.25% is equivalent to a gross interest (assuming the interest is taxable) of 2.81% for a basic-rate taxpayer, 3.75% for a higher-rate taxpayer, and 4.5% for an additional-rate taxpayer. At the time of writing (July 2012), no issues were on general sale.

- *Premium Bonds* – These are £1 bonds that are issued and administered by the NS&I department. The public can hold between £100 and £30,000 in premium bonds. Premium bonds do not offer interest or capital growth. The bonds are entered into a prize draw, which takes place twice in each month. The prize draw distributes 1.5% of the fund annually. At the time of writing, each draw has a £1 million main prize and over 500,000 other smaller prizes, which start at £25. The prize winnings are tax-free. It is highlighted that the capital portion of this investment will decrease over time, and winnings are not guaranteed.

- *Children's Bonus Bonds* – Anyone who is over 16 can invest between £25 and £3,000 in children's bonus bonds for terms of five years, which end on the child's 21st birthday. The £3,000 applies to each issue, not to the child. If there are four issues in a year, an adult can invest a maximum of £12,000 for each child. The interest rate is fixed for each five-year period at the outset, and a bonus is payable at the end. In the July 2012 issue (number 34), the NS&I department was offering an annual equivalent rate of circa 2.5%. The return is tax-free to both parent and child, so long as the investment is held for five years, or until the child's 21st birthday. No interest is payable if the bond is liquidated within the first year.

Other taxable products on offer from the National Savings and Investments Department (UK) include the following:

- *Guaranteed Income Bond* and the *Guaranteed Growth Bond* – The *guaranteed income bond* has a guaranteed return for amounts invested over either one, three or five years. The interest varies depending on the duration of the bond and is taxable. The interest is paid net of tax. The interest is paid monthly, and the original capital remains intact. Individuals can invest between £500 and £1 million in these bonds. In July 2012, no issues were on general sale, though interested individuals could sign up to be alerted about the next issue. The *guaranteed growth bond* is similar in every respect, except that the monthly net interest is added to the capital value of the bond and not returned to the investor until the bond matures. Both bonds can be cashed in early, but a penalty equal to 90 days interest applies.

- *Income Bonds* – An income bond provides a monthly income to the investor. An initial capital lump sum of between £500 and £1 million can be invested to provide a monthly interest income over a term (no set term). The interest rates awarded by the NS&I department are tiered, depending on the size of the savings. At the time of writing (July 2012), interest rates ranged from 1.46% APR for investments of under £25,000 to 1.76% APR for investments of over £25,000. The interest rate is variable, taxable and is paid gross. The capital element of this investment is secure, and it can be cashed in with no notice and no penalty at any time. Income bonds can be purchased for children aged seven and over.

- *Investment Account* – The NS&I department also offer a postal 'Investment Account' (from 21 May 2012 this account became postal only; before this date individuals could access the account through the post office). Between £20 and £1 million can be invested. There is no set term. Interest rates are variable and, in July 2012, the rates were 0.75%.

- *Easy Access Savings Account* – The NS&I department offered an instant access deposit account called the 'Easy Access Savings Account'. However, this account closed on 27 July 2012.

- *Direct Saver Account* – The direct saver account is an online account which is suitable for any individual who does not require a branch presence to manage their account. Anyone over 16 years of age can open this type of account and can invest between £1 and £2 million into the account. Interest is calculated daily, but is credited yearly. The interest rate is variable and, in July 2012, the rate on offer was 1.5%. The interest is taxable, but is paid gross so the investor has to declare the interest income in their tax return if they are subject to taxation.

Conclusion

Good financial management involves being able to save funds on a regular basis. Just as liquidity is important for companies, it is equally important for individuals. All individuals should hold, at a minimum, a safety level of easily obtainable funds, called an emergency fund. This ensures that individuals do not leave themselves vulnerable to financial distress. Though an individual may have a number of investments, they will still damage their wealth if they do not ensure that they retain liquidity at the correct level. Investments that are cashed early usually incur penalties. Having a sufficient level of funds in savings ensures that this does not happen.

Savings should be managed to maximise the return being earned on them (interest). This means holding appropriate levels of cash in a current account, in an instant access deposit account and in a fixed-term deposit account. Good financial planning with the use of cash flow budgets should allow an individual to manage this efficiently. The use of Internet banking has made cash and savings management quick, flexible and easy.

Key Terms

Childcare save account
Children's bonus bonds
Child Trust Fund (CTF)
Current account
Deposit account
Deposit account plus
Deposit Interest Retention Tax (DIRT)
Deposit Protection Scheme
Direct ISA account
Direct saver account
Easy access savings account
Emergency fund
Fixed interest savings certificates
Guaranteed growth bond
Guaranteed income bond
Household saving
Household saving ratio
Income bonds
Index linked savings certificates
Individual Saving Account (ISA)
Instalment savings scheme
Instant access savings account

Investment account
Junior ISA (JISA)
National Savings and Investments Department (NS&I)
National solidarity bond
National Treasury Management Agency (NTMA)
Pension save account
Post office savings bank deposit account
Precautionary motives
Premium bonds
Prize bonds
Savings goal
Special Savings Investment Account (SSIA)
Special Term Account
Speculative motive
State guaranteed savings bonds
State guaranteed savings certificates
State savings
Transactions motive

WEBSITES THAT MAY BE OF USE

- For information on savings products on offer from the National Treasury Management Agency (ROI government-backed products) visit (rates are subject to change): *www.statesavings.ie/products*
- For information on products on offer from the National Savings and Investment Department (UK government-backed products) visit: *www.nsandi.com*
- If you Google any bank you will be able to see a wide range of savings products.

REVIEW QUESTIONS

(Suggested solutions to **Review Questions** are provided in **Appendix 4**.)

Question 7.1

It is considered that individuals might hold cash for transactions motives, precautionary motives or speculative motives.

Required: Explain what this means and provide an example of each motive.

Question 7.2

Outline the main differences between a current account and a deposit account.

Question 7.3

List the savings products available in your jurisdiction that have tax breaks (UK/ROI)?

Question 7.4

Should an individual invest funds for emergency expenditures in the stock market, government bonds, property, a savings deposit account or in their current account?

Question 7.5

Find the values for the following:

(a) An initial €/£1,000 compounded for 2 years at 8 per cent.
(b) An initial €/£1,000 compounded for 4 years at 8 per cent.

(c) The present value of €/£1,000 due in 2 years at a discount rate of 8 per cent.
(d) The present value of €/£1,000 due in 4 years at a discount rate of 8 per cent.

Question 7.6

Which grows to a larger future value:

(a) €/£10,000 invested for 10 years at 5% per annum or
(b) €/£5,000 invested for 10 years at 10% per annum.

Question 7.7 (Challenging)

(Suggested Solutions to **Challenging Questions** are available to lecturers.)

(a) Clarissa Fox is now 25 years old, and she wants to buy her own house. Her aunt, Matilda, started a bank account on her behalf when she was born and put €/£1,000 in the account on that date. For the first eight years, the interest rates were very favourable at 8%, but then it dropped to 6% and remained at that rate up to today. She is now trying to get the deposit in order to buy her house, and she wants to cash in her savings account. How much is the deposit now worth? (Tax can be ignored.)

6 Marks

(b) Clarissa has been advised to wait another four years before she invests in a house as she does not have sufficient savings at this point in time and the property market may fall even lower, making her dream house more attainable. If Clarissa saves €/£3,000 per annum at the start of each of the next four years, how much additional savings will she have at the end of that period? She expects to be able to earn 8% interest on this investment as she can lock her savings into a high yield account.

4 Marks

(Based on Chartered Accountants Ireland, CAP 1, Autumn 2011, Q6(a) and (b))

Question 7.8 (Challenging)

Which grows to a larger future value, €/£10,000 invested for two years at:

(a) 8% each year,
(b) 4% the first year and 12% the second year, or
(c) 12% the first year and 4% the second year?
Explain your answer.

Question 7.9 (Challenging)

Which is worth more at 10%, compounded annually:

(a) €/£10,000 in hand today, or
(b) €/£20,000 due in five years?

Question 7.10 (Challenging)

A lottery jackpot of €/£1 million is paid out at €/£25,000 a year for 40 years. At a 10% required return, what is the present value of this payoff? Assume that the first payment is paid immediately.

Question 7.11 (Challenging)

At an interest rate of 10%, what is the present value of €/£1 million to be received in:

(a) 10 years
(b) 50 years
(c) 100 years
(d) 150 years?

Question 7.12 (Challenging)

(a) If Seamus placed €/£20,000 in the bank today earning 6% interest per annum, what would this sum amount to in one year's time and in two years' time?
(b) If Seamus placed €/£20,000 in the bank today earning 5.2% interest per annum, what would this sum amount to in 18 months' time and in 42 months' time?

Question 7.13 (Challenging)

The bank offers interest at the rate of 5% for ordinary deposits, or 7% for term deposits, which cannot be withdrawn for five years. What will this difference in interest rates mean in five years, given that the value of the investment now is €/£25,000.

Question 7.14 (Challenging)

You put €/£10,000 into a fixed interest deposit account that earns 5% per annum immediately, €/£2,000 is lodged at the start of the next year and €/£5,000 at the start of the following year. The deposit account will mature in six years' time.

(a) What is the terminal value that you expect to receive?
(b) What is the present value if your cost of capital is 8%?

CHAPTER 8

INVESTMENTS

LEARNING OBJECTIVES

Upon completion of this chapter, readers should be able to:

- explain the meaning of the key terms listed at the end of the chapter;
- explain the relationship between investment risk and return;
- discuss the impact of inflation, debt, portfolio theory and liquidity on personal investment decision-making;
- describe the ways in which an individual can invest in equity;
- explain the differences between gilts and bonds;
- calculate the yield/return on an investment in bonds/gilts;
- describe factors that should be considered when investing in property;
- list at least four mortgage products;
- explain how a repayment mortgage works;
- explain how an endowment mortgage works;
- calculate the monthly instalment on a repayment and an endowment mortgage;
- describe collective funds; and
- explain the difference between unit trusts, investment trusts and life insurance investment bonds.

Introduction

As part of every financial plan, the *investment decision* should be considered. The relevance of this section to an individual depends on the extent of disposable income available. The more funds that are available, the greater the flexibility when it comes to the investment decision – hence the greater the potential to generate more wealth. This chapter starts by discussing the factors that influence an individual's choice of investment such as attitude to risk, inflation, liquidity and debt levels. Then the main types of personal investments are explained including equity shares, government gilts, corporate bonds, investment property, collective funds and tangible assets. Deposit accounts are not included in this chapter as they were discussed in **Chapter 7**, 'Savings'.

Risk and Personal Investment

Putting all an individual's excess cash into savings only is considered to be an inefficient investment strategy, though not risky. Risk and return are related. *Return* encapsulates income received on capital invested, a rise in the value of capital invested, or both. In simple terms, *risk* is the likelihood that the actual returns received will differ from the expected returns on an investment. It is measured as the standard deviation of actual returns from expected returns (average returns). A larger standard deviation indicates that there is greater risk and vice versa. To compensate for uncertainty in returns, higher risk investments usually have higher expected returns relative to investments which have no/little risk. In addition, there is a chance that a risky investment will provide an abnormal return in addition to the higher expected average return; conversely, a high-risk investment also runs the risk of providing a low or even a negative return. In most high-risk investments the capital element of the investment can fall as well as rise. It is important to gauge an individual's attitude to risk and return before deciding on an appropriate investment portfolio.

ASSESSING AN INDIVIDUAL'S ATTITUDE TO RISK

Questions to ask might include:

1. The current real return on your risk-free savings is, for example 1% (net rate after tax less the weighted average inflation rate for the period). Are you happy with this return or do you wish to invest in products that provide a higher return?
(Note: *the majority of investments that offer a return in excess of the risk-free rate are subject to risk.*)
2. Are you willing to risk a fall in the capital value of your investment? Most investments with higher returns are available when the cash invested is prone to capital increases and decreases.
3. Many high-risk, high-return investments require a long-term commitment to fully benefit from the investment. How long are you willing to commit funds for?
4. Have you a specific funding requirement in the future that you wish to coincide with the maturity of this investment? What is the specific sum required?
5. Given your future financial requirement target, what are you willing to invest now to achieve this? (*This information can be used to determine the growth and return required, to achieve the planned financial target. This will help to determine the type of investment product to suggest.*)
6. Are you happy to lock away funds that cannot be accessed, without incurring penalties or a reduced return?
7. If there are no specific financial targets, what growth/return do you wish to achieve (ideally and realistically) from the investment in more risky investments?

When evaluating an individual's risk profile it is good practice to get the individual to specify the risk they are willing to accept for each of their objectives. To this end, a scale of risks could be prepared and individuals should be asked to specify their willingness to invest in different types of products that have different risk characteristics. They should identify their liquidity requirement and highlight the proportion of their capital that they are willing to invest in a particular product. For example, a simple deposit account or government bond would be classed as having *low* or *no risk*. Deposit accounts typically have different levels of liquidity and the specific products to be suggested will be influenced by the individual's liquidity preferences.

Low risk usually means there will be no loss of capital, but there may be some inflationary risk to the real value of the capital that is invested. This is likely to occur where the income is pegged to the performance of, for example, the stock market, but the capital is protected. The premium is usually capped at a set level for the total period. The concern here is that, were the stock market index not to meet the predefined target, then the individual might only be entitled to the capital and possibly a smaller return than anticipated. If this return ended up at a rate below inflation, then the individual's wealth has been damaged in real terms. Fixed-return investments are the same. An investment that guarantees a return of 5% per year is only increasing an individual's wealth if inflation remains below the individual's net return (after tax). The net return might be 3% (5% (1 - 40%)) where the individual is a 40% taxpayer. If inflation is 4%, the individual has made a loss on this investment in real terms.

Modest risk is where there is a small risk that the capital value will be eroded by a capital loss in the value of the investments. This type of investment would typically include an equity investment in blue chip securities, or unit trusts or an investment in corporate bonds. In general these types of investment incur a short-term loss in capital value which is generally reversed in the longer term.

Relatively high risk is where there is a higher level of risk that the investment might suffer a capital loss; conversely there is a higher chance that the investment will reap higher returns relative to an investment in lower risk products. These investments typically include owning a carefully selected portfolio of shares that is deemed to be reflective of the market. Again, this type of investment requires a more long-term view if high returns are to be expected, so should not be considered if the investment is to be liquidated in the short-term. The return on this type of investment is usually linked to the success of the economy.

High risk refers to investments that have a high chance of there being a loss in the capital invested. However, these investments, if managed well and if the investor is skilled and lucky, can reap the highest rewards. This may involve investing in certain types of company securities, such as new starts, high technology companies, or may include investing in hedge funds, or junk bonds. Individuals who are financially secure, who have their future funding requirements well covered, and who have excess funds are more likely to 'gamble' with high-risk investments.

Inflation and Personal Investment

As mentioned in the last section, an investment's net returns should exceed inflation. If this is not the case then the investment is actually eroding an individual's wealth. Hick's income theory is relevant here. If the purchasing power of capital at the end of a particular period is less than the purchasing power of capital at the start of that period, even though the absolute amount is more, then an investor's wealth is damaged. Hick's income theory regards income as the difference between the opening capital position in real terms and the closing capital position in real terms plus any capital, or income that has been consumed from the investment in the period being considered.

Depending on the inflation rate, *risk-free investments* such as monies invested in a deposit account or in government bonds sometimes damage wealth in real terms. Historically long-term investments in the equity markets provide real gains in capital wealth, though these investments are regarded as the most risky. This historical pattern of higher returns is why pension and insurance companies commit substantial funds to this type of investment.

Debt and Personal Investment

In some instances, it is impossible to get access to a particular type of investment unless debt is used to source some of the funds. This might occur where the investment requires a minimum amount of funds. The best example is an investment in property. The general rule is that so long as inflation is positive and property price increases exceed inflation and the cost of financing the purchase of the property, then using debt to obtain the investment is recommended (so long as the yearly servicing of the debt does not lead to liquidity problems).

Liquidity and Personal Investment

If an investment provides yearly cash distributions that cover the servicing of the related debt and the costs of running the investment then the investment is *self-liquidating*. This is an attractive investment, and is even more attractive if the investment is also rising in value each year. Where an investment requires a yearly cash contribution from an individual then, regardless of how attractive the future returns are, the investment should not be taken if it leaves the individual with insufficient cash to cover their normal running expenses. Liquidity problems can cause an individual to become bankrupt, which will result in the investment having to be encashed before its maturity date, probably at a loss to the individual. There is also the personal aspect to consider; becoming bankrupt is likely to cause stress to an individual, which may result in health problems.

Portfolio Theory and Personal Investment

An individual should aim to hold a *diversified portfolio of investments*. The adage 'it is not wise to put all your eggs in one basket' is very relevant to the investment decision process. If an individual keeps all their investment funds in interest bearing investments then the value of their income and possibly their capital will fall when interest rates decline. Likewise, if an individual keeps all their investment funds in equity shares, then the value of their income and their capital will fall when the stock market takes a downturn. When an individual's investment pot is of sufficient size the individual should be encouraged to invest a proportion in property, in equity shares, in bonds, in interest bearing accounts and in tangible assets such as antiques or gold. When the performance of shares or bonds and interest bearing accounts start to decline, the capital gains on property and/or the price of gold usually start to increase and vice versa. Indeed in 2008, the equity market in the ROI suffered a serious decline in value. In contrast, the bond markets had one of the best years in terms of performance. Even so, bond returns are considered to be uncorrelated to equity returns. Some investments are *negatively correlated* with each other, in other words an inverse relationship exists between their returns. Even within equities the risk of an individual's equity returns being different to market average returns can be minimised by selecting equities that have returns that are negatively correlated to each other, for example, selecting shares in an ice-cream company and an umbrella company. The financial crises and subsequent economic downturn that started in 2007 led to a decline in the value of most investment assets. Gold is one of the exceptions, its price soared as many investors transferred their funds into gold to diversify their risk exposure to the markets.

To conclude, a portfolio that contains a variety of investments is more likely to provide a steady, less risky return for an individual.

The Investment Decision Process Summarised

The fundamental principles underlying investment choice need to be applied to each and every investment decision. At the outset it is important to specify the aim or purpose of the investment and the term of the investment (including an estimate of the future financial requirement from the investment). The amount that can be invested by the individual both initially and periodically should be ascertained. An evaluation of these facts will help to determine the return that the investment needs to make to achieve the financial aim. At this point the feasibility of the aim will be discussed and the risk of the type of investment required to achieve the return explained. If this risk exceeds the risk identified in the initial assessment of the individual, this should be pointed out and an alternative plan prepared showing the expected investment return from an investment in the type of product more suited to the individual's risk profile. The additional contributions required to achieve the aim should also be highlighted. As with all investments, the tax implications of the investments being suggested should be highlighted.

Investment Types: Equities, Gilts and Bonds

Equities

How to Buy and Sell Equities: Equity investments are usually bought or sold by a stockbroker or an investment manager on behalf of an individual. A stockbroker provides an *execution only service* (the broker buys and sells without communicating with the investor). This is usually the cheapest way to obtain an equity investment. When an investment manager takes responsibility for an equity investment fund the level of individual involvement in the investment decision process varies, depending on the amount of control an individual wishes to retain over the investment. The arrangement with an investment manager can be *discretionary* (wherein the investment manager ultimately makes the decisions), *advisory* (wherein the investment manager provides advice on investment types but the decision-making is shared) or *self-select* (wherein the individual specifies the equities to invest in and conducts the trade). Self-selection can be done online, without getting clearance from the investment manager. Advances in telecommunications (broadband and the Internet) allow an individual to invest in shares from the comfort of their own home using the trading platform of the investment manager's firm. Most of these trading platforms are very sophisticated, providing real-time information on share prices and share price changes. They usually highlight the movers, chart the price movement of shares, provide minute-by-minute coverage of relevant news stories on companies and allow the user to set price targets, automatic sales prices or purchase prices. One leading UK banking institution provides an online buying and selling service for £6.95 per transaction (as long as 11 trades are conducted within a month, if not, this can increase to £12 per trade). However, it is not good practice to trade just to maintain low transaction costs. It is better to purchase shares that you expect to hold on to for a long time. Prices fluctuate and commission is payable every time a transaction occurs reducing the return on the share. Equity share investment is suited to an individual who is willing to lock their funds away for five to ten years (or more) and who will have the flexibility at the end of the period to leave the funds invested in the event of their being a stock market downturn.

Before purchasing equity shares it is important to set investment goals in terms of generating income or capital growth. When selecting shares, there are some patterns than an individual can look out for. Old companies that have shares with generous dividends typically have low capital growth. New fast growing companies, that pay a small or no dividend, may generate high levels of capital growth or may fail!

How to Find Out Equity Price Performance: The *Financial Times* (UK) and the *Irish Times* (Ireland) provide up-to-date information on equity share performance in the London (*Financial Times*) and the Irish (*Irish Times*) stock exchanges by industry classification. The Internet also provides up-to-date information on the performance of equities. The information provided is quite detailed and an investor needs to be able to read the tables that are provided. The tables typically disclose the following information:

SHARE INFORMATION PROVIDED IN FINANCIAL NEWSPAPERS

Pharmaceuticals and Biotech

Notes	Price	Chng	52 week High	Low	Yld	P/E	Vol. '000
Drug Co. ♣	112	−½	134	22	2.0	18.9	556
Medicine	150xd	+¾	190	135	3.2	16.8	678

(Format taken from Financial Times *disclosures)*

The *notes section* states the name of the company and uses playing cards symbols to provide information. A club indicates that a free annual report is available, a diamond that the company is subject to a takeover bid, merger or reorganisation, a spade indicates an unregulated investment scheme, whereas a heart indicates that the company is an overseas incorporated company. The *price column* provides the average market price of an individual share, as quoted by the market traders at 4.30 pm on the previous day. This also uses signage to provide information to the reader. When a share has the letters *xd after the price*, this signifies that the share price is *ex-dividend* (i.e. though a dividend has been announced, new buyers will not be entitled to the dividend). If the share price has a *(#) symbol* after it, this means that trading in the share is suspended and the price disclosed is the price before suspension. The *Chng column* details the *price change* in the 24 hours ending at 4.30 pm yesterday. The *52-week high and low columns* highlight the range in price movements over the past 52 weeks by disclosing the highest and lowest prices recorded for the shares.

The *Yld column* discloses the **dividend yield** on the share. It signifies the percentage dividend return on the share (gross dividend divided by current market share price). The *P/E column* provides information on the **price-earnings ratio**. This ratio provides an indication of the number of times the market price of the share covers the earnings made per share. It provides an indication of market confidence and, the higher the price-earnings ratio, the happier investors are with the company's performance, as they are paying a higher price for the company's earnings, relative to companies that report a lower price-earnings ratio. Finally, the *Vol. column* reports the turnover in shares in the previous day, rounded to the nearest thousand. If a dash appears in this column, this means that there either was no trading the previous day, or the information is not available.

Gilts

Gilts are another name for government issued bonds. These investments typically have a fixed interest rate with a set capital repayment at the end of a pre-agreed term. Gilts are regarded as being **risk-free investments** as the return is guaranteed by the government. The risk assessment depends on the country! The return earned on gilts is regarded as revenue income by the tax authorities, not capital gains. Therefore, the demand for gilts is impacted on by changes in tax rates. Individuals can purchase gilts through their bank, through the **Bank of England's Brokerage Service Direct** (UK gilts only), or through a stockbroker (UK and the ROI). Specialist stockbrokers who trade in gilts are known as **Gilt-Edged Market Makers**. Information on the performance of gilts can be obtained from the financial press (as discussed under equity above) and the Internet.

Bonds

Bonds are corporate issued debt that can be purchased by investors. Bonds are typically redeemable or irredeemable. *Redeemable bonds* normally have a maturity of between seven and 30 years, though the period can be shorter or longer. *Irredeemable bonds* do not have a maturity date, though commonly can be redeemed at the borrower's request. Bonds can be sold by way of a *public issue* (the company will have to prepare a prospectus, apply to the stock exchange and provide financial statements to the lenders, at least annually) or by a private issue. Publicly-traded bonds are traded in the secondary market of the London Stock Exchange (UK) and in the official list of the Irish Stock Exchange (ROI). A *private issue* is normally administered by a financial intermediary. They purchase the bonds from a company and sell them to a limited number of investors. These bonds are not tradable on the secondary markets of the stock exchange, but can be traded in private deals between bond brokers.

The risk associated with investing in a particular bond depends on the strength of the underlying corporation. A good indication of bond risk can be obtained from the *bond's credit rating*, which is usually performed by rating agencies like Moody's, Standard and Poor's and Fitch IBCA. Companies with publicly-traded bonds are required to keep their credit rating up-to-date. Bonds are usually given a credit rating which ranks from a triple A score (strongest) to a D which stands for Default (some only rate as far as BBB). There are varying ratings between these scores including AA, A, BBB, BB, B, C and so on. Anything graded BBB or above is considered to have hit the *investment grade* and any bond rated below BBB is regarded as being a *junk bond*. Junk bonds are considered to be risky investments.

Like gilts, the return earned on bonds is considered by the tax authorities to be revenue income. Bond values are negatively correlated with changes in the bank base rate. When interest rates rise, the value of bonds fall, as the coupon (interest) attached to the bond is usually fixed. Like gilts, an individual can purchase bonds through their bank, through the Bank of England's Brokerage Service Direct (UK bonds only), or through a stockbroker (specialist stockbrokers who trade in gilts are known as *Bond Market Makers*). Information on the performance of bonds can be obtained from the financial press (as discussed under equity) and the Internet.

Calculating the Yield/Return on bonds

Bonds have common characteristics. In the UK and in the ROI they typically have a nominal value (also called par value) of €/£100 but are bought and sold for whatever price market forces dictate. An asset backed bond issued by a strong blue chip company will have a low return, whereas an unsecured bond issued by a technology company will offer a high return. Most bonds have a coupon attached to them. This is the name for the interest that is paid on the bond. It is typically a set percentage of the nominal value. The interest income is taxable but there is no capital gain on the sale of most straightforward bonds. Bonds can either be secured or unsecured and can be redeemable or irredeemable. When they are irredeemable the bond is never redeemed (purchased back) by the company. The annual yield on an irredeemable bond can be calculated using the following formula:

$$r_b = \frac{I(1 - t)}{P_o} \times 100$$

where r_b is the after tax yield on the bond to the investor, I is the coupon amount, t is the investor's marginal rate of tax and P_o is the market value of the bond just purchased by the investor.

WORKED EXAMPLE 8.1: YIELD ON AN IRREDEEMABLE BOND

Smith purchased 1,000 €/£100 bonds for €/£95,000. They are irredeemable bonds with a 4% coupon. Smith pays tax at the marginal rate of 20%.

Required:

(a) Calculate the yearly after-tax yield earned by Smith on the bonds at the current market price.
(b) Calculate the annual after-tax yield if Smith paid tax at the marginal rate of 40%.
(c) Calculate the after-tax annual yield if you were told that the bond paid out 2% every six months. For this part, assume Smith has a marginal rate of tax of 20%.

Solution:

(a) The after-tax yield to Smith on the bond is:

$$r_b = \frac{I(1 - t)}{P_o} \times 100$$

$$\text{where } I = €/£4 \; (€/£100 \times 4\%)$$

$$t = 20\%$$

$$P_o = €/£95$$

$$r_b = \frac{4(1 - 0.2)}{95} \times 100 = 3.37\% \text{ per annum (after-tax)}$$

Continued

(b) The after-tax yield to Smith could change to:

$$r_b = \frac{4(1 - 0.4)}{95} \times 100 = 2.53\% \text{ per annum (after-tax)}$$

(c) The annual rate is now 4.04% $(1.02^2 - 1)$

And the after-tax yield to Smith is:

$$r_b = \frac{4.04(1 - 0.2)}{95} \times 100 = 3.4\% \text{ per annum (after-tax)}$$

When a bond is redeemable, it has a finite life. These are fixed-term bonds. They can be issued for a short period of about 5 years or a long period of about 30 years. On maturity they are redeemed for a set amount. This is usually the nominal value per bond of €/£100; however, this is not always the case. The conditions (as set out in the trust deed for the bond) will detail the redemption value of the bond. If a question does not tell you this assume redemption is at nominal value.

The following formula can be used to provide a close approximation of the yield on the bond to maturity taking into account the coupon received (net of tax) and the change in the price of the bond (capital appreciation or depreciation).

$$r_b = \frac{I(1 - t)}{P_o} + \frac{(R - P_o)/n}{P_o} \times 100$$

Where I is the annual coupon paid by the company on the bond, t is the investor's marginal rate of tax, P_o is the market value of the bond, R is the redemption value and n is the number of years to maturity/redemption. The calculation is covered in **Worked Example 8.2**.

WORKED EXAMPLE 8.2: YIELD ON A REDEEMABLE BOND

Mildred purchased 100 €/£100 bonds with a five-year duration to redemption, for €/£8,000. They have an annual 6% coupon. Mildred pays tax at the marginal rate of 41%.

Required:

(a) Estimate the after-tax annual yield to maturity that Mildred will generate on this bond investment at current rates. Assume the redemption value is the nominal value.

Continued

(b) Calculate the after-tax annual yield to maturity for Mildred, assuming the redemption value was €/£70.

Solution:

(a) The after-tax yield to Mildred on the bond is:

$$r_b = \frac{I(1-t)}{P_o} + \frac{(R-P_o)/n}{P_o} \times 100$$

where I = €/£6 (€/£100 × 6%)

t = 41%

P_o = €/£80

R = €/£100

n = 5 years

$$r_b = \frac{6(1-0.41)}{80} + \frac{(100-80)/5}{80} \times 100$$

$$r_b = \frac{3.54}{80} + \frac{4}{80} \times 100$$

$$r_b = 4.425\% + 5\% = 9.425\%$$

(b) The after-tax yield to Mildred is now:

$$r_b = \frac{6(1-0.41)}{80} + \frac{(70-80)/5}{80} \times 100$$

$$r_b = \frac{3.54}{80} + \frac{-2}{80} \times 100$$

$$r_b = 4.425\% - 2.5\% = 1.925\%$$

When the investor does not plan to hold the bond to maturity, the return earned on the investment can be calculated using the following formula:

$$\text{Rate of return} = \frac{\text{Coupon income (net of tax)} + \text{price change}}{\text{Investment}}$$

The calculation of the return earned is provided in **Worked Example 8.3**.

> ### WORKED EXAMPLE 8.3: RETURN EARNED ON A BOND
>
> Frank invested €/£9,750 in 100 bonds with eight years to redemption. The bonds have a 5% coupon rate. Frank pays taxation at 22%.
>
> **Required:**
>
> What rate of return (net of tax) has Frank earned on the bonds if he sells them for €/£10,400 (after commission costs) after one year? Frank has received one year's coupon.
>
> **Solution:**
>
> The rate of return on the €/£9,750 investment in bonds is as follows:
>
> $$\text{Rate of return} = \frac{\text{Coupon income (net of tax)} + \text{price change}}{\text{Investment}}$$
>
> $$\text{Rate of return} = \frac{€/£500\ (1 - 0.22) + (€/£10,400 - €/£9,750)}{€/£9,750}$$
>
> $$\text{Rate of return} = 10.67\%$$

Investment Types: Property

An investment in property is very illiquid. An individual will not be able to obtain quick access to the funds that are tied up in properties, particularly when the market is in a downturn or stagnant.

Two major decisions face an investor when the decision is taken to invest in property. The first involves selecting a property, the second financing the investment. *Property investment* involves a major capital outlay. The individual purchasing the property usually requires debt to finance the purchase.

Buy-to-let Property Investment

An individual might choose to purchase a property for *buy-to-let* purposes. When individuals purchase buy-to-let properties they usually expect the rent from the property to exceed the costs of the property (costs include all running, management and finance costs) and to provide a yearly surplus. In addition, capital appreciation is expected.

When selecting a buy-to-let property, an individual should be advised to choose a property based on its price, the quality of the location, its condition, funds required to make it rentable, the availability of local amenities and facilities (for example, schools, leisure centres, play areas, shops), closeness to public transport and expected maintenance. For example, large gardens are attractive to tenants; however, they require high maintenance. It is likely that a large garden will not add to the rental premium that can be obtained from a property; however, the costs of maintenance will increase (landlords are usually responsible for the upkeep of the external parts of a property, with tenants being responsible for the upkeep of the internal parts of the property).

There is also a chance that the property will not be rented for several months if a tenant is to leave. Additional repair costs also usually have to be incurred as tenants rarely return the property in the condition they received it in.

Mortgage lenders may restrict the type of property an individual can purchase. For example, they may insist that the property has a fire escape or one kitchen (so that the property is not converted into bed-sits).

The *management of a property* can be taken on by the individual themselves, or can be contracted to a letting agency. These typically charge 10–15% of the rent for managing the property (including finding and vetting tenants, collecting rent and dealing with repairs – with the cost of repairs and maintenance not forming part of the commission). Care should be taken when setting up the agreement with a letting agency. The timing of rent reimbursements should be agreed up front. Letting agents can hold on to rent for a long time before reimbursing it, if the terms are not stipulated in advance. It should be policy for the letting agent to gain permission to incur certain costs and to prove that they are using a competitive source for the repairs. All rentals should be backed up using a legal rental agreement, which should be renewed yearly.

The net income from a buy-to-let property is subject to income tax and any capital growth in the value of the property is subject to capital gains tax, if sold.

Costs Associated with Directly Owning a Property (UK)

Capital Depreciation/Appreciation: Historically, property prices typically increase in value year on year; however, this is not guaranteed. In the period up to the credit crunch huge gains were made on property with average residential property prices rising by 235% from the first quarter in 2000 to the third quarter in 2007 in the UK, though there were vast regional differences. In particular, the property market in Northern Ireland saw unprecedented house price increases amounting to 344% over the same period. However, the credit crunch caused a slump in the property market with UK house prices falling by 17.8% from the third quarter in 2007 to the first quarter in 2009 before starting to rise again in the second quarter of 2010. UK house prices have actually fallen again since 2010 by 2.3% (Quarter 2, 2012) though the deflation/inflation in price is regional. Indeed, the property market in NI is still experiencing a fall in value. Since the third quarter of 2007 residential house prices in NI have fallen by 51.44% (to quarter 2, 2012), the most serious price reductions of any region in the UK (*Nationwide Seasonal Regional Quarterly Index*, 2012).

Initial Costs: There are considerable up-front costs associated with purchasing a property. These costs include legal fees, mortgage booking fee, valuation fee, telegraphic transfer fee and stamp duty. In 2012/13, the *Stamp Duty Land Tax (SDLT)* rates and thresholds were as follows:

Table 8.1: Stamp Duty Land Tax (SDLT) Rates and Thresholds (UK)

Consideration	SDLT rate
Less than £125,001	Zero
Between £125,001 and £250,000	1%
Between £250,001 and £500,000	3%
Between £500,001 and £1,000,000	4%
Between £1,000,001 and £2,000,000	5%
Greater than £2,000,001	7%

A tax incentive is afforded to individuals who invest in government designated disadvantaged areas. In these areas, SDLT is not payable on properties that have a value of less than £150,000.

On-going Cost: Most properties have yearly running costs which include repairs and maintenance, renewals, buildings and contents insurance, public liability insurance, water rates, rates (in Northern Ireland only[1]), ground rent (if leasehold), letting agents' fees (if used), mortgage interest,

---

[1] From October 2011 local councils in Northern Ireland started to charge rates on all properties whether the property was vacant or not.

taxation, accountancy fees, legal fees (for contracts, renewing leases), cleaning and gardening and other ad hoc expenses such as advertising, telephone and stationery. The extent of these running expenses will depend on the contract agreed with the tenant.

Exit Costs: When properties are sold, there are also costs associated with selling the property, estate agent fees, legal fees, capital gains tax and an early mortgage redemption fee (depending on the mortgage contract).

Costs Associated with Directly Owning a Residential Property (ROI)

Capital Depreciation/Appreciation: Historically, property prices typically increase in value year on year; however, this is not guaranteed. In the period from the end of 1993 to October 2006 property prices in the ROI experienced steady price increases; moreover, house prices tripled in the period 2001 to 2006. The house price increases spurred additional building activity with approximately 75,000 new properties being built each year (Finfacts Ireland, 2010). At this time (2006) the Central Statistic Office reported that 15% of housing stock in Ireland (266,000 homes) was unoccupied, yet building continued. A recent report by Williams *et al.* (2010) has estimated that about 345,000 homes, representing 17% of the country's total housing stock, are unoccupied (this includes holiday homes). The OECD and most economists pre-empted the fall in house prices and were publishing warnings that house prices at that time (2006) were inflated; however, few predicted the seriousness of the credit crunch which was to follow. House prices in Ireland started to fall by small amounts at the end of 2006 and in 2007. For example, the monthly reduction in the value of an average property fell by 0.6% in March 2007 and by 0.8% in April 2007.

However, the scale of the drop in house prices began to escalate during the last quarter of 2007 as the credit crunch started to take hold. This coupled with the onset of recession led to a crash in the property market. At its height in October 2006, the average house price in Ireland was €311,078. This has fallen by 49.9% by 2012 (Finfacts Ireland, 2012). House prices fell by higher proportions in Dublin relative to the rest of the country (Finfacts Ireland, 2012).

Initial Costs: There are considerable up-front costs associated with purchasing a property. These costs include legal fees, mortgage booking fee, valuation fee, telegraphic transfer fee and stamp duty. In 2012, the stamp duty rates and consideration thresholds on the purchase of residential property were as follows:

Tables 8.2: Stamp Duty Rates and Thresholds (ROI)

Consideration	Rate (%)
Less than €1,000,000	1
Balance	2

On-going Costs: Most properties have yearly running costs which include repairs and maintenance, renewals, buildings and contents insurance, public liability insurance, environmental management charges, refuse charges, ground rent (if leasehold), letting agents' fees (if used), mortgage interest, taxation, property tax household charge, accountancy fees, legal fees (for contracts, renewing leases), cleaning and gardening and other ad hoc expenses such as advertising, telephone and stationery. The extent of these running expenses will depend on the contract agreed with the tenant. Only 75% of the mortgage interest expense is considered allowable and a wear and tear allowance of 12.5% per annum for eight years is allowable for capital expenditure on fixtures and fittings.

Exit Costs: When properties are sold, there are also costs associated with selling the property including, estate agent fees, legal fees, capital gains tax and possibly an early mortgage redemption fee (depending on the mortgage contract).

Commercial Property Investment

Private investors can also invest in *commercial property*. As the amounts involved are typically very large this type of investment is usually only possible through collective funds such as unit trusts. Most investment, pension and insurance companies own commercial properties and several partnerships purchase offices using a '*self-investment pension plan*'.

Other Property Investment: Second Home

Other investments in property might include purchasing a *second home* or a *property overseas*. Second homes are not usually rented;

hence have a direct impact on an individual's monthly cash position. Second homes usually have fixed costs that have to be covered, such as ground rent, water rates, rates, second house tax (ROI), insurance, maintenance and utility costs. These costs are regarded as personal costs. The income to be made on a second home is usually the capital gain on the property. The tax authorities will only accept one property as the main residential property, so it is important to inform them, within two years of the purchase of the second property, which one should be regarded as the main residence. The choice should be the most tax efficient one. The property with the highest expected capital gains should be classified as the main residence (capital gains on a person's main residence are tax-free). In the ROI, the availability of mortgage interest relief on an individual's principal private residence will affect this decision.

Other Property Investment: Property Abroad

When purchasing a second home overseas, the issues to be faced are the same as those facing properties purchased in Ireland or in the UK, though in addition there is the added complication of having to get to know and to comply with local laws, taxes and currency fluctuations. Rent on a foreign property (net of expenses) and any capital gain made on a sale is subject to tax in both countries (the country of the property and the country of the owner – where these differ), though, where a double taxation agreement exists, the foreign tax is usually taken off the individual's tax bill for the rent or capital gain with the difference being paid to the tax authorities. Though attractive gains are possible from investing in property overseas, the risks are greater (as are the costs) than the risks associated with investing in the local property market. It is advisable to obtain legal and taxation advice from an expert who resides in the country where the property is located. This advice should cover the local land laws (in Spain many individuals saw their holdings diminished as the local Spanish authorities took back land) and inheritance laws (in Spain the law determines how an estate should be divided, not an individual's will). Discussion of the tax treatment of overseas property is beyond the scope of this book.

Property – Type of Ownership

Properties are usually of two types – freehold and leasehold. *Freehold* property means that the property and the land on which the property is situated forms the total property. *Leasehold* on the other hand involves purchasing the right to lease the buildings and gardens that are on the land for a set period of time. The investor becomes a lessee. The lease period of leasehold properties typically range from 99 years to 999 years. When the lease expires the right to use the property reverts to the lessor (the legal owner).

Taxation of Gains Made on Investment Properties (UK)

Yearly Income: Profits made on rental properties are subject to income tax. There are some restrictions on losses incurred, which can usually only be carried forward against future rental profits. There is one exception – profits made from furnished holiday letting properties. In this instance, losses can be used within that year against income/profits from other sources.

Capital Gains: Gains on the sale of properties are subject to capital gains tax. Individuals are eligible for an annual exempt amount, which in 2012/13 amounted to £10,600 (after losses and reliefs have been adjusted for). Capital gains tax is payable at the rate of 18% when the individual's total taxable income is less than £34,370 (up to this threshold). Where the capital gain takes the individual's total taxable income to above £34,370, capital gains tax of 28% is payable on the excess.

Taxation of Gains Made on Investment Properties (ROI)

Yearly Income: Profits made on rental properties are subject to income tax. There are some restrictions on losses incurred, which can usually only be used against rental profits made on other properties in the same year or carried forward against future rental profits.

Capital Gains: Gains on the sale of properties are subject to capital gains tax. Individuals are eligible for an annual exempt amount, which in 2012 amounted to €1,270 (after losses and reliefs have been adjusted for). Capital gains tax is payable at the rate of 30%. The 2012 Budget brought in an incentive to stimulate property sales wherein relief from CGT will be given for properties purchased between budget night and the end of 2013 that are held for at least seven years. Hence, if a property is purchased and held for eight years it will only be subject to CGT on 1/8 of the capital gain, a CGT exemption being available for the first seven years (7/8). If the property is sold after six years, the whole gain is chargeable to CGT.

Financing Property Investment

Debt

Most properties are purchased using a mortgage. A *mortgage* is a long-term *secured loan* which allows the lender to have a legal charge encumbered on the property. The legally binding contract which sets out the terms and conditions of the loan and the restrictive covenants that the purchaser has to adhere to is called a *mortgage deed*.

> ### TYPICAL CONTENTS OF A MORTGAGE DEED
>
> 1. The address of the property subject to the mortgage.
> 2. The names of the purchaser/s and the lender.
> 3. The amount being loaned, the set-up fees, repayment amounts, how they are calculated and the interest rate and type.
> 4. The granting of the legal charge over the property (the property deeds are usually retained by the bank).
> 5. The minimum insurance requirements and restrictions/conditions on the alterations that can happen to the property, or restrictions/conditions on how the property can be used by the purchaser. The lender usually insists that the purchaser keeps the property in a good state of repair, so that its value is not diminished and their security put at risk.
> 6. The steps that will be taken if the agreement is breached.
> 7. The purchaser's signature to confirm that they have received the loan and agree to the conditions.

Lender's Perspective

Mortgage debt on property is relatively low-risk for lenders as property values typically increase, making the security stronger over time[2]. As the lender has a *legal charge* over the property this means that they have to be repaid out of the proceeds of the property first and in addition, because the loan is *secured*, the lender can force the sale of the property if the conditions of the mortgage deed are not adhered to.

---

[2] The current economic climate is an exception to the general rule. Property prices typically increase in value hence the security improves over time.

In general, lending institutions have a number of set criteria which they apply when deciding on whether or not to give a mortgage. The most common criteria applied by financial institutions are as follows:

MORTGAGE LENDING CRITERIA

1. *General criteria*: Lending institutions will be interested in the credit standing of the borrower, the reputation of the borrower, the relationship they have had with the borrower in the past (for example, have they complied with all prior loan agreements), the proportion of funds being contributed by the borrower, the amount of debt already being serviced by the borrower, the amount of equity amassed by the borrower and the security on offer.

2. *The loan-to-value ratio*: How much of the investment is being contributed by the purchaser and how much is being contributed by the bank. A low '*loan-to-value ratio*' is seen as being less risky. Typical ratios range from 75% to 90%. Before the credit crunch the 'loan-to-value ratio' regularly exceeded 100% wherein the lender was providing additional finance for the purchaser to take payment breaks, to pay stamp duty or refurbish the property. However, mortgages of over 100% are no longer available due to the current credit climate as banks are experiencing capital rationing and are less willing to increase their exposure to credit risk by providing loans that are not 100% secured by a property, etc.

3. *The ratio of 'loan size-to-income'*: Traditionally this was set at about three times an individual's gross salary or 2.5 times a couple's gross salary (or three times the higher salary plus two times the lower salary), less other debt commitments. Before the credit crunch a higher multiple of four or five times became quite common. However, the downturn in the sub-prime market has caused lending institutions to tighten their lending criteria and the traditional more restrictive multiples have become the norm again.

4. *The percentage of net income required to service the loan*: Lending institutions normally place a cap on the percentage of an individual's net income that should go towards paying off the debt. This is normally between 30% and 35%. This cap will restrict the repayment amount which will either restrict the amount of debt that the individual can obtain, or increase the acceptable term of the loan.

Continued

5. *Evidence*: A lending institution will typically wish to see sight of at least three months' pay slips (or the financial statements for two years), and three months' bank statements (including the most recent statements) from all bank accounts. The mortgage process usually involves a lengthy interview at which all these details are recorded and conditions, such as having house insurance, mortgage protection insurance, etc., are discussed.

Individual Borrower's Perspective

From an individual borrower's perspective, the mortgage decision should factor in the individual's liquidity, age and health (income generating ability and longevity), income (stability and variation) and how the investment and mortgage fit in with the individual's overall financial plan and their financial objectives. The wealthier and more cash rich an individual, the more likely they are to get the best deal to cater for their needs.

Parental Loan Guarantees

Many financial institutions will provide a mortgage to an individual on more relaxed terms than their normal products if the individual can provide a guarantor. *Parental loan guarantees* are guarantees provided by parents or close family relatives over the mortgage repayments of the individual obtaining the mortgage. The guarantee typically enables the individual to purchase more than their standard income multiple would typically allow. The mortgage advance can vary but is typically limited to 4 or 4.25 times the guarantor's income and the amount loaned is up to a maximum of 80% to 90% of the property value. A parent/close family relative is typically only eligible to become a guarantor if they are under 60 years of age. If the individual fails to make a monthly payment, the parent/close family relative becomes liable for the arrear.

Types of Mortgage

There are typically two different types of mortgage: repayment and interest only. A *repayment mortgage* involves an individual paying a pre-agreed monthly repayment for a set period of time (this will depend on the age of the individual, their financial aim in respect of the mortgage and their ability to meet the repayments). The repayment includes the month's interest and a portion of the capital. At the start of the mortgage most of the repayment is interest. Over time as the outstanding debt balance reduces, the capital element of each repayment increases and the interest portion reduces. The following equation can be used to determine the monthly repayment, given the interest rate and term of the mortgage:

$$P = \frac{M \times r}{1 - (1/(1 + r)^t)}$$

where P is the periodic payment, M is the initial size of the mortgage, t is the number of payments and r is the periodic interest rate (the annual interest rate divided by the number of payments per year).

WORKED EXAMPLE 8.4: (REPAYMENT MORTGAGES)

Alex wants to borrow €/£250,000 to purchase a property. She wants a repayment mortgage. Her bank can offer an interest rate of 6%. This is competitive and Alex is very interested. She is thinking about paying the mortgage off in 20 years, though may have to agree to 25 years.

Required: As a trainee in the bank you have been asked to determine the monthly repayments required to pay off the €/£250,000, assuming the mortgage term is:
  (a) 20 years
  (b) 25 years
  (c) Show the pattern of interest and capital repayments for the first five years assuming the 20-year option is taken.

Solution:

  (a) The periodic payment can be calculated using the following formula:

$$P = \frac{M \times r}{1 - (1/(1 + r)^t)}$$

Where P is the periodic payment (to find)
M is the initial size of the mortgage (€/£250,000)
t is the number of payments 240 (20 × 12)
r, the periodic interest rate, is 0.5% (6%/12)

Continued

Therefore

$$P = \frac{€/£250,000 \times 0.005}{1 - (1/(1+0.005)^{240})}$$

$$P = €/£1,791.08$$

(b) Where P is the periodic payment (to find)
M is the initial size of the mortgage (€/£250,000)
t is the number of payments 300 (25 × 12)
r, the periodic interest rate, is 0.5% (6%/12)

Therefore:

$$P = \frac{€/£250,000 \times 0.005}{1 - (1/(1+0.005)^{300})}$$

$$P = €/£1,610.75$$

(c)

Year	Opening Balance	Interest (6%)	Capital repayment	Closing balance
	€/£	€/£	€/£	€/£
1	250,000.00	15,000.00[1]	6,492.96[2]	243,507.04[3]
2	243,507.04	14,610.42	6,882.54	236,624.50
3	236,624.50	14,197.47	7,295.49	229,329.01
4	229,329.01	13,759.74	7,733.22	221,595.79
5	221,595.79	13,295.75	8,197.21	213,398.58

1. The interest for the year is calculated on the opening balance: €/£250,000 × 6%
2. The capital repayment is €/£6,492.96 ((€/£1,791.08 × 12) – €/£15,000)
3. The closing balance is €/£243,507.04 (€/£250,000 – €/£6,492.96)

As can be seen from the solution to part (c) above the yearly repayment remains the same at €/£21,492.96 (€/£1,791.08 × 12), but the proportion of this that goes to pay interest on the mortgage reduces and the capital amount increases each year.

The alternative type of mortgage is the *interest only mortgage*. As the name stipulates, the repayment is interest only. The capital amount does not reduce over the life of the loan. If Alex (above example) were to opt for an interest-only mortgage then her yearly repayments would be €/£15,000 or €/£1,250 per month (€/£15,000/12). Individuals might opt for an interest only mortgage for an initial period of time for liquidity reasons.

When an individual purchases a new property there are many costs, the individual may wish to reduce their debt servicing costs in the initial period so that they have sufficient liquid cash to cover the initial bills.

In the 1980s and early 1990s many individuals took out *endowment mortgages*. These mortgages were interest-only mortgages with a set monthly amount also being directed into an endowment investment fund. The theory was that the endowment fund would increase in value and would be of sufficient size by the end of the loan period to repay the capital balance outstanding. In most cases these mortgages did not provide sufficient funds to repay the capital. Individuals had to increase their contributions, and in many cases the endowment fund still did not cover the outstanding loan. Many financial advisers were considered to have mis-sold the mortgages and millions of pounds were paid out in compensation. The following equation can be used to determine the amount to pay into an endowment type mortgage to ensure that the policy matures with sufficient funds to cover the mortgage liability:

$$M = \frac{p((1 + y)^t - 1)}{y}$$

where M is the target maturity amount, p is the periodic payment, t is the number of periods and y is the rate of return expected to be earned by the fund. The target maturity fund will only be achieved if the fund earns the expected rate of return.

WORKED EXAMPLE 8.5: (ENDOWMENT MORTGAGES)

Alex wants to borrow €/£250,000 to purchase a property. She wants an endowment mortgage. Her bank can offer her the €/£250,000 at an interest rate of 6% and an endowment product which is expected to earn a return of 8%. She is thinking about paying the mortgage off in 20 years, though may have to agree to 25 years.

Required: As a trainee in the bank you have been asked to determine the monthly repayments required to pay the interest and to pay into the endowment fund so that it will have a maturity value of €/£250,000, assuming the mortgage term is:
  (a) 20 years
  (b) 25 years

Continued

Solution:

(a) The interest payment each month to the bank will be €/£1,250 ((€/£250,000 × 6%)/12).

The periodic payment to the endowment can be calculated using the following formula:

$$M = \frac{p((1 + y)^t - 1)}{y}$$

Where M, the target maturity amount, is €/£250,000
p is the periodic payment (to find)
t, the number of periods, is 20
and y, the rate of return expected to be earned by the fund, is 8%.

$$€/£250,000 = \frac{p((1 + 0.08)^{20} - 1)}{0.08}$$

$$€/£250,000 = p \times 45.762$$

$$€/£250,000/45.762 = p$$

$$€/£5,463.05 = p$$

Therefore the monthly payment to the endowment policy will be €/£455.25 (€/£5,463.05/12).

The total monthly payment will be €/£1,705.25 (€/£1,250 + €/£455.25)

(b) Where p is the periodic payment (to find)
M is the initial size of the mortgage (€/£250,000)
t is the number of payments, 25
r, the periodic interest rate, is 8%

Therefore:

$$€/£250,000 = \frac{p((1+0.08)^{25}-1)}{0.08}$$

$$€/£250,000 = p \times 73.106$$

$$€/£250,000/73.106 = p$$

$$€/£3,419.69 = p$$

Therefore the monthly payment to the endowment policy will be €/£284.97 (€/£3,419.69/12).

The total monthly payment will be €/£1,534.97 (€/£1,250 + €/£284.97).

A similar option which is available at the moment is called a *lifestyle fund*. Under this fund the contributions in the early stages of the mortgage are invested in equity. As the investment reaches maturity, the funds are transferred into bonds and finally into deposit accounts – so that the final balance cannot be affected by a fall in the equity markets shortly before the fund is to mature.

Mortgage Terms: Interest Rates

Mortgage lenders have to quote their interest rates as APRs or *Equivalent Annual Rates (EAR)*. This allows comparison across financial institutions. However, most financial institutions use other costs to gain revenues. For example, a mortgage lender may charge a set-up fee, they may insist that their house insurance product is purchased, or they may factor in a redemption fee.

There are two main types of interest rate: fixed-rate and variable-rate. *Fixed-rate mortgages* fix the interest rate being charged by the lending institution for a set period of time (typically one to two years, though terms of up to 10 years have been used in the past). This type of mortgage suits an individual who has a high debt-to-income ratio. They will be more risk averse and will be attracted to this type of mortgage as it hedges their exposure against increases in interest rates. This will also be seen as attractive to an individual who believes that interest rates will increase. These mortgages normally involve a high redemption penalty if the mortgage is redeemed within a specified period of time.

In a *variable-rate mortgage* the interest charged is usually pegged to the bank's base rate. In the ROI, banks' base rates are pegged to the European Central Bank base rate or Euribor. In the UK, banks' base rates are pegged to the Bank of England base rate or the London Interbank Offered Rate (LIBOR). When the base rate increases by 0.25%, so does the interest being charged on the mortgage. This product is commonly referred to as a 'tracker mortgage'.

Mortgage Terms: Introductory Offers

To attract mortgage customers, most financial institutions who provide mortgages offer introductory inducements. For example, variable rate/tracker mortgages usually come with an introductory discount on their variable rate. This discount is typically between 0.5% and 3% and ranges for a period of between six months and two years. Like fixed rate mortgages, a redemption fee will be payable if the mortgage is altered/repaid within a fixed period of time. In addition to this, it is possible that the lender will provide some cash back or pay legal fees. These incentives are attractive for individuals who wish to keep the cash outflows to a minimum in the initial years. The incentives are usually repayable if the loan were to be redeemed within a specified term (usually two to five years).

Other Mortgage Products

The competition between lending institutions over the past two decades has resulted in a variety of types of mortgage products being available. The most commonly sourced types are now outlined briefly.

Cap and Collar Mortgages

A *cap* mortage combines the benefit of having interest rate risk hedged as under a fixed-rate mortgage and allowing the borrower to benefit when interest rates fall as under a variable-rate mortgage. A *collar* mortgage is slightly different. The interest rate on this product moves freely in line with the bank's base rate between two limits. The *cap* is the predetermined upper interest rate limit and the *floor* is the lower interest rate limit. If mortgage rates fall below the predetermined floor level, the lender benefits from the arrangement; if the rates rise above the cap level, the borrower benefits.

Offset Mortgage

An *offset mortgage* involves pooling an individual's mortgage account with their savings and current accounts into one pot for the purpose of determining the interest to be charged for the period. The individual bank accounts are separate and have their own unique account number. The savings and current accounts do not earn interest, as their daily balances are used to save interest on the mortgage amount. The arrangement can be set up to have a fixed repayment, which means that an additional repayment caused by the interest saving will be used to repay the capital – hence the mortgage debt will be paid off quicker, or the monthly mortgage repayment could be reduced by the amount of interest saved. When an individual has liquidity needs the latter option is likely to be preferable. This product usually allows capital repayments to be made at any time. On the downside this product typically incurs a higher interest rate relative to straightforward variable-rate mortgages.

Current Account Mortgages

Current account mortgages are similar to offset mortgages except there is only one account that has an overall lending limit. The interest is charged on the amount borrowed. When this type of mortgage is being utilised, it would make sense not to have a separate deposit account but to lodge all funds in the current account, to reduce the net debt.

Flexible Mortgage

A *flexible mortgage* allows variation in the repayment schedule (there will be limits), additional capital draw-downs (to a limit) and the ability to make capital repayments without incurring a penalty (to a limit).

Shared Appreciation Mortgages

Shared appreciation mortgages were started by the Bank of Scotland in 1996, primarily as equity release vehicles for elderly people who wish to access some of the equity built up in their property. This involved the bank advancing 25% of the value of the property with no repayment in exchange for 75% of the appreciation in the property's value when the individual sells the property or dies. Therefore, if an individual's house is worth €/£50,000, they will be entitled to borrow €/£12,500 against the value of the property. If it is assumed that the individual sells the property in ten years' time for €/£150,000, then the bank will be entitled to claim €/£87,500 of the proceeds made up by the €/£12,500 originally advanced and €/£75,000 being 75% of the gain in the property's value (€/£150,000 − €/£50,000).

Co-ownership mortgages (Northern Ireland)

In Northern Ireland, a co-ownership scheme is supported by the government and is administered by Northern Ireland Co-ownership Housing Association Limited. The scheme aims to help first-time buyers who cannot afford to purchase their own property. The individual must purchase greater than 50% of the value of the property and the scheme covers properties with a market value of up to £175,000. The bank does not typically require a deposit for lower loan-to-value mortgages provided, but does require a 5% deposit when the loan-to-value ratio increases to about 80% (the deposit rates may vary across financial institution). The scheme helped 492 mostly first-time buyers to purchase properties in the year to 31 March 2012.

The monthly repayments include a mortgage repayment to the bank that advanced the funds and a rent to Northern Ireland Co-ownership

Housing Association Limited for the portion that is not owned. When the individual wishes to purchase the remainder of their property at some future date, it is the capital value at that date that is applied to determine the price. There may be issues in respect of improvements. The individual may undertake improvements which add value to the property as a whole, yet will still have to purchase the remainder at the higher market value, with no reduction in amounts owing to compensate for the monies spent on the improvements.

Re-Mortgaging

Most individuals are advised to re-mortgage their property as soon as the lock-in period is over. The *lock-in period* is a condition of most mortgages. The individual obtaining the mortgage agrees to meet the repayment terms in full during this period. It is a fixed term, typically the first two, three or five years of a mortgage. Re-mortgaging within the lock-in period can result in heavy penalties which reduce the attractiveness of re-mortgaging. After the lock-in period an individual might be in a position to repay part of the mortgage debt (reducing the monthly cash outflow) or may wish to extend the mortgage to finance something else (mortgages are typically the cheapest form of debt). If the mortgage is being extended to pay back bad debt this should be regarded as a short-term requirement, which the individual should aim to clear in full at the next re-mortgage. An individual should aim to clear their mortgage debt fully by the time they retire.

Mortgage Interest Relief (ROI only)

Mortgage interest relief is a tax relief that is given at source to home owners. This is known as 'Tax Relief at Source' (TRS). This relief is available for seven years, therefore has expired for any individual who purchased their property from 2004 onwards. The relief will end for all in 2017 and no mortgage taken out after 31 December 2012 will qualify for the relief. This relief is given by the lender either as a reduced mortgage payment or as a credit to the individual's account. This tax relief only applies to mortgage debt that is secured on an individual's main residence, so long as it is located in the ROI.

Different rates of relief apply to first-time buyers and other buyers.

First-time buyers: At the time of writing qualifying first-time buyers are allowed 25% mortgage interest TRS for the first two years of the mortgage falling to 22.5% for years 3–5 after which relief is provided at 20%. The relief is given to an interest ceiling of €10,000 for a single person, or €20,000 for a married couple, or a widowed individual. This equates to cash savings of €2,500 for an individual or €5,000 for a married couple on their mortgage repayments (for the first two years). The 2012 budget brought in a special relief rate of 30% for the remaining years to 2017 for first-time buyers who purchased their sole or main property in the period 2004 to 2008 (at inflated prices).

Other individuals: Other individuals quality for mortgage interest relief at the rate of 15%. The ceiling amount that interest can be claimed on for all other individuals is €3,000 for a single person and €6,000 for a married couple or a widowed individual. This equates to cash savings of €600 for an individual or €1,200 for a married couple on their mortgage repayments.

These reliefs also apply to extensions to mortgages that were in existence before 1 January 2004, so long as the extensions were entered into in the qualifying period – between 1 January 2004 and 31 December 2012. In addition the additional loan had to meet the qualification criteria (monies used to buy/repair/extend/improve the individual's main residence, which is located in the ROI). (Revenue Website, 2012.)

Property Market Risk Indicators

When house prices rise, individuals typically obtain larger mortgages and their *household debt to disposable income ratio* rises. After a long spell of house price increases the population in the UK and the ROI typically have higher debt levels relative to their disposable income. This ratio provides an indication of the liquidity risk that households face. The higher this ratio the greater the risk that financial distress can occur. In 2009 average household debt exceeded 176% (ROI)/170.7% (UK) of disposable income and *mortgage interest payments to gross income ratio* amounted to about 20%. This had increased from a ratio of 11% in 2003. The risk involved with these high ratios is reduced if the housing market is bullish, with rising prices and lots of liquidity as individuals can sell their property quickly. In this environment banks are more likely to be lenient when an individual has liquidity problems as the debt is secured on the value of the property. This was the case up to 2007. The *house price to income ratio* in 2003 in the UK was 3.36 times; however, this had increased to 5 times by 2008. However, during 2007 the property market started to stumble causing many households in the UK and Ireland to have negative equity and rising liquidity issues. A high house price to income ratio can lead to:

- A property price crash as continuing house price rises above income increases is not sustainable.

- Labour shortages and social immobility as people are unwilling to work in certain areas as they cannot afford to purchase a property in the area.

- Reduction in the liquidity of the housing market. First-time buyers will find it more difficult to obtain finance as the amount they are requesting is a greater multiple of their disposable income and the banks are less likely to provide finance, resulting in the property chain coming to a halt.

- A riskier banking system as banks provide larger loans to people who have to use greater proportions of their disposable income to repay the debt (www.mortgageguideuk.co.uk. 2012).

Before investing in property, it is recommended that individuals calculate their property to income multiple, their household debt to income ratio and their mortgage interest to gross income ratio. This will make them more aware of the liquidity risk involved in investing in property.

Collective Funds (In Brief)

Collective funds, otherwise known as *mutual funds, managed funds, investment funds* or just simply *funds*, are investment vehicles that combine a wide range of assets to create a diversified investment portfolio. They allow individuals to participate in a wider range of investments than they normally would, were they to invest in the underlying assets on an individual basis.

The most common types of collective funds are unit trusts, investment trusts and life assurance funds. These products are invested in by many investment companies, including pension companies.

Unit Trusts

Unit trusts are 'open ended' investments that have a specific aim. The term *'open ended'* means that the trust managers can create or cancel units depending on demand for the units. This means that, when an individual invests funds in the unit trust the manager purchases more investments and, when the individual wants to cash in their units, the manager sells some of the underlying assets to meet the individual's needs.

The value of the units is linked to the value of the underlying portfolio of asset investments which make up the fund. The underlying assets are predominately property, equity and bonds. The returns on these different classes of asset are not considered to be correlated and are assumed to hedge the overall return of the trust. However, this is not always the case. In the current financial crisis all three of these investment assets experienced a deterioration in value.

Unless part of a government tax break scheme, unit trust gains are subject to capital gains tax when they are sold/redeemed.

The value of the units can fluctuate, depending on the performance of the underlying assets. Therefore an individual's capital is subject to risk and can go up as well as down.

Investment Trusts

Investment trusts are usually British companies that are listed on the London Stock Exchange. They specialise in investing in equity shares (quoted and unquoted) and in other investment trusts both in the UK and overseas. Investment trusts are examples of closed-end funds. *Closed-end funds* are collective investment funds that have a limited number of shares. Unlike open-end funds, the share capital in closed-end funds rarely changes. If an individual wants to invest in a closed-end fund then they typically have to purchase shares in the company that manages the fund. Therefore, an investment in an investment trust company is possible by buying their shares on a stock exchange. This means that the value of this investment is influenced by the performance of the underlying equity assets that are held by the investment trust company and by demand for the investment trust company's shares in the market. If they are trading at an amount which is below the value of the underlying company assets then they are more attractive to an investor than if they were trading at a value which is greater than the value of the underlying assets.

Like unit trusts, gains on investment trust shares that are sold are subject to capital gains tax, unless they are included in a Government tax break scheme.

The value of this type of investment is likely to fluctuate in line with the equity markets. The capital invested is not protected. There is a possibility of negative returns as well as positive returns. This investment is suited to an individual who can tie the funds away for long periods and who has the flexibility to liquidate the funds when the conditions are right (the market is high), or to hold on to their investment when the market is low.

Life Insurance Investment Bonds

Life insurance investment bonds invest in similar types of assets to those invested in by investment trusts, though are sold for a specified term (this is why they are referred to as 'bonds'). They are similar to unit trusts in their make-up. An individual who invests in a life insurance bond gets a set number of units which reflect the value of the underlying assets. However, a portion of the investment is used to provide life cover. The taxation of these investments is complicated. As this investment is being covered only very briefly in this text, the author recommends that any potential investor investigates the tax consequences very carefully. In simple terms, fund holders pay the income tax and capital gains tax on the gains made on the underlying investments at the lower rate of tax. The bonds can be either regarded as qualifying or non-qualifying by Revenue and Customs/ Revenue Commissioners. On maturity, a *qualifying* policy has no further tax to pay. However, higher-rate taxpayers who have invested in a *non-qualifying* policy may have to pay additional tax on maturity. Steps can be taken to manage/reduce the potential liability. *Endowment mortgage policies* are examples of qualifying life assurance investment bonds.

Collective funds can be '*with profits*' (wherein the policy-holder is able to reap the benefits of the returns made by all the company's businesses – or the losses), '*protected funds*' or '*guaranteed funds*'. Protected or guaranteed funds are usually linked to an index. The growth rate advertised may be guaranteed, but the capital value is not – for example, a total return of 20% over three years may be guaranteed, but the capital value might fall by 70%. In this case the guaranteed return is 20% of the 30% remaining capital balance. The capital loss more than outweighs the guaranteed return earned!

Tangible Assets

Many investors choose to purchase tangible assets as part of their investment portfolio. Assets typically invested in include artwork, wine, forestry, precious metals, antiques and classic cars. Any collectable item can have the potential to result in gains. The gains may be subject to capital gains tax, duty and value added tax (VAT). In each instance, the investor should clarify the current taxation situation (across all the taxes) before investing. In addition to the financial reward, an individual can also gain pleasure from having the item (for example, art, antiques, gold or wine) or can feel satisfaction from the act of promoting environmentally friendly activities (if purchasing/creating forests). The advantages and disadvantages of some of the main tangible asset investments are now outlined.

Art/Photography/Antiques

The value of artwork, photographs and antiques can rise and fall in value. Over the past 20 years, investments in these items have, if carefully selected, outperformed the markets (A. Bawden, 2002). An excellent example is the sale by actor Hugh Grant of his Andy Warhol 1963 painting of Elizabeth Taylor, called *Liz (coloured Liz)*. Hugh Grant purchased the painting in Sotheby's in 2001 for a reported $3.6 million (Ivory, 2007) and sold it in November 2007 for $23.7 million (the actor is reported to have received around $21 million after commission (circa 12%)).

Investing in art/photography/antiques can be risky; the value of an item may fall in line with the world economy (the credit crunch in America may prolong; the current oil price has reached an all-time high and may rise higher); an investor may purchase a fake; an investor may pay over the odds for the item at the time of purchase because of lack of knowledge. In addition, there are the high costs that are involved in buying, insuring, housing the items securely, transporting and selling the items. Auction houses can charge up to 20% of the sale value for commission and insurance while the item is on their premises.

Gold and Gemstones

There is a readily available market for gold and, since the start of the credit crunch and the onset of recession, gold has become very popular with its value breaking price records every year since 2007. Gold was trading at £798 in July 2010 by July 2012 this had increased to £1,017.58 per ounce (www.24hrgold). Gold is sometimes used to hedge an investment portfolio as its value is usually negatively correlated to the performance of the equity markets. Investors who have investments that are exposed to foreign currency risk also use gold to diversify their risk, and the recent economic uncertainty with Greece, Spain, Ireland, Portugal and Italy will keep the demand for gold high.

Investment in gemstones can also be lucrative, but this market is attractive to fraudsters and care needs to be taken if gemstones are being considered for an individual's investment portfolio.

Wine

Sometimes referred to as **liquid gold**, investing in wine has become more attractive, though is risky for the uninformed individual. There are win-win stories that stimulate the interest of the investing community, such as the purchase of a case of 'Le Pin' for €/£150 in 1982 that is worth over €/£18,000 in today's market (Heartwood, 2006); however, there are many pitfalls. First, only certain types of wine are regarded as investments by the market. The Bordeaux region of France comprises about 94.41% of the *Liv-ex 100 index* (the fine wine benchmark index). Bordeaux (red) wine accounts for 93.4% with Bordeaux (white) accounting for 1.01% of the Liv-ex 100 index value. In June 2010 the index value was 343.86; by June 2012 this had fallen to 265.12 (www.liv-ex.com, accessed July 2012). Many investors expand their portfolio of investments to include wine to reduce their overall investment risk. Skilled knowledge of wine is vital for successful investment. The value of wine is influenced by vintage, chateau, classification system, taste and longevity, quantity produced, storage conditions and the ongoing cost of maintenance. In addition, the value of wine is susceptible to trends. It becomes fashionable to invest in wine and this changes over time. *Fine wine* is classed as a wasting asset by Revenue and Customs/Revenue Commissioners, hence is not subject to capital gains tax but is subject to income tax. The gains on wine are subject to capital gains tax in some instances – this is where Revenue and Customs/Revenue Commissioners consider a wine's life to be greater than 50 years, or they decide it is a business asset on the grounds that it is being used for trade.

Forestry

Investing in forestry is attractive in the UK and in the ROI because it is supported by both Governments as part of their environmental policies. To this end, the Governments do not charge capital gains tax on the increase in value of the tree crop if sold (though the increase in value of the underlying land is taxable). They do not charge inheritance tax on the value of the forest (so long as held for two years prior to death) and the sale of felled timber is free from income tax (restricted to 20 years in the ROI) and capital gains tax. Forestry grants are also available (though may be taxable). On the downside a forest takes over 20 years to mature (this depends on the type of tree, with oak trees taking over 100 years to mature) and is subject to damage by nature (fire, winds and disease).

Conclusion

Long-term investments should form part of every individual's financial plan. An individual is more likely to earn higher returns from long-term investments than from short-term investments. Indeed, many short-term investments can actually damage an individual's wealth as the return earned may not exceed inflation. Yet purchasing long-term investments has disadvantages, as funds are locked away and heavy penalties are incurred if the investments are cashed in earlier than planned or are cashed in when the underlying investments are performing poorly due to cyclical economic downturns. In some instances, potentially lucrative long-term investments can be loss-making in the short term. The equity market is a good example. If an individual were to invest funds in shares for a six-month period, they run the chance of making a loss, whereas if they were to purchase a balanced portfolio of shares for 20 years, it is more likely that good returns would be made. The risk-return relationship is also relevant. The equity markets are regarded as risky, hence a strong return is possible, as is a loss.

Individuals should always ensure that sufficient liquidity is retained, yet try to ensure that funds are not invested inefficiently – for example, kept in low-return bank accounts.

Most individuals, at some stage in their life, purchase their own home. This is a long-term investment and should be properly planned. There are a variety of mortgage products and this chapter has introduced a number of the more common types. Whether to opt for a repayment or endowment type mortgage with either a fixed or variable rate of interest will depend on individuals' preferences and views on how the equity markets will perform and how interest rates will move.

KEY TERMS

Advisory arrangement

Bank of England's Brokerage Service Direct

Bond market makers

Bond credit rating

Bonds

Buy-to-let properties

Cap

Cap and collar mortgages

Closed-end funds

Collective funds

Commercial property

Current account mortgage

Discretionary arrangement

Diversified portfolio of investments

Dividend yield

Endowment mortgage

Equivalent Annual Rates (EAR)

Ex-dividend

Liv-ex 100 index

Loan-to-value ratio

Loan-size-to-income ratio

Lock-in period

Low-risk investments

Managed funds

Management of a property

Mutual funds

Modest-risk investments

Mortgage

Mortgage deed

Mortgage interest payments to gross income ratio

Negatively correlated

No-risk investments

Offset mortgage

Overseas property

Open ended funds

Execution only service

Fine wine

Fixed-rate mortgage

Flexible mortgage

Floor

Freehold property

Gilts

Gilt-edged market makers

Guaranteed funds

High-risk investments

House price to income ratio

Household debt to disposable
  income ratio

Interest only mortgage

Investment funds

Investment grade

Investment trusts

Irredeemable bonds

Junk bonds

Leasehold property

Legal charge

Life insurance investment bond

Lifestyle fund

Liquid gold

Parental loan guarantees

Price–earnings ratio

Private issue

Property investment

Protected funds

Public issue

Redeemable bonds

Relatively high-risk investment

Repayment mortgage

Return

Risk

Risk-free investments

Second home

Secured loan

Self-investment pension plan

Self-liquidating investments

Self-select service

Shared appreciation mortgage

Stamp duty

Stamp Duty Land Tax (SDLT)

Tracker mortgage

Unit trusts

Variable-rate mortgage

With profits

WEBSITES THAT MAY BE OF USE

There are many sites that are geared towards giving advice on investment management. A couple have been highlighted here, though a Google search would provide you with a wealth of information.

- For information on purchasing properties through co-ownership visit: *www.co-ownership.org*
- Information on personal finance products in the ROI can be obtained from the following website: *www.itsyourmoney.ie*
- Information on personal finance products in NI can be obtained from: *www.moneymadeclear.fsa.gov.uk*

REVIEW QUESTIONS

(Suggested Solutions to **Review Questions** are provided in **Appendix 4**.)

Question 8.1

What are the differences between bonds and equity shares?

Question 8.2

What is a risk-free investment?

Question 8.3

Geoffrey requires a mortgage facility of €/£280,000 to purchase a property. He would like to be able to repay this over 15 years. He is wondering how much the monthly repayment would be, given that interest rates on this type of product are currently about 5%.

Required: Calculate the expected monthly repayment for Geoffrey.

Question 8.4

Geoffrey is also looking at an endowment type mortgage. He has been told that funds invested are currently earning 7%. The mortgage costs 5%. He feels that he would be better off if he opted for the endowment mortgage.

Required:

(a) Calculate the expected monthly mortgage repayment that Geoffrey will have to make.
(b) What factors should Geoffrey take into consideration when deciding on whether to opt for a repayment or an endowment type mortgage?

Question 8.5

List three differences between unit trusts and investment trusts.

Question 8.6

What are the benefits of investing in collective fund products from an investor's viewpoint?

Question 8.7

You need €/£25,000 in three years' time. How much will you have to invest now, given interest rates are 7% to ensure that you get the €/£25,000 in three years' time?

Question 8.8

During a recent game of golf, a colleague stated that 'admittedly, both property and equity shares had a bad year in 2008 and 2009, but the evidence shows equity shares as providing the best long-term growth performance compared to cash, bonds or property'.

Required:

(i) Prepare a table summarising the relative merits of the four types of investment on a scale of '1' = bad to '5' = excellent with regard to: growth (performance), security (risk) and access (liquidity).

5 Marks

(ii) Comment, giving reasons, as to whether you agree with the opinion that equity is the best long-term investment for all investors.

5 Marks

Total: 10 Marks

(Source: Chartered Accountants Ireland, CAP 1, Autumn 2009 (Extract from Q6))

Question 8.9

(Knowledge of IRR is required to answer this question.)

Your client, Mr Black, is a risk averse investor who is recently retired. Consequently he is no longer paying income tax at the high rate and expects to be liable to income tax at 25% from now on.

The interest rate receivable on his deposit accounts has recently decreased significantly and he is considering transferring some of his savings into government bonds.

Mr Black has identified a government bond with a nominal face value of €/£100 which has 12 more years to run before it matures. The bond pays an annual coupon of 8% interest which has just been paid. The redemption value is tax free, with only the interest being subject to tax. It is currently selling at a price which gives a gross redemption yield of 12% per annum.

Required: Calculate the market price of the government bond and the net redemption yield to a 25% taxpayer.

7 Marks

(Source: Chartered Accountants Ireland, CAP 1, Autumn 2009 (Extract from Q7))

Question 8.10

Jim Maddox is a self-employed butcher aged 61 with no mortgage loan on his residence. Jim was recently widowed and has two grown up children who are financially independent. He has a family history of heart disease and is reluctant to increase his pension contributions but, having inherited €/£22,000 from a deceased sister, he is considering investing it in low to medium-risk shares. Jim has no investment expertise, but believes the shares in Southern Bank plc at 30 c/p (22 c/p last year) are undervalued. However, a friend suggests he consider a collective fund product such as a unit trust or an investment trust.

Required: Advise Jim on the relative benefits of investing in the collective fund products detailed above instead of buying shares in Southern Bank plc.

5 Marks

(Source: Chartered Accountants Ireland, CAP 1, Summer 2009 (Extract from Q6))

Question 8.11

Joan and Jim have a newborn child and are considering investing funds to pay for their child's education. Which one of the following investment products would you recommend, and why?

  (i) A current account
 (ii) A deposit savings account
(iii) An indexed equity mutual fund
(iv) Government gilts
 (v) Fine wine
(vi) Gold

Question 8.12

George is currently renting in Dublin but is considering moving to London in the near future. Which of the following options is most appropriate for George given his current circumstances:

  (i) George should purchase a property in Dublin if he can get a mortgage where the repayment is less than his current rental expense.
 (ii) George should continue renting in Dublin because there will not be any tax relief for the interest payments he will have to make on the mortgage in the future.
(iii) George should purchase a property in Dublin because property prices always rise in value over time.
(iv) George should continue renting as buying and selling properties is costly and the investment is very illiquid.

Question 8.13 (Challenging)

(Suggested Solutions to **Challenging Questions** are available to lecturers.)

A personal client has asked your advice as to whether to increase her investment in the ordinary shares of Acorn plc which recently published very disappointing results. However, the company chairman made very positive comments that it was a 'one-off' problem and reassured investors that the company's prospects for the next year were excellent. Your client expected a significant decrease in the value of the shares and is confused as to whether to sell or to buy more.

Required:

In order to assist your client, comment on the possible meaning of the following information, supporting this with the calculation of any further relevant ratios.

Year:	2009	2010	2011
Earnings per share (EPS)	10c/p	15c/p	4c/p
Dividend per share (DPS)	2c/p	3c/p	3c/p
Share price	120c/p	195c/p	150c/p

7 Marks

(Based on Chartered Accountants Ireland, CAP 1, Summer 2012, Question 4(b))

Question 8.14 (Challenging)

A friend is considering investing a small lottery win in shares. Give this friend advice in simple terms (and using examples if necessary) as to how a shares price earnings (P/E) ratio and its dividend yield can be used as indicators to interpret whether a company's shares are under-valued or over-valued by the stock market.

6 Marks

(Based on Chartered Accountants Ireland, CAP 1, Autumn 2010, Q6(b))

Question 8.15 (Challenging)

Jane obtained a mortgage loan in 2006 at a variable interest rate. Because Jane had a substantial deposit saved, the loan of €/£240,000 was less than 70% of the cost of her house which cost €/£350,000. Consequently, with a loan-to-value Ratio (LTV) of less than 70%, she paid interest of only 5% rather than 6.5% for a higher LTV. Jane has read that mortgage interest rates are expected to rise by up to 2% over the next 12 months. She has been advised that the current market value of her house has fallen €/£100,000 to €/£250,000. Jane is considering switching her loan on which the capital sum outstanding is now €/£231,000 to a fixed-rate loan at 5.75% for 3 years. Jane does not qualify for tax relief on her mortgage.

Required:

Advise Jane on the advantages and disadvantages of switching from her current variable-rate mortgage to the fixed-rate mortgage.

7 Marks

(Based on Chartered Accountants Ireland, CAP 1, Finance, Autumn 2010, Q7(a))

Question 8.16 (Challenging)

A paper company invests €/£4 million to clear a tract of land and plant some young pine trees. The trees will mature in 10 years, at which time the forest will have a market value of €/£8 million.

Required:

What is the expected rate of return for the paper company's investment?

Question 8.17 (Challenging)

A 2012 advertisement in the *Belfast Telegraph* solicited offers on a 1992 Austin Martin (Collectable) that had been stored undriven in a climate controlled environment for 20 years.

Required:

If the original owner paid €/£4,000 for this car in 1992, what price would he have to receive in 2012 to obtain a 10 per cent annual return on his investment?

Question 8.18 (Challenging)

In 1960, your grandfather put €/£1,000 into a trust to be paid to a future grandchild (you) 60 years later, in the year 2020.

Required:

(a) How much will this trust be worth in the year 2020 if it has been earning 8%?

(b) How much will this trust be worth in the year 2020 if it earns 12%?

Question 8.19 (Challenging)

You have been hired as a financial advisor to David Bockham. He has received two offers for playing professional football and wants to select the best offer, based on considerations of money only. Offer A is a €/£10 million offer for €/£2 million a year for 5 years. Offer B is a €/£11 million offer of €/£1 million a year for four years and €/£7 million in year 5.

Required:

What is your advice? (Hint: compare the present value of each contract by assuming a range of interest rate, say 8% – 14%.)

Question 8.20 (Challenging)

Vincent van Gogh sold only one painting during his lifetime for about €/£20. A sunflower still-life he painted in 1888 sold for €/£26.57 million one hundred years later in 1988. At this time this was the highest priced painting ever sold.

Required:

If this painting had been purchased for €/£20 in 1888 and sold in 1988 for €/£26.57 million, what would have been the annual rate of return?

Question 8.21 (Challenging)

What is the present value of a 5 year €/£1,000 annuity, when the rate of discount is 6%?

Question 8.22 (Challenging)

The time value of money is 6%. You owe €/£15,000 which has to be paid in 3 years' time. What is the maximum sum you would be prepared to pay now to settle this liability?

Question 8.23 (Challenging)

Assume it is now 1 January 2000, and someone offers the following deal: starting from year 2000, you will be paid each year the amount of pounds equal to the year, i.e., €/£2,000, €/£2001, €/£2,002, ... until year 3000 inclusive.

Required:

(a) If payments occur at the year end and the interest rate remains at 10%, what is the PV of such a deal?

(b) What is the PV if the payments cover only the years from 2000 to 2050 inclusive?

(c) What can you conclude from the comparison?

Question 8.24 (Challenging)

You win a major prize and have the choice of a perpetuity of €/£25,000 per year with the first payments being made immediately or €/£420,000. You think that investments should earn a return of about 5%. Which option should you take?

CHAPTER 9

PENSIONS

Upon completion of this chapter, readers should be able to:

- explain the meaning of the key terms listed at the end of the chapter;
- discuss the merits of having a pension;
- describe the way the public/state pension works in your jurisdiction;
- explain the difference between a public/state and a private pension;
- explain the difference between a personal and an occupational pension scheme;
- calculate the value of a pension fund;
- explain the difference between a defined contribution and a defined benefit pension scheme; and
- detail how tax relief is given on pensions in your jurisdiction.

Introduction

Most young people look towards retirement as a positive thing, imagining golf, holidays and a life of comfort. A life where they are able to do all those things that they could not do because of work. However, many individuals who are in their fifties and early sixties are anxious about retirement. To them retirement means withdrawing from active working life. This means leaving their occupation, their status, their position and their link to the working social network. There is also the realisation that their income level will fall and there is uncertainty as to how they will be able to finance their current lifestyle. Many have to accept a reduction in lifestyle.

The problem has been accentuated by the increase in the longevity of individuals, the inability of the government to finance current public pension expectations and the reduction in the number of company defined benefit schemes.

Longevity of Individuals

The average life expectancy of a person born in 1900 was 47. The Office for National Statistics (ONS) estimate that males aged 65 in 2010 can expect to live until they are 78.2 years of age (on average); whereas females, aged 65 in 2010, have an average life expectancy of 82.3 years (ONS, 2011).

This is expected to increase by a further three years by 2020. Therefore, some individuals may be in retirement for periods that equal the period of time they spent working. This means that financing retirement is a growing problem.

Pensions

Pensions are monies that are paid to an individual or their spouse usually on retirement or when they reach retirement age. There are two types of pension: state public pensions and private pensions. Both pensions operate in a different manner. State public pensions are considered first.

State Pensions (ROI)

A common misconception individuals have is that when they pay their *Pay-Related Social Insurance (PRSI)* a portion is put aside to cover their pension. This is not the case. The Irish Government currently adopts a *'pay-as-you-go' policy*. Current employed individuals' PRSI contributions pay for current pension expenditure, though a Pension Reserve fund had been established to help fund future public pension commitments (discussed in **Chapter 2**). There are three state pensions available in the ROI: the contributory pension, the transition pension and the non-contributory pension.

Contributory State Pension

The *contributory state pension* is not means-tested and is payable to individuals who have paid sufficient social insurance contributions over their lifetime. These individuals can continue in work and still receive this pension. At the time of writing the maximum contributory state pension is €230.30 per week for an individual, topped up by a further €206.30 for a qualified adult i.e. partner/spouse (SW 19 – *Rates of Payment 2012*). This rate has not increased since 2010. This pension is available to any individual who is aged 66 or over and who has paid at least 520 weekly full-rate employment insurance contributions and a yearly average of at least 48 paid or credited weekly full-rate insurance contributions from 1979 to the end of the tax year when the individual reaches 66 years of age. The qualifying age will increase to 67 in 2021 and to 68 in 2028. Full-rate contributions are PRSI contributions at classes A, E, F, G, H and N and class S for self-employed individuals. The level of state pension (contributory) available depends on the extent of the annual average insurance contributions paid by the individual since 1979. It is important for individuals to keep their social insurance record active. Employers typically pay the social insurance contribution (PRSI); however, when an individual becomes unemployed, they may be able to get credited social security contributions as they are payable on some social welfare payments. Voluntary contributions can also be made. The rates paid by the Government in 2012 are provided in the following table:

Table 9.1: Rates of Payment 2012

Yearly average contributions	Personal pension rate per week	Increase for qualifying adult* aged < 66	Increase for qualifying adult aged 66 or over*
48 or over	€230.30	€153.50	€206.30
20 – 47	€225.80	€153.50	€206.30
15 – 19	€172.70	€115.10	€154.70
10 – 14	€115.20	€76.80	€103.20

*The qualifying adult pension reduces for every €10 earned by the qualifying adult in excess of €100. No qualifying adult pension is receivable if the qualifying adult earns over €310 per week.

(Source: SW19 *Rates of Payment 2012*)

In addition, €29.80 per week can be claimed for each dependent child, so long as the qualifying adult living in the house is eligible for the pension. If they are not, then a reduced claim of €14.90 per child is available. From 6 July 2012, no payment for a dependent child will be made where the qualifying adult earns in excess of €400 per week. The personal pension can also be increased by €7.70 per week if the individual is living alone, by €10.00 if the individual is over 80 years of age and by €12.70 if the individual is living on an offshore island.

The rates of payment are being reduced in September 2012 for individuals who have not paid the maximum required yearly average contributions. The rates are as follows:

Table 9.2: Rates of Payment from September 2012

Yearly average contribution	Pension rate per week (€)	Increase for a qualifying adult aged < 66*	Increase for a qualifying adult aged >66*
48 or more	230.30	153.50	206.30
40–47	225.80	146.00	196.00
30–39	207.00	139.00	186.00
20–29	196.00	130.00	175.00
15–19	150.00	100.00	134.00
10–14	92.00	61.00	83.00

*Means-tested (no change since before September 2012).

(Source: SW19 *Rates of Payment 2012*)

Transition State Pension

A *transition state pension* is available to persons who are 65. This is available for just one year and is only available to people who are retired or who earn less than €38 per week (see www.citizensinformation.ie, 2012 rates) and satisfy certain social security contribution conditions (an average of over 24 contributions yearly). The pension available until September 2012 depends on the average yearly contributions and is the same as that outlined in the first two rows of **Table 9.1**. For individuals reaching the age of 65 after September 2012, the rates are as outlined in the first four rows of **Table 9.2**. Individuals automatically transfer to the contributory pension when they reach the age of 66. It is worth noting that people who are 66 can take up employment again without suffering a loss in their contributory pension. The contributory pension for the individual who built up the contributions is not means-tested, though the pension for any related qualifying adult may be reduced, as their pension is means-tested. The transition state pension will no longer be available for people retiring after 1 January 2014.

Non-contributory State Pension

The *non-contributory state pension* is a means-tested pension that is available to all ROI habitual residents who are over 66, who have a valid personal public service (PPS) number, who do not qualify for the contributory pension and who satisfy a means test. The less an individual has, the higher the non-contributory state pension that is receivable. Any individual who has other cash income, income from employment of over €200, income from self-employment, or capital assets such as property (except for the individual's permanent residence), investments or savings, will have their non-contributory state pension reduced.

The individual's capital value is also converted to reflect a weekly income. Each €1,000 is converted to a euro income equivalent. The first €20,000 of capital is free, the next €10,000 is considered to equate to a weekly income of €10 (€1 for each €1,000 held above the threshold), the next band of €10,000 is converted at the rate of €2 for every €1,000 held, with the final band (capital held amounting to more than €40,000) considered to be equivalent to a weekly income of €4 for each €1,000 held. The maximum non-contributory state pension receivable in 2010 is €219 for an individual with €144.10 available for a qualifying adult who lives with the individual and who is less than 65 years of age (this increases to €219 if they also are 66 or over as they are entitled to make their own claim); an additional €29.80 is available per week for a qualifying child. The first €30 per week of means as assessed by the Department of Social Protection does not affect the rate of pension. After that the pension is reduced by €2.50 each week for every €2.50 of means. The pension payout diminishes depending on income level and is zero where the individual is deemed to have a weekly 'means' income of over €245.00 per week. (Rates can be found in the publication SW19 *Rates of Payment 2012, Payments for Retired or Older People.*) The rates have not increased since 2010. An extract from the state pension (non-contributory) pension payment rates for 2012/2013 is set out in **Table 9.3** below:

Table 9.3: Rates of Payment 2012/2013: Payments for Retired or Older People

Weekly income as assessed by the Department of Social Protection	Personal pension rate per week	Increase for qualifying adult aged < 66*
Up to €30	€219.00	€144.70
Over €30 and up to €32.50	€216.50	€143.00
Over €32.50 and up to €35.00	€214.00	€141.40
Over €35.00 and up to €37.50	€211.50	€139.70
...		
...		
...		
Over €240 and up to €242.50	€6.50	€4.30
Over €242.50 and up to €245.00	€4.00	€2.60
Over €245	Nil	Nil

*When the qualifying adult reaches 66 they are entitled to make their own claim.

(Source: SW19 *Rates of Payment 2012/2013, Payments for Retired or Older People*)

The value of partner/spouse income and capital is also included when calculating the weekly means income. The individual's means are taken to be half of the total means of the individual and their spouse/partner.

WORKED EXAMPLE 9.1: NON-CONTRIBUTORY PENSION: ROI

S. Moke, who is 66, has just retired. He is entitled to the non-contributory pension in the ROI. He is currently employed with a weekly income of €220, has farm income on land that he lets at €30 per week. He has €15,000 in the bank and a property worth €60,000 (this is in addition to his home).

Required:

(a) Provide an estimate of the non-contributory pension that S. Moke will be entitled to, given the above information.
(b) You are subsequently told that S. Moke has a partner, who is aged 64. She has savings of €55,000 and has no income.
Recalculate the non-contributory pension payable to S. Moke and his partner.

Solution:

(a) The starting point is to work out S. Moke's weekly means.

		€
Income from employment over the €200 threshold		20
Income from self-employment		30
Capital *(weekly means assessed)*		
Bank	€15,000	
Property	€60,000	
Total	€75,000	
Exemption	(€20,000)	
Balance	€55,000	

Assessed as:	€	
€10,000 × €1 per €1,000	10	
€10,000 × €2 per €1,000	20	
€35,000 × €4 per €1,000	140	170
Weekly means		220
State pension (non-contributory) per week		€29.00

(Source: Rates obtained from SW19 Rates of Payment 2012, Payments for Retired or Older People)

Continued

(b) S. Moke has a partner who also has savings of €55,000. As they are cohabiting the Department of Social Protection treats the capital as being jointly owned. Therefore the new pension is:

			€
Income from employment over the €200 threshold			20
Income from self-employment			30
Capital weekly means assessed			
Bank	€70,000		
Property	€60,000		
Total	€130,000		
Assessable (1/2)	€65,000		
Exemption	(€20,000)		
Balance	€45,000		
Assessed as:			
€10,000 × €1 per €1,000		€10	
€10,000 × €2 per €1,000		€20	
€25,000 × €4 per €1,000		€100	€130
Weekly means (for each person)			€180
State pension (non-contributory) per week			€69.00
State pension payable to the partner			€45.60

(Rates obtained from SW19: *Rates of Payment 2012, Payment for Retired or Older People*)

Other Benefits (ROI)

Other benefits available to retired persons in the Republic of Ireland include increases to the state pension (as mentioned there is a living alone allowance, an age 80 allowance, a fuel allowance, an island allowance, an allowance for a qualified adult or qualified children) or other schemes for the retired (a free travel pass; an electricity, natural gas or bottled gas refill allowance; a free television licence; a free telephone allowance; a carer's allowance; a medical card (conditions apply for most of these allowances)). As mentioned previously, retired people who are over 65 years of age may be exempt from paying DIRT, if their total income is below €18,000 for single/widowed persons or €36,000 for a married couple (2012 rates).

State Pensions (UK)

When the Welfare State was introduced in post-war Britain (after suggestions by Beveridge in 1942), a cradle to grave approach was adopted, with the government vowing to look after its citizens from birth to death. The state pension was part of this policy and was considered to be favourable at that time. However, in the late 1970s the state pension started to fall in value relative to the UK population's income levels, and limits on the amount that would be paid as a state pension were imposed in 2002 when the 'State Earnings Related Pension Scheme' was closed (discussed below). It would seem that current government policy is paving the way for further reductions in the value of state pensions in the future. The most recent change is an increase in the pension age. The state pension is currently available to women who reach the age of 60 and men who reach the age of 65. However, the pension age for women will increase to 65 by 2018 and both the male and female age limits will increase to 66 by 2020 and to 67 by 2026–2028. The coalition Government is set to link the state pension age to life expectancy. Therefore, it is likely that the state pension age will rise to 70 and beyond! Prior to April 2011, many individuals had to retire at 65; this has now been abolished. There is no compulsory retirement age; it is now entirely up to the conditions of the contract of employment. Pension increases from 2012 will be linked to the higher of 2.5%, earnings increases, or cost increases as measured by the RPI.

The public state pension is paid out of *national insurance contributions (NICs)*. This tax provides various benefits for an individual. The individual's entitlement to the benefits depends on their prior contribution record (at least 30 qualifying years). The benefits that can be claimed by individuals who pay NICs are weekly income benefits and some lump-sum benefits upon unemployment, maternity, disability, retirement and death.

A common misconception individuals in the UK have is that when they pay their NICs a portion is put aside to cover their pension. This is not the case. The Government adopts a *'pay-as-you-go' policy*. Current employed individuals' NICs pay for current pension expenditure. In addition, the current ethos is that benefits are more *means-tested* (not *universal*); therefore, employed individuals who pay higher levels of NICs do not benefit to the same extent as they used to. Indeed, individuals who save for their retirement are actually penalised when it comes to being able to claim a pension credit. A brief synopsis of the state pension is now provided.

There are two main pensions available, both of which rise with inflation and are taxable: the basic state pension and the state second pension.

The Basic State Pension

The *basic state pension*, which is a flat-rate pension, is payable to a single individual at the rate of £107.45 per week for the year 2012/13 (this can be topped to £142.70 per week with a pension credit). Civil partners are also entitled to a pension that is related to the other partner's NI contributions. They can get up to 60% of the basic state pension. This amounted to £64.40 in 2012/13, bringing married couple/civil partnership state pension income up to £171.85. This can be topped to £217.90 per week with a pension credit, so long as the individual paid NICs for a set number of years. Couples who are both entitled to full state pensions will receive £214.90 between them. From 6 April 2010, men born after 6 April 1945 and women born after 6 April 1950 have to have contributed for 30 years to qualify for the full basic state pension. Women and men born before these dates need to have contributed for 44 and 39 years respectively. When an individual is on benefits, is a carer, is in training or receives family allowance, the Government pays a notional NIC so qualifying years are recorded. It is only when someone is not on the system that the NICs fail to be accumulated. An individual can make voluntary NICs even if not working. If an individual has fewer than 30 qualifying years, they will get less than the full amount of basic state pension.

Pension Credits

A *pension credit* strives to ensure that individuals receive a minimum weekly income. The minimum amount was £142.70 per week in 2012/13 for a single person and £217.90 for a couple. Savings over £10,000 will reduce the pension credit as will most other sources of income, including the state second pension (there are some exemptions).

Additional State Pension

The *additional state pension* (formerly called the *State Second Pension (S2P)*) is an additional pension that is available to people who pay compulsory NICs over and above those required for the basic state pension. There is no cap on the number of years that can be built up, and contributions can be made up to retirement age, after which NICs are no longer payable. The amount that is paid under the additional state pension is capped at £161.94 per week (in addition to the basic state pension) for individuals who retired between 6 April 2012 and 5 April 2013.

At the current time, an individual can opt to *contract out* of the additional state pension and have the relevant NICs paid into a private pension scheme.

However, from 6 April 2012, this will no longer be permissible where the transfer is to a personal/stakeholder pension or a company/occupational pension scheme which is contracted out on a 'money purchase' or a 'defined contribution' basis (discussed below). The additional State pension (or S2P) replaced the *State Earnings Related Pension Scheme (SERPS)* in 2002. SERPS was established in 1978. It initially provided a pension equal to 25% of the average indexed excess earnings on which NICs are paid (over and above the amount required for the basic state pension) by an individual over their working life (this is reduced when the 90% rule is not fulfilled).

Over the last two decades, the SERPS pension has been reduced and eventually replaced. Pensions payable on the average excess earnings prior to 1988 still remain at 25%; however, a separate calculation is prepared for the indexed average excess earnings earned between 1988 and 2002 when the new S2P came into play. The rate used to calculate the SERP pension depends on the date at which an individual becomes a pensioner. The rate tapers from 24.5% for a person who becomes a pensioner in 2000/01 to 20% for an individual who becomes a pensioner in 2009/10. SERPS is protected, so anyone who contributed NICs prior to 2002 is entitled to the SERPS state pension amount that was running at that time.

The additional state pension (formerly S2P) applies for NICs earned after 6 April 2002. The additional state pension gives a more generous additional state pension to low and moderate earners, carers and people with a long-term illness or disability.

Future Directions (Universal Pension)

A universal flat pension rate of £140 will start in 2016 in England, Wales and Scotland for new pensioners with a 30-year NIC record. This will replace the basic state pension, the pension credit and the additional state pension. This will benefit low income individuals and will be detrimental to high income individuals who can currently obtain more on both pensions. Any individual who has already accrued SERPS and S2P benefits at the point of implementation of S2P contributions will still benefit from them (this may change).

Other Benefits

Retired people in the UK are also entitled to claim grants to undertake works that improve the energy efficiency of their homes and are entitled to claim a winter fuel allowance of £200 per individual living alone or £100 each per couple (2012/13) if over 60 years of age and to claim £300 if over 80 years of age and living alone, or £150 each if living with another qualifying individual. The qualifying age for this allowance is expected to increase to 65 over the period to 2020. When an individual reaches pension age, they typically qualify for bus and travel concessions, though this differs across England, Scotland, Wales and Northern Ireland. When they reach the age of 75, they are entitled to a free television licence. If born before 2 September 1929, a pensioner qualifies for a free 10-year British passport. Pensioners may also be entitled to a reduction in council tax (Britain) and a 10% reduction in their rates bill (NI).

Tax implications (UK)

State pensions (basic and additional) are subject to income tax, though retired individuals have higher tax-free bands that typically cover the state pension with some excess. The Government is taking action to reduce the preferential tax treatment afforded to pensioners. The 2012 budget increased the age-related allowance for individuals aged between 65 and 74 in 2012/13 to £10,500. For those aged over 75, this was increased to £10,660. The increases to the age-related allowances are at much lower rates than those announced for younger individuals. The personal allowances do not change for 2013/14, though the age bands do.

Individuals who are over 75 years of age also qualify for a Married Couples Allowance (a minimum allowance of £2,960 to a maximum allowance of £7,705) for 2012/13. This provides relief at 10%.

Tax implications (ROI)

State pensions (contributory and non-contributory) are subject to income tax, though individuals aged 65 and over are entitled to an income exemption limit which exempts them from income tax. This is set at €18,000 for a single widowed person and €36,000 for a married couple. The exemption limit can be increased if dependent children reside with the pensioners. Where income received marginally exceeds the exemption threshold, the individual can elect to pay tax at the marginal rate of 41% on the excess, or they can re-enter the tax system.

Private Pensions (UK and ROI)

Non-state pension schemes operate differently to state pension schemes. As mentioned, state pensions in the UK are funded from current NICs, in the ROI they are funded from the USC. This means that state pensions are susceptible to changes in Government policy and the economy (if the economy goes into recession, NICs fall and governments are less likely to award pension increases, resulting in the value of the state pension diminishing in real terms). There are typically two types of private pension scheme; personal schemes and company pension schemes. These are now discussed in turn.

Personal Pension Schemes

In a *personal pension scheme* an individual's expected pension payout is wholly dependent on:

- the specific contributions made to the pension pot;
- the performance of the administrator in the investment of the contributions over the contributing life of the individual; and
- the expected performance of the pension fund that will be purchased from the accumulated pension pot.

Personal pension funds are usually administered by financial organisations such as banks, insurance companies, unit trusts or building societies. They charge for starting up, investing and administering the pension investment (these charges are taken out of the pension funds). At retirement age, the built-up monies are used to purchase a separate pension fund from a pension company.

An individual's pension will be paid from this fund. A *pension fund* is a pool of assets that is established (when an individual comes of pension age) for the sole purpose of providing a pension. The pension fund is legally independent from the pension company and all the other funds.

Though this textbook does not examine all the different pension products available in the marketplace, one pension is worth a mention, lifestyle pensions, as they are popular.

Lifestyle pensions provide the investor with the flexibility to change the components of their pension fund as their lifestyle changes. The common view is that people who are young can take a higher degree of risk, hence the pension might start off by investing in equities, then as the individual progresses through life and gets older, they may wish to crystallise gains made in the earlier years by transferring their funds into less risky type investments, such as bonds, when they approach retirement age (say in their 50s). Then in the years coming up to retirement, the funds are transferred into risk-free/low risk investments, such as government gilts or deposit accounts. The potential for return is higher in the earlier years, but the risk is also higher. Typically, the different phases have different names, such as adventurous, balanced and cautious.

The format of a pension is typically:

- a cash annuity (taxable on the individual at their normal income tax rate);
- a lump sum; or
- some combination of both.

In both the ROI and the UK, there are tax breaks for *Pension Commencement Lump Sums (PCLS)*[1]. The *lifetime allowance* is a Government-set, tax-free limit on the total value of an individual's pension fund. The value of amounts held beyond this target limit are subject to taxation. In many instances, the individual who will receive the pension has some say over the format of the pension to be received.

INDIVIDUALS WHO SHOULD CONSIDER A PERSONAL PENSION SCHEME INCLUDE:

1 Self-employed people.
2 Unemployed people who can afford to pay contributions.
3 Employees who do not have a company pension scheme (either the company does not run one, or they do not contribute to the company scheme).
4 Employees who do pay into a company pension scheme but at a low level, as their income is moderate *(Note: It is considered better to make additional voluntary contributions to the company scheme or to consider a stakeholder pension).*

The different tax treatments for pensions for both the ROI and the UK are now outlined.

Tax Relief on Personal Pension Contributions (ROI)

In the ROI, the amount of tax relief depends on an individual's age and their earnings. An individual who pays tax at the standard rate will be entitled to a tax relief at 20% up to the limits outlined in **Table 9.4**. A higher rate taxpayer will be entitled to relief at 41%. The tax relief limits

---

[1] This is a Single Lump Sum payout that occurs when the pension commences.

on yearly contributions (which apply to private and occupational pension schemes) are as follows:

Table 9.4: Tax Relief Limits on Yearly Contributions Applying to Private and Occupational Pension Schemes

Age	Percentage of earnings
Under 30 years	Up to 15% of earnings*
Aged 30 to 39 years	Up to 20% of earnings*
Aged 40 to 49 years	Up to 25% of earnings*
Aged 50 to 54 years	Up to 30% of earnings*
Aged 55 to 59 years	Up to 35% of earnings*
Aged 60 or over	Up to 40% of earnings*
*Where annual earnings are capped at €115,000 (July 2012)	

For PAYE employees, the tax relief is given at source, with the pension contribution being deducted from the taxable income before the tax liability is calculated. From 1 January 2011, individuals pay PRSI and the Universal Social Charge (USC) on their pension contributions. Self-employed persons can claim the relief against their gross taxable income.

The maximum pension fund (from all sources) that an individual can have for tax-free status is €2.3 million (2012 rates). The fund value can be valued using the following formula:

$$(\text{Pension} \times 20) + \text{PCLS} = \text{Pension Fund Value}$$

Any pension funds that exceed the €2.3 million limit are taxable at the rate of 41% (income tax) when the funds are drawn down. An individual is entitled to receive up to €200,000 as a tax-free PCLS lump sum. PCLSs are taxed as follows:

Table 9.5: PCLS Taxation Rates

Amount of lump sum (€)	Income tax rate
0 to 200,000	Exempt
200,001 to 575,000	20%
Over 575,000	Taxpayer's marginal rate of tax
(Data obtained from www.citizensinformation.ie, accessed July 2012).	

Two examples of pension funds with values below and above the lifetime allowance are now prepared to further explain the tax treatment.

WORKED EXAMPLE 9.2: PENSION FUND BELOW THE LIFETIME ALLOWANCE LIMIT

Roger's private pension company has just written to him telling him that he is entitled to a PCLS of €200,000 on retirement and an annual pension of €60,000 thereafter. He has no other pension schemes.

Required:

Determine if Roger will be subject to a tax charge on crystallisation of his pension fund.

Solution:

Roger's fund is valued using the formula:

$$(\text{Pension} \times 20) + \text{PCLS} = \text{Pension Fund Value}$$

$$(€60,000 \times 20) + €200,000 = €1,400,000$$

As the €1,400,000 is less than the lifetime allowance of €2.3 million, Roger will not be subject to a lifetime allowance charge.

The €200,000 is tax free, as it is below the threshold (€200,000).

The €60,000 yearly pension will be chargeable to income tax each year.

WORKED EXAMPLE 9.3: PENSION FUND VALUE IN EXCESS OF THE LIFETIME ALLOWANCE LIMIT

Jennifer retires and becomes entitled to a PCLS of €800,000 and an annual pension of €120,000 from her employer's registered pension scheme.

Required:

(a) Estimate the value of Jennifer's pension rights.
(b) Describe the likely taxation treatment of the pension on crystallisation (show all calculations).

Continued

Solution:

(a) The Revenue will estimate the value of Jennifer's pension using the formula:

(Pension × 20) + PCLS = Pension Fund Value

= (€120,000 × 20) + €800,000

= €2,400,000 + €800,000

= €3,200,000

(b) Jennifer will have to pay tax on crystallisation of the pension fund on the excess amount of €900,000 (€3,200,000 − €2,300,000).

This will mean a tax charge of €369,000 (€900,000 × 41%) when the funds are drawn down.

The following formula is sometimes used to determine if an individual's pension scheme value is above the lifetime allowance:

$$LTA\% = \frac{(\text{Annual pension} \times 20) + \text{Lump sum}}{\text{Lifetime allowance}} \times 100$$

The LTA% is the Lifetime Allowance Percentage. If this equation works out at over 100%, then the pension fund built up will have exceeded the lifetime allowance percentage, and a tax charge will be payable on the excess.

WORKED EXAMPLE 9.4: LIFETIME ALLOWANCE PERCENTAGE

Jane is told that her occupational pension scheme will provide a pension of €90,000 per annum and a lump sum of €200,000.

Required:

Estimate the value of Jane's pension fund relative to the Lifetime Allowance Limit.

Continued

Solution:

Jane's pension fund relative to the Lifetime Allowance Limit is:

$$\frac{(\text{Pension} \times 20) + \text{PCLS}}{\text{Lifetime Allowance}} \times 100 = \text{LTA}\%$$

$$= \frac{(€90,000 \times 20) + €200,000}{€2,300,000} \times 100$$

$$= \frac{€1,800,000 + €200,000}{€2,300,000} \times 100$$

$$= 87\%$$

As Jane's percentage is less than 100%, she will not be subject to a LTA charge on the excess.

An individual no longer has to purchase an annuity with the remaining proceeds of a personal pension policy. However, this does not apply to occupational pension schemes, though may apply to additional voluntary contributions paid through occupational pension schemes. An individual can take 25% of their pension fund tax-free (subject to the limits outlined earlier), but the individual must then set aside a minimum €119,800 of the fund into an *Approved Minimum Retirement Fund (AMRF)* unless they have a guaranteed annual income from other sources of over €18,000. The balance on the AMRF cannot fall below €119,800 at any time before the individual reaches 75 years of age. Withdrawals from the fund are subject to income tax. An Approved Retirement Fund (ARF) can simply be a bank account with a regulated financial institution. An individual has to pay tax on 5% of the asset value of the fund if that amount is not drawn down. Where the ARF has an aggregate asset value of over €2 million, this increases to 6%.

Flexible Private Retirement Fund (ROI)

The *Personal Retirement Savings Account (PRSA)* is a retirement plan that is flexible, convenient and offers value for money (it has tax benefits). It is linked to an individual and, hence, follows that person between employments and if self-employed. When an employer does not have an occupational pension scheme, they can elect to contribute to their employees' PRSA. Tax relief for contributions, if relevant, are similar to that outlined in **Table 9.4**. The growth in the value of the fund is tax-free. The fund can be realised when an individual is between 60 and 75 years old. Like other pensions, it can be set up to provide a lump sum, an annuity or a combination of both.

Tax Relief on Personal Pension Contributions (UK)

As an incentive to promote personal pensions, the UK Government allows tax relief on contributions made to personal pension schemes. An individual can pay into any number and type of registered pension scheme and avail of the relief. In the UK, personal pension contributions attract tax relief at either 20% (if a basic rate taxpayer) or at 40% (if a higher rate taxpayer). The maximum amount on which an individual can claim tax relief in any tax year is the greater of the individual's UK relevant earnings, up to a limit, and £3,600. The £3,600 limit is typically applied where an individual does not have any relevant earnings. In the tax year 2012/13, individuals can contribute up to £50,000 per year from their relevant earnings into a pension fund and obtain tax relief. Any contribution above this does not obtain tax relief. This limit does not apply in the year that full pension benefits are taken.

Relevant earnings are emoluments that are chargeable to Schedule E taxation (including benefits-in-kind) and profits from a trade, vocation or profession chargeable under Schedule D.

The way an individual can get tax relief on pension contributions depends on whether they pay into an 'occupational', 'public service' or 'personal' pension scheme.

In a *personal pension scheme* the individual pays the net amount and the Government provides a tax credit to the pension provider worth 25% of the net amount paid to the pension company (this equates to 20% of the gross contribution). For example, where an individual has no relevant earnings, they can only contribute £3,600 to their pension fund. This is gross. In this instance, they pay £2,880 (£3,600 × 80%) to the fund and the Government pays £720 (£3,600 × 20%). Where the individual is a higher rate taxpayer, they have to contact the Revenue directly to claim the additional tax relief available to them (the Government only credits 20% to personal pension funds).

> **WORKED EXAMPLE 9.5: THE TAX TREATMENT OF PERSONAL PENSION SCHEMES**
>
> B. Good is self-employed. He earned £15,000 last year. He is 62, is wealthy and has no liquidity problems.
>
> **Required:**
>
> What is the maximum amount that B. Good can contribute to his personal pension scheme, relating to the income he earned last year?
>
> **Solution:**
>
> B. Good can contribute a gross amount of £15,000 to his personal pension scheme. This means that he should pay a cheque to the pension scheme administrators of £12,000 (£15,000 × 80%). The government will then contribute £3,000, taking the total contribution up to £15,000 (his net relevant earnings).

Furthermore, there is a lifetime allowance on the value of a pension fund of £1.5 million (tax year 2011/12). PCLSs are tax-free if they are less than 25% of the pension fund. The tax-free amount is further limited to 25% of the lifetime allowance where the pension fund has a fund value that is greater than the lifetime fund allowance.

Where the fund exceeds £1.5 million in value, the excess can be taken out as a lump sum – taxed at 55% (recovery charge), or the individual can withdraw the excess as income. This will be taxed at source at the rate of 25%. The remaining 75% that is paid to the pensioner is also subject to income tax.

The fund can be valued using the following formula:

$$(\text{Pension} \times 20) + \text{PCLS} = \text{Pension Fund Value}$$

Therefore, at present, an annual pension of about £75,000 is deemed to reflect a fund of about £1.5 million (where no PCLS is taken). A pensioner will only receive 75% of any pension income paid above the £75,000 limit, and will then also be taxed on the full pension received under income tax. **Examples 9.6** and **9.7** show the pension and tax consequences of having a pension fund with a value that either lies within or exceeds the lifetime allowance.

WORKED EXAMPLE 9.6: PENSION FUND BELOW THE LIFETIME ALLOWANCE LIMIT

Roger has a pension fund worth £100,000 at June 2012. He has no other pension schemes. Roger decides to take out the maximum lump sum possible.

Required:

Given Roger's requirements, describe the pension that he is likely to obtain (assume the lifetime fund value formula reflects market values).

Solution:

Under current taxation arrangements, Roger can take 25% of this pension fund (£25,000) as a tax-free PCLS. The remaining £75,000 will be used to purchase a pension annuity (a lifetime annuity). The Revenue would currently suggest a value on this of £3,750 (£75,000/20 – assuming the pension fund value formula applies in practice).

As the £100,000 is less than the lifetime allowance of £1.5 million, Roger will not be subject to a lifetime allowance charge. The £3,750 will be chargeable to income tax each year, though may be covered by Roger's personal allowance.

WORKED EXAMPLE 9.7: PENSION FUND VALUE IN EXCESS OF THE LIFETIME ALLOWANCE LIMIT

Jennifer retires and becomes entitled to a PCLS of £400,000 and an annual pension of £85,000 from her employer's registered pension scheme.

Required:

(a) Estimate the value of Jennifer's pension rights.
(b) Describe the likely taxation treatment of the pension (show all calculations).

Continued

Solution:

(a) The Revenue will estimate the value of Jennifer's pension using the formula:

$$(\text{Pension} \times 20) + \text{PCLS} = \text{Pension Fund Value}$$
$$= (£85,000 \times 20) + £400,000$$
$$= £1,700,000 + £400,000$$
$$= £2,100,000$$

(b) Jennifer will be subject to a Lifetime Allowance Charge on £600,000 of her Pension Fund (£2,100,000 – £1,500,000).

Pension Commencement Lump Sum
The maximum tax free lump sum is £375,000 (£1,500,000 × 25%)
The remaining lump sum of £25,000 (£400,000 – £375,000) will be taxed at source by the pension company at the rate of 55%.
Therefore, Jennifer will receive a lump sum of £386,250 being the tax-free element £375,000 and the taxed element of £11,250 (£25,000 (1–0.55)).

Pension Annuity
The remaining excess of £575,000 (£600,000 − £25,000 lump sum element) will be converted to an equivalent yearly pension of £28,750 (£575,000/20).
This will be taxed at source at the rate of 25% by the pension company.
Hence, Jennifer will receive a yearly pension of £77,812 being the £85,000 minus the tax deducted at source of £7,188 (£28,750 × 0.25).

Thereafter
The PCLS is tax free, but the yearly pension of £77,812 is subject to normal income tax rules.

The following formula is sometimes used to determine if an individual's pension scheme value is above the lifetime allowance:

$$\text{LTA\%} = \frac{(\text{Annual pension} \times 20) + \text{Lump sum}}{\text{Lifetime allowance}} \times 100$$

The LTA% is the lifetime allowance percentage. If this equation works out at over 100% then the pension fund built up will have exceeded the lifetime allowance percentage and a tax change will be payable on the excess.

WORKED EXAMPLE 9.8: LIFETIME ALLOWANCE PERCENTAGE

Jane is told that her occupational pension scheme will provide a pension of £60,000 per annum and a lump sum of £350,000.

Required:
Estimate the value of Jane's pension fund relative to the Lifetime Allowance Limit.

Solution:
Jane's pension fund relative to the Lifetime Allowance Limit is:

$$\frac{(\text{Pension} \times 20) + \text{PCLS}}{\text{Lifetime Allowance}} \times 100 = \text{LTA\%}$$

$$= \frac{(£60,000 \times 20) + £350,000}{£1,500,000} \times 100$$

$$= \frac{£1,200,000 + £350,000}{£1,500,000} \times 100$$

$$= 103.33\%$$

As Jane's percentage exceeds 100%, she will be subject to an LTA charge on the excess.

In an 'occupational' or 'public service' pension scheme the employee usually takes the pension contribution from the individual's pay before deducting tax (but not NIC). In this way, full tax relief (either at the basic or higher rates) is received immediately.

Flexible Private Pension (UK)

Stakeholder pensions are a form of personal pension. The difference between stakeholder pensions and other personal pensions is that they have to meet government standards. The requirements are that they should be flexible (have the ability to stop and start repayments) and have limited management charges. In all other respects, they are the same as personal pensions.

Occupational/Company Pension Schemes (UK and ROI)

Company pension schemes are sometimes referred to as *occupational pension schemes*. When a company offers a company pension scheme, this usually means that they will contribute to the pension scheme on an individual's behalf, so long as the individual also contributes to the scheme. The tax treatment of company pension schemes is similar to that in a personal pension scheme except that the employer deducts the pension contribution from the individual's relevant earnings before determining their tax for the year. This is how the Government provide their tax relief to the individual. Therefore, only the individual and their employer place funds in the scheme, not the Government. The treatment is best explained using an example:

WORKED EXAMPLE 9.9: TAX TREATMENT OF COMPANY PENSION SCHEMES

B. Good is employed. He earns €/£5,000 each month. He is a member of the company's pension scheme, in which employees pay 6% of their earnings and the employer pays 4%.

Required:

(a) Determine the monthly salary that will be subject to taxation under PAYE.
(b) Determine the monthly contribution to the pension scheme on behalf of B. Good.

Solution:

(a) B. Good will pay €/£300 (€/£5,000 × 6%) each month into the pension scheme. This means that B. Good will only be taxed on €/£4,700 (€/£5,000 − €/£300). Therefore, the tax relief is given at source.
(b) The total contribution to the pension scheme each month on behalf of B. Good is €/£500 (€/£300 + (€/£5,000 × 4%)).

Tax Relief in the ROI for Company Pension Schemes

An individual who pays tax at the standard rate will be entitled to tax relief of 25% up to the limits outlined previously in the personal pension section. A higher rate taxpayer will be entitled to relief at 41%.

Tax Relief in the UK for Company Pension Schemes

In the UK, pension contributions attract tax relief at the 20% tax band level and at 40% if a higher rate taxpayer. Relief is not available for National Insurance Contributions (NICs); however, if the company comes to an arrangement with the Revenue to treat the pension payment as a salary sacrifice, both PAYE and NICs are saved. This will amount to a total saving of 32% (20% PAYE and 12% NIC) for the employee and 13.8% (employer's NIC) for the employer for lower rate taxpayers and 42% (40% PAYE and 2% NIC) for higher rate taxpaying employees with the employer saving 13.8% employer's NIC.[2] The tax relief available is the same as that outlined in the personal pension scheme section. The difference is that relief is given through the PAYE system.

National Employment Savings Trust ('NEST') Pensions (UK)

From 1 October 2012, employers in large companies have to set up *National Employment Savings Trust (NEST)* pension schemes for employees who earn over a certain threshold (£8,105 in 2012/13) and who are over 22 years of age. The pension scheme will be phased in for employers of all sizes over the period 1 October 2012 to 2016. The NEST pension scheme will involve the employer automatically enrolling their employees (who qualify) in a qualifying pension arrangement. The employer and employee will have to contribute to the scheme with an overall yearly contribution limit being set at £4,400 (2012/13 rate). The contribution limit will be adjusted annually in line with average earnings (www.nestpensions.org.uk). The contributions will start low, at 2% (1% from the employer and 1% from the employee) and are expected to increase to 8% (3% from the employer and 5% from the employee) by 2017.

Types of Company Pension Scheme

Company pension schemes are of two types:

- defined benefit; and
- defined contribution schemes.

Defined Benefit Schemes

Defined benefit schemes are also referred to as *'salary related'* pension schemes. Defined benefit schemes are usually guaranteed. The pension

---

[2] 2012/13 rates.

amount being calculated is either a fraction or percentage of an employee's final salary, a fraction or percentage of their average salary over the final three to five years, or a fraction or percentage of the average salary of the employee over their full career. The latter is referred to as the *Career Average Re-valued Earnings (CARE) scheme*. The fraction is usually calculated with reference to the number of years and months of service given to the employer (i.e. number of years and months that the employee has contributed to the pension scheme divided by the maximum number of years as set by the pension scheme – this is commonly 80).

WORKED EXAMPLE 9.10: DEFINED BENEFIT SCHEMES

R. Hood has been working for the University of Ireland for the past 15 years and four months. He earns €/£60,000 per annum and has contributed to the pension fund since joining the university. The university's pension scheme is a final salary defined benefit scheme. It pays an annual pension related to the number of years and months that the employee contributed to the scheme, divided by 80. In addition to this, the scheme pays out a lump sum of three times the amount of the standard pension.

Required:

(a) Assuming that R. Hood's final salary is €/£60,000, calculate the annual pension he should expect to receive from the university's pension scheme.

(b) Advise R. Hood of the amount of the PCLS that he should expect to receive.

Solution:

(a) R. Hood's annual pension can be calculated using the following formula:

$$\frac{\text{Year and days}/365}{80} \times \text{pensionable salary} = \text{Annual pension}$$

$$\frac{15\text{plus}122/365}{80} \times €/£60,000 = €/£11,500$$

This equates to a monthly pension of €/£958 (€/£11,500/12). This is subject to income tax.

(b) In addition R. Hood will receive a lump sum equal to:
€/£pension × 3 = €/£lump sum
€/£11,500 × 3 = €/£34,500

Defined benefit company pension schemes that are administered by companies have become unpopular over the past 20 years. From a company's perspective, defined benefit schemes are too expensive. When the stock market fell in the 1990s so did the value of pension assets, and companies were left with large pension deficits for which they were liable.

The current accounting regulations insist that a company's pension liability be shown on the company's statement of financial position. This is deemed to be unattractive to company directors. Then there is the actual annual cost, with some companies having to pay 20% of employee salaries into the company's pension scheme. There has also been the problem of security.

This issue first came to the public's attention in 1991 with the Robert Maxwell scandal. After his death, it emerged that he had used £440 million of the pension fund to purchase shares in his own companies to boost their share price. This fraudulent behaviour affected 32,000 pensioners. Four years later, the investment banks (including Goldman Sachs and Lehman Brothers) and the accountants (Coopers and Lybrand) agreed to fund part of the deficit, the Government provided £100 million and the remaining Maxwell companies provided the rest in an out-of-court settlement. The total reimbursement was estimated at £376 million. This was still a loss to the pensioners, as Robert Maxwell used £440 million that should have been invested to earn a return for the pensioners. Gordon Brown's UK Government (December 2007) pledged that it would guarantee 90% of failed company pension schemes.

Defined Contribution Schemes

Defined contribution schemes (otherwise known as *money purchase schemes*) operate in a similar manner to personal pension schemes. A company contributes to the scheme on behalf of their employees and pays this along with the employee's contribution to the pension fund administrator. The employee's contribution is deducted from their salary before the tax is calculated on their earnings. The contribution is normally a set percentage of an employee's salary, though most companies allow their employees to make *Additional Voluntary Contributions* (AVCs). Like a private pension, the final pension will depend on the level of contributions made and the performance of the investment manager. When an employee leaves a company, they usually cannot contribute to the scheme and become known as *deferred members*. In some instances, the fund built up may be transferable to a new company scheme, or to a personal scheme. However, charges will be incurred if this happens.

Contracting Out (UK)

In the UK, employed people can opt out, called *contracting out*, of the additional state pension. In this case, the employer pays lower NICs to the Government, and puts the balance into the company pension scheme instead (these individuals still qualify for the basic state pension, based on the lower NICs still being paid). This option is only available for defined benefit schemes (since 6 April 2012).

Conclusion

Pensions have historically been used to provide funds for individuals when they retire. There are two versions of pension: public pensions and private pensions. Most public state pensions are paid by the Government from current NICs (UK)/social security contributions (ROI) to people who have contributed these taxes in the past. The level and type of public/state pension depends on the level of contributions made in the past.

In the ROI, individuals can either qualify for a contributory or a non-contributory state pension (non-contributory state pensions are means-tested and are payable to individuals who have not contributed sufficient social security contributions in the past).

In the UK, everyone who has paid the minimum level of NICs qualifies for the basic state pension, with people who contributed over the basic state level qualifying for a second state pension. In both cases, a minimum level of income is guaranteed, and an individual's income will be topped up to this level with a pension credit. At the present time, three public pensions are in existence; from 2016, these will replaced with a universal flat rate pension.

The other type of pensions are private pensions. Private pensions involve the build-up of a fund over an individual's life. This fund is then used to provide income for the retired individual. Pensions typically have three options, a Pension Commencement Lump Sum (PCLS), a monthly payment (an annuity) or a combination of both – 25% of the pension can be received in the form of a PCLS (usually, tax-free – to set limits).

There are two types of private pension; personal pensions and occupational pensions. Individuals usually set up and contribute to a personal pension when they do not have an occupational pension. Personal pensions are always contribution schemes (money purchase schemes). Their final value is reliant on the performance of the fund. The individual bears all the risk. Most of the institutions who manage personal pensions invest heavily in the stock markets, so there is quite a bit of risk associated with the funds.

Occupational pension schemes are set up by employers. Employees and the employer contribute to the pension. There are two types: defined contribution (money-purchase type scheme) and defined benefit (final salary). When the pension is a defined contribution scheme, the individual bears all the risk (just like a personal pension scheme); when it is a defined benefit, the employer bears the risk, as they guarantee the pension. If the pension fund built up is not large enough, they have to make up the difference out of their reserves.

Regardless of the type of pension (public, personal or occupational), all pension income received by an individual is taxable (except the lump sum that can be paid when retirement starts), subject to the usual tax allowances and tax bands.

Due to public demand, many pension schemes now offer ethical options, wherein they guarantee pensions that have not been built up by investment in what are deemed to be unethical businesses. These sorts of funds will not invest in companies that, for example, deal in arms, tobacco, alcohol, gambling, pornography, animal testing, exploitation of poor people or that cause environmental damage.

Because of the poor performance of pension funds over the past two decades, confidence in pensions has decreased. Most individuals no longer rely solely on their pension for their retirement. Many individuals build up other investments, deposit accounts, properties, etc., for their retirement years.

KEY TERMS

Additional Voluntary Contributions (AVCs)

Additional state pension

Approved Minimum Retirement Fund (AMRF)

Basic state pension

Career Average Re-valued Earnings schemes (CARE)

Contracted out

Contributory state pension

Deferred members

Defined benefit scheme

Defined contribution schemes

Lifestyle pension

Lifetime allowance

Means-tested

Non-contributory state pension

Occupational pension schemes

Pay-as-you-go policy

Pay-Related Social Insurance (PRSI)

Pension credit

Pension Commencement Lump Sum (PCLS)

Pension fund

Pensions

Personal pension schemes

Personal Retirement Savings Accounts (PRSAs)

Relevant earnings

Salary related pension

Stakeholder pensions

Money purchase schemes
National Insurance Contributions
  (NIC)
National Employment Savings Trust
  (NEST)

State Earnings Related
  Pension Scheme (SERPS)
State second pension (S2P)
Transition state pension
Universal benefits

WEBSITES THAT MAY BE OF USE

- For more information on pensions in the UK,
  visit: *www.direct.gov.uk/*
- For information on pensions in the ROI, visit: *www.welfare.ie*
- For information on personal finance and pensions in the ROI,
  visit: *www.citizensinformation.ie*
- For information on National Employment Saving Trusts,
  visit: *www.nestpensions.org.uk/*

REVIEW QUESTIONS

(Answers to **Review Questions** are provided in **Appendix 4**.)

Question 9.1

What is a pension?

Question 9.2

Explain the differences between a public and a private pension.

Question 9.3

Explain the differences between a personal and an occupational pension scheme.

Question 9.4

Explain the differences between a defined contribution and a defined benefit scheme.

Question 9.5

How is pension income taxed on a retired individual?

Question 9.6

Thomas earns €/£4,000 per month working for AIJ Ltd. He is a member of their occupational pension scheme. He contributes 10% per annum and the company contributes 3% per annum.

Required:

(a) Calculate the amount of Thomas's salary which will be subject to taxation.
(b) Calculate the amount that will be paid into the pension scheme each month by AIJ Ltd.

Question 9.7

Thomas has been working for AIJ Ltd for the past 22 years and 10 months. The pension is a final salary defined benefit pension which pays an annual pension related to the number of years and months that the employee contributed to the scheme, divided by 80. In addition to this, the scheme pays out a lump sum equal to three times the annual pension.

Required:

(a) Given the information in **Question 9.6**, calculate the expected monthly pension that Thomas should receive from the company's pension scheme.
(b) What lump sum should Thomas expect to receive?

Question 9.8

Thelma earns €/£3,000 per month working for Surething Ltd. She is a member of the company's final salary defined benefit pension scheme. She contributes 8% of her gross pay while the company pays 10%. The benefit entitlement to Thelma is 1/80th of her final salary for each year of service – maximum 40/80ths, and a lump sum of 30/80ths maximum 120/80ths, i.e. a lump sum equal to three times her final salary.

Required: If Thelma retires after 28 years of service, calculate the lump sum and annual pension that she will receive under the terms of her pension scheme.

5 Marks

(Source: Chartered Accountants Ireland, CAP 1, Autumn 2009 (Extract from Q6))

Question 9.9 (Challenging)

(Suggested Solutions to Challenging Questions are available to lecturers.)

Briefly explain four of the following terms to someone who knows very little about pensions (candidates should answer in accordance with their relevant laws and practice below):

Republic of Ireland:

(i)   Contributory state pension
(ii) Non-contributory state pension
(iii) Defined benefit company scheme
(iv) Defined contribution company scheme
(v)   Additional voluntary contributions (AVCs)

United Kingdom:

(i)   Additional state pension
(ii) Basic state pension
(iii) Defined benefit company scheme
(iv) Defined contribution company scheme
(v)   Additional voluntary contributions (AVCs)

8 Marks

(Source: Chartered Accountants Ireland, CAP 1, Summer 2011, Q7b)

Question 9.10 (Challenging)

Peter is approaching his retirement in 2 years' time and has been reading that pension funds were badly affected by the stock market crash in 2008, but some analysts regard increasing inflation as the main risk in 2011 and 2012.

Peter has been advised that his pension fund (sometimes called a 'lifestyle fund') automatically acts so that an increasing proportion of his fund will have been switched from equity investments into cash and fixed interest gilt loan stock in the five years before his retirement age, when it is assumed that he will be purchasing an annuity pension with his pension fund at the annuity rate at that date.

Required:

Identify and explain two advantages and two disadvantages of an automatic switching from equities into cash and gilt loan stock by a pension fund as Peter approaches his retirement age.

8 Marks

(Source: Chartered Accountants Ireland, CAP1, Autumn 2010, Q7b)

CHAPTER 10

REGULATION OF THE FINANCIAL SERVICES MARKETS

Learning Objectives

Upon completion of this chapter, readers should be able to:

- explain the meaning of the key terms listed at the end of the chapter;
- describe the regulation of financial services in the ROI/UK; and
- describe the steps to take when negligence is suspected.

Regulation (ROI)

The Central Bank of Ireland (CBI) is responsible for the regulation of all financial services providers in Ireland under the terms of the Central Bank Reform Act of 2010. The aim of the CBI's regulation is to promote a safe and fair financial services market for consumers, to promote sound and solvent financial institutions, thereby giving depositor and other consumers of financial products confidence that their deposits and investments are safe. The CBI regulates the activities of credit institutions, investment intermediaries, stockbrokers, financial exchanges, collective investment schemes, funds, investor compensation and related consumer issues, life insurance, general insurance, insurance-related consumer issues, money lenders, mortgage and credit intermediaries and related credit consumer issues, and credit unions (citizensinformation.ie, 2012).

The CBI monitors and enforces the consumer protection guidance, conduct of business and the prudential requirements of financial institutions as set out in the CBI's codes of practice. The codes of practice require financial institutions to act in a fair and transparent manner and to act in the best interests of their customers. The CBI also audits and monitors the practices of financial service firms and takes punitive action if required. It undertakes on-site inspections and has an enforcement department that takes matters further if issues are found by the auditing team. The most notorious investigations undertaken by the CBI involved Allied Irish Banks (AIB) and National Irish Bank, when it found that these banks were overcharging customers in certain cases.

Negligence Suspected

Negligence occurs when a financial adviser does not exercise due care, or fails to do what is reasonable and prudent under the circumstances. When an individual feels that they were misled by a financial adviser when being sold a financial services product, they can contact the National Consumer Agency (or the Central Bank of Ireland) for advice on how to proceed. All financial services firms in the ROI have to comply with the CBI's Code of Conduct (i.e. to act in a fair and transparent manner). Steps to take when a customer is unhappy with the advice received (suspects negligence) are outlined, in brief, in the following insert.

STEPS TO TAKE WHEN NEGLIGENCE IS SUSPECTED

1. *Initial contact:* Contact the firm who sold the product, explain the concerns and state clearly the required outcome.
2. *Formal complaint:* If the problem is not resolved, contact the firm in writing with a formal complaint. Include all details and specify the outcome required.
3. *Ombudsman:* If unhappy with the response received from the firm, contact the relevant ombudsman (an independent complaint scheme that is free of charge for consumers). They can recommend a solution or pay out compensation. In the ROI, there are two ombudsman services for financial products: the Financial Services Ombudsman Bureau and the Pensions Ombudsman.
4. *Courts:* If unhappy with the decision of the ombudsman, an individual can appeal their decision in the High Court.

The *Financial Services Ombudsman* (FSO) is a free, independent and impartial service, which was established by the Central Bank and Financial Services Authority of Ireland Act (2004). It became operational on 1 April 2005. The FSO is a statutory officer who deals with complaints from consumers about their individual dealings with financial services providers, where the complaint has not been resolved by the provider. The FSO deals with complaints about financial service providers and personal pensions. They investigate, mediate and adjudicate the unresolved complaints of customers. Complaints in respect of occupational pension schemes and PRSAs are dealt with by the Pensions Ombudsman.

The *Pensions Ombudsman* is also a free, independent and impartial service. Complaints are restricted to instances where the consumer considers that they have suffered financial loss because the pension scheme or PRSA was not managed properly (administration issues).

Regulation (UK)

Historically, the financial services in the UK were self-regulated under the Financial Services Act (1986) and the Securities and Investment Board (SIB). However, there were many scandals in the mid-1990s which suggested that self-regulation was not protecting the public. The main issue was *mis-selling*. Mis-selling is where an advised sale does not meet the Financial Services Authority's (FSA) standards. Examples of mis-selling during the early to mid-1990s included:

- encouraging people to leave occupational pension schemes and join personal pensions;
- encouraging people to take out endowment mortgages without highlighting the risks;
- selling split-capital investment trusts as low-risk when they are not; and
- encouraging individuals (particularly the elderly) to take out equity release mortgages when the individual was not made aware of the consequences.

On investigation, it became clear that some of the main perpetrators of mis-selling were the most influential entities under the self-regulatory system. Therefore, in 1997, an independent body was established to regulate the sector under the FSA. This system changed again in December 2001. The FSA itself received statutory powers under the Financial Services and Markets Act (2000) to regulate the financial services industry in the UK directly.

At the time of writing, regulation of the financial services industry is still under the remit of the FSA; however, legislation is in the pipeline which will result in the winding up of the FSA and the formation of three separate agencies to regulate the financial services industry using a more macroeconomic approach, rather than regulation on an individual institution basis. This change is being brought about because of the financial crisis. The OECD suggested that bank regulation not only did not protect the banking system, but contributed to the crisis (Hosking, 2009). Regulation was also highlighted as a problem by the International Monetary Fund (IMF), who commented in a paper that:

> 'neither market oversight nor prudential supervision were able to stem excessive risk-taking or take into account the interconnectedness

of the activities of regulated and non-regulated institutions and markets. This was due in part to fragmented regulatory structures and legal constraints on information sharing.' (See Cortavarria *et al.*, 2009)

The FSA conducted its own investigation (the Turner Review) published in 2009, and it also concluded that the 'light touch' approach to regulation had not worked and that more intrusive and systemic approaches were required. Turner also strongly recommended that a macro approach be adopted to bank regulation. The current regulatory body, the FSA, is now examined, followed by a brief outline of the expected new agencies and their roles.

The Financial Services Authority

The *Financial Services Authority* (FSA) is an independent non-governmental body. It is a company limited by guarantee and financed by the financial services industry. It is accountable to Treasury Ministers and, through them, parliament. It regulates the financial services industry in the UK. All firms that wish to undertake financial service activities have to be registered with the FSA. Indeed, it is a criminal offence to give advice without being authorised by the FSA. Financial advisers must demonstrate competence (by holding a relevant qualification), honesty and financial soundness. If a financial adviser is called 'independent', they must advise across a range of providers (*depolarisation*).

The FSA has four statutory objectives under the Financial Services and Markets Act (2000):

- to maintain confidence in the UK financial system;
- to contribute to the protection and enhancement of stability of the UK financial system;
- to secure the appropriate level of protection for consumers; and
- to reduce the opportunity for regulated business to be used for a purpose connected with financial crime.

To assist individuals, the FSA provides information on all the financial products that are available in the UK and will also provide advice/guidance when an individual considers that they have been treated negligently by a financial adviser.

Negligence Suspected

Negligence occurs when a financial adviser does not exercise due care, or fails to do what is reasonable and prudent under the circumstances. The steps to take when negligence is suspected are as follows:

STEPS TO TAKE WHEN NEGLIGENCE IS SUSPECTED

1. *Initial contact:* Contact the firm who sold the product, explain the concerns and state clearly the required outcome.
2. *Formal complaint:* If the problem is not resolved, contact the firm in writing with a formal complaint. Include all details and specify the outcome required. The firm has eight weeks to investigate the complaint.
3. *Ombudsman:* If unhappy with the response received from the firm, contact the relevant ombudsman. They can recommend a solution, or pay out compensation.
4. *Courts:* If unhappy with the decision of the ombudsman, an individual can appeal their decision in the High Court.

In the UK, the ombudsman is the *Financial Ombudsman Service (FOS)*. The ombudsman will help solve disputes between customers and *regulated* firms (Financial Ombudsman Service website, 2012). The FSA requires that all financial advisers have professional indemnity insurance. If an entity is found guilty of mis-selling, then their professional indemnity insurance can be claimed against. The result is that, in the future, the yearly premium will increase (FSA website, 2012). The financial adviser may also have to pay a fine, court costs and/or compensation to the victims. In addition, the financial adviser may lose their regulated status. If the offence is regarded as being fraudulent, the relevant financial advisers could even end up going to jail. When the professional indemnity insurance company does not investigate the claims of a customer, or does not meet a compensation claim, then the *Financial Services Compensation Scheme (FSCS)* may investigate (this is only available to those entities that are regulated by the FSA and is limited to individuals and small companies). The FSCS may provide compensation where the financial adviser is in financial difficulty (FSCS website, 2012). Individual consumers are not charged for use of the FSCS service.

The FSA is very active in pursuing claims and taking action against any individual or any institution that does not act properly when providing financial services advice, and details of hundreds of cases can be found on their website. For example, the Enforcement and Financial Crime Division's annual report for 2010/11 concluded that they had imposed a record total of £98.5 million in fines, including the highest fine against a firm of £33.3 million (against JP Morgan Securities), and the highest fine against an individual of £2.8 million (against Simon Eagle). They obtained five criminal convictions, secured over £100 million in redress for consumers and prohibited 71 individuals from the financial services industry.

The Proposed Regulation (UK)

The outgoing Chancellor, Alistair Darling, suggested in 2009 that:

> 'the quality, skills and judgement of individual regulators that failed to examine the connections between institutions led to a weakness in the regulation which failed to act to head off the financial crisis.' (Vina, 2010)

In addition, the current Chancellor (George Osbourne) in a speech on 16 June 2010 contributed some of the blame to the FSA:

> 'At the heart of the crisis was a rapid and unsustainable increase in debt that our macroeconomic and regulatory system utterly failed to identify, let alone prevent.' (Vina, 2010)

Over the next period, the responsibilities of the FSA are to be taken over by three new agencies under the auspices of the Bank of England. Each of these agencies is to work together and to take an overall macroeconomic view of financial institutions and how they impact on the financial system overall. The new structure has received support from the British Bankers Association. The proposed agencies are now outlined:

Financial Policy Committee

An interim *Financial Policy Committee (FPC)* has already been established by the Treasury and the Bank of England until the required legislation is enacted. It is chaired by Mervyn King, Governor of the Bank of England, and is made up of independent members. In addition, it is scrutinised by Parliament's Treasury Committee. When formalised by legislation, it will have executive power over financial supervision and will focus on macroeconomic issues. It will consider the impact of banking and financial services across the economy and will direct the Prudential Regulatory

Authority (PRA) to take action to avert deteriorations in the financial stability of the financial services industry and the economy. This will involve identifying risks and taking action by directing the PRA to reduce or mitigate the risks identified.

The other two bodies, the Prudential Regulatory Authority and the Financial Conduct Authority will be created to focus on the regulation of financial firms at a micro level.

Prudential Regulatory Authority

The *Prudential Regulatory Authority (PRA)* is to be created as a subsidiary of the Bank of England. It is to be responsible for the day-to-day supervision, called *micro-prudential supervision*, of financial firms, including banks, investment banks, building societies and insurance companies (HM Treasury, 2012). The PRA will adopt a more judgemental, focused approach to regulation so that business models can be challenged, risks identified and action taken to preserve financial stability (HM Treasury, 2012). The chief executive of this agency is expected to be a deputy governor of the Bank of England, with Mervyn King, Governor of the Bank of England, acting as Chairman.

Financial Conduct Authority

This regulatory body will take a tough approach to regulating how firms conduct their business. It will promote confidence and transparency in financial services and will give greater protection to financial service customers. It will promote competition in the financial services sector (HM Treasury, 2012).

KEY TERMS

Depolarisation
Financial Conduct Authority
Financial Policy Committee (FPC)
Financial Ombudsman Service (FOS)
Financial Services Authority (FSA)
Financial Services Compensation Scheme (FSCS)
Financial Services Ombudsman (FSO)
Micro-prudential supervision
Mis-selling
Negligence
Pensions Ombudsman
Prudential Regulatory Authority (PRA)

Websites that may be of use

- For information on regulation of personal finance in the ROI, visit: *www.centralbank.ie*
- For information on the role of the Financial Services Ombudsman (FSO) in the ROI, visit: *www.financialservicesombudsman.ie*
- For information on the role of the Pensions Ombudsman in the ROI, visit: *www.pensions.ombudsman.ie*
- For information on regulation of personal finance in the UK, visit: *www.fsa.gov.uk*
- For more detail on the role of the FOS, visit: *www.financial-ombudsman.org.uk*
- For more detail on the financial services compensation scheme available in the UK, visit: *www.fscs.org.uk*

Review Questions

(Answers to **Review Questions** are provided in **Appendix 4**.)

Question 10.1

What steps should an individual take when they suspect that they have been dealt with negligently by their financial adviser?

Question 10.2

Outline the current regulatory regime for financial services in your region (ROI/UK).

Question 10.3 (Challenging)

(Suggested Solutions to Challenging Questions are available to lecturers.)

Describe the financial services regulatory environment and in particular the steps that can be taken when a financial adviser is suspected of negligence in their dealings with a client.

7 Marks

(Source: Chartered Accountants Ireland, CAP 1, Summer 2011, (Question 7a))

APPENDICES

APPENDIX 1

CASE STUDIES

(Suggested Solutions to the **Case Studies** are available to lecturers.)

Case A: Debt Management: 'Martin'

Martin is 30 years of age. He has approached you to help him to manage his debt. He informs you that he has just received a pay rise that equates to €/£500 per month. However, up to this point he was actually overspending his take-home wages by €/£100 per month (this €/£100 is being spent on cash consumables). Therefore, he only has €/£400 to tackle his debt problem.

Martin informs you that he has a mortgage which has 15 years left to run. This mortgage is being repaid at €/£1,200 per month, payable on the first of the month. The last statement showed an outstanding balance of €/£135,000 (the mortgage interest rate is 6.25%). Martin has a 10% car loan, which he repays at the rate of €/£400 per month (on the 6th of each month). This loan has an outstanding balance of €/£6,000. He also has a 13% personal loan which is repayable at the rate of €/£200 per month (on the 4th of each month). There is an outstanding balance of €/£10,000 on this loan. He also has two credit cards. He owes €/£4,000 on the first (A) and €/£5,500 on the second (B). The minimum repayment on A is €/£70 per month, while the minimum repayment on B is €/£110 per month. These payments are due on the 15th and 16th of each month. Martin pays €/£250 off each card, every month. The balances have not been decreasing as Martin is still using both cards. The interest rate on credit card A is 1.4% per month and is 1.75% per month on credit card B. Credit card A has a credit limit of €/£5,000 and credit card B is at its limit.

Martin has historically paid his car insurance monthly. Last month, the final payment on last year's premium was paid. Martin is considering paying his car insurance over 12 months again. The yearly premium is €/£1,000. If he elects to take the finance option, he would have to pay €/£94.56 per month for the year. The payment date is the 10th of each month. Martin has €/£2,000 in his current account earning 1% per year and €/£1,000 in a savings account earning 5% per year.

Required:

(a) Prepare a 'debt schedule' for Martin based on the information provided.

15 Marks

(b) Classify the different types of debt into 'good debt' and 'bad debt'.

2 Marks

(c) Advise Martin as to the most appropriate steps to take to tackle his debt problem and to become financially healthy. Show calculations to back up your advice.

(Martin informs you that, apart from the €/£100 that he spends in cash, all his other consumable expenditures are paid for using the credit cards.)

33 Marks

Total: 50 Marks

Case B: Personal Financial Plan

A self-employed local businessman approaches you for advice on his personal finances. He supplies you with the following list of his investments, insurances and debt.

Investments
Credit union share account (4%)	€/£3,000
Deposit account at bank (2.5%)	€/£35,000
Government tax-free deposit account (5.5%)	€/£15,000
Current account	€/£15,000
Personal pension (€/£500 per month)	€/£45,000
Investment property (cost)	€/£70,000
Share portfolio value	€/£18,000

Annual insurances – yearly premiums
Life assurance	€/£800
Permanent health insurance	€/£750
Voluntary health insurance	€/£500
Mortgage protection insurance	€/£450
Loan protection insurance	€/£300

Debt
Mortgage outstanding	€/£180,000
Loan on vehicle	€/£18,000

Other Information
- The small share portfolio has returned on average 10% per annum over the past five years.
- The businessman informs you that his private home has a market value of about €/£400,000 and the investment property is worth €/£150,000. The investment property has been increasing in value each year. The businessman is aware of the strong return it is making and has not rented the property as he would have to spend €/£10,000 now to make it attractive to tenants. The property

could only be rented for €/£500 per month and the businessman considers that it would not be worthwhile undertaking the initial investment. The mortgage is secured on the private home.

- The businessman has just signed a loan agreement to purchase a vehicle (the agreement gives a 14-day withdrawal period). The loan on the vehicle is repayable at the rate of €/£1,400 per month for 15 months. The payments do not include loan protection insurance, which is being paid for separately at the rate of €/£30 per month. The businessman was able to purchase the car for €/£18,000, so long as he took the finance deal, otherwise the car would have cost €/£19,000. He reckons he got a great deal!
- The life assurance is being paid over the year at the rate of €/£80 per month.
- The permanent life insurance is being paid at the rate of €/£70 per month.
- The voluntary health insurance is being paid at the rate of €/£43.75 per month.
- The mortgage protection insurance is being paid at the rate of €/£37.50 per month.
- The mortgage repayment is €/£900 per month. This is an interest only mortgage. The businessman has been paying it for the past five years.
- The businessman informs you that his take-home salary from his business is €/£3,500.
- The general household costs are all purchased using the Visa card and amount to about €/£1,500 per month. The businessman pays €/£1,200 each month off the Visa bill. The outstanding balance has crept to €/£12,000. The Visa card company charges 1% per month on outstanding balances. The businessman regards this as not bad value.
- Inflation is currently at 2% per year.

Required:

(a) Prepare an opening statement of affairs for the businessman from the information provided above.

5 Marks

(b) Prepare a schedule of debt to be utilised by the businessman during the year showing the cost of each source.

12 Marks

(c) Prepare a personal cash budget for the businessman for the coming year based on the above information.

8 Marks

(d) Provide advice on how the businessman could better manage his finances and his investments. Highlight other information you would be interested in finding out about the businessman and specify how this might influence your advice.

25 Marks

(e) Prepare a statement to show the new expected statement of affairs at the start of the year assuming the advice given in part (a) is acted on immediately. In addition, prepare a revised typical yearly personal cash flow budget for the businessman assuming your advice is acted on.

25 Marks

Total 75 Marks

Case C: Preparing a Financial Plan

Veronica lives in her own home (worth €/£300,000). She has a €/£220,000 mortgage, which she is repaying at €/£1,200 per month (€/£650 is capital). The mortgage is converting to a variable-rate mortgage in six months' time (halfway through the year). The bank is offering base rate plus 3.5%. The same capital repayment is expected. Base rate is expected to be 0.5%. She will incur no penalties at this stage for extending or paying off part of the mortgage.

She has €/£2,500 in an instant access deposit account which earns a negligible amount of interest, €/£3,000 in the local credit union, €/£15,000 in savings and a rental property valued at €/£130,000 (debt of €/£50,000 being repaid at the rate of €/£200 per month (interest only)). She has an overdraft in her current account of €/£2,000. She pays interest at the rate of 10% per annum on this overdraft.

Veronica's net salary is €/£2,600 per month from her employment. She also gets an income of €/£650 per month from the rent of the rental property but has to pay out €/£120 per month on rates and insurance. She receives a dividend of 3% on her credit union share account and 2% interest (net) on her deposit account balance. She spends €/£150 per week on consumables (clothing and food, etc.) and €/£200 per month on household bills.

She pays two insurances: one at €/£35 per month (annual premium is €/£380) and the other at €/£40 per month (annual premium is €/£450).

Veronica has a car worth €/£1,000. She is thinking of changing the car and purchasing a new car worth €/£16,000. The bank has quoted her a five-year loan for the €/£15,000 required. The repayment is to be five annual payments of €/£4,265 (payable at the end of each period). Car expenses (tax, insurance and petrol) amount to about €/£240 per month.

Veronica received a legacy of €/£25,000 from her grandfather and has not decided what to do with the cheque.

Veronica pays tax at the 40% band on her rental profits (assume all the other income is received after tax).

Required:

(a) Prepare a statement of Veronica's net worth (at present).

5 Marks

(b) Prepare a statement of Veronica's projected cash flows for the coming year (based on the current financial situation).

12 Marks

(c) Show how purchasing the car with bank debt will impact on Veronica's statement of net worth and on her projected cash flows for the year.

3 Marks

(d) Prepare a debt schedule for Veronica from the information provided.

9 Marks

(e) Prepare a statement of Veronica's projected net worth at the end of the year (assume that the capital value of the properties have fallen by 10% in the year and that the car has been purchased using the bank loan).

10 Marks

(f) Identify any changes that you would suggest in her assets and liabilities that might increase her personal net worth. Re-prepare the amended cash budget and expected net worth assuming your suggestions are implemented. *(Note: a variety of outcomes are possible but all should specify how the legacy should be used).*

10 Marks

(g) Identify questions that you, as her financial adviser, would need answered before analysing the situation further.

10 Marks

(h) What insurances would you advise Veronica to consider? Assume she is single, is aged 40, has no children and is in good health.

6 Marks

(i) What other issues would you advise on?

5 Marks
Total 70 Marks

APPENDIX 2

PRESENT VALUE DISCOUNT FACTOR TABLE

Present value of 1, i.e. $(1 + r)^{-n}$. Where r is the discount rate and n is the number of periods until payment.

Periods (n)					Discount rates (r)					
	1%	2%	3%	4%	5%	6%	7%	8%	9%	10%
1	0.990	0.980	0.971	0.962	0.952	0.943	0.935	0.926	0.917	0.909
2	0.980	0.961	0.943	0.925	0.907	0.890	0.873	0.857	0.842	0.826
3	0.971	0.942	0.915	0.889	0.864	0.840	0.816	0.794	0.772	0.751
4	0.961	0.924	0.888	0.855	0.823	0.792	0.763	0.735	0.708	0.683
5	0.951	0.906	0.863	0.822	0.784	0.747	0.713	0.681	0.650	0.621
6	0.942	0.888	0.837	0.790	0.746	0.705	0.666	0.630	0.596	0.564
7	0.933	0.871	0.813	0.760	0.711	0.665	0.623	0.583	0.547	0.513
8	0.923	0.853	0.789	0.731	0.677	0.627	0.582	0.540	0.502	0.467
9	0.914	0.837	0.766	0.703	0.645	0.592	0.544	0.500	0.460	0.424
10	0.905	0.820	0.744	0.676	0.614	0.558	0.508	0.463	0.422	0.386
11	0.896	0.804	0.722	0.650	0.585	0.527	0.475	0.429	0.388	0.350
12	0.887	0.788	0.701	0.625	0.557	0.497	0.444	0.397	0.356	0.319
13	0.879	0.773	0.681	0.601	0.530	0.469	0.415	0.368	0.326	0.290
14	0.870	0.758	0.661	0.577	0.505	0.442	0.388	0.340	0.299	0.263
15	0.861	0.743	0.642	0.555	0.481	0.417	0.362	0.315	0.275	0.239

PRESENT VALUE DISCOUNT FACTOR TABLE (continued)

Discount rates (r)

Periods (n)	11%	12%	13%	14%	15%	16%	17%	18%	19%	20%
1	0.901	0.893	0.885	0.877	0.870	0.862	0.855	0.847	0.840	0.833
2	0.812	0.797	0.783	0.769	0.756	0.743	0.731	0.718	0.706	0.694
3	0.731	0.712	0.693	0.675	0.658	0.641	0.624	0.609	0.593	0.579
4	0.659	0.636	0.613	0.592	0.572	0.552	0.534	0.516	0.499	0.482
5	0.593	0.567	0.543	0.519	0.497	0.476	0.456	0.437	0.419	0.402
6	0.535	0.507	0.480	0.456	0.432	0.410	0.390	0.370	0.352	0.335
7	0.482	0.452	0.425	0.400	0.376	0.354	0.333	0.314	0.296	0.279
8	0.434	0.404	0.376	0.351	0.327	0.305	0.285	0.266	0.249	0.233
9	0.391	0.361	0.333	0.308	0.284	0.263	0.243	0.225	0.209	0.194
10	0.352	0.322	0.295	0.270	0.247	0.227	0.208	0.191	0.176	0.162
11	0.317	0.287	0.261	0.237	0.215	0.195	0.178	0.162	0.148	0.135
12	0.286	0.257	0.231	0.208	0.187	0.168	0.152	0.137	0.124	0.112
13	0.258	0.229	0.204	0.182	0.163	0.145	0.130	0.116	0.104	0.093
14	0.232	0.205	0.181	0.160	0.141	0.125	0.111	0.099	0.088	0.078
15	0.209	0.183	0.160	0.140	0.123	0.108	0.095	0.084	0.074	0.065

PRESENT VALUE DISCOUNT FACTOR TABLE (continued)

Discount rates (r)

Periods (n)	21%	22%	23%	24%	25%	26%	27%	28%	29%	30%
1	0.826	0.820	0.813	0.807	0.800	0.794	0.787	0.781	0.775	0.769
2	0.683	0.672	0.661	0.650	0.640	0.630	0.620	0.610	0.601	0.592
3	0.565	0.551	0.537	0.525	0.512	0.500	0.488	0.477	0.466	0.455
4	0.467	0.451	0.437	0.423	0.410	0.397	0.384	0.373	0.361	0.350
5	0.386	0.370	0.355	0.341	0.328	0.315	0.303	0.291	0.280	0.269
6	0.319	0.303	0.289	0.275	0.262	0.250	0.238	0.227	0.217	0.207
7	0.263	0.249	0.235	0.222	0.210	0.198	0.188	0.178	0.168	0.159
8	0.218	0.204	0.191	0.179	0.168	0.157	0.148	0.139	0.130	0.123
9	0.180	0.167	0.155	0.144	0.134	0.125	0.116	0.108	0.101	0.094
10	0.149	0.137	0.126	0.116	0.107	0.099	0.092	0.085	0.078	0.073
11	0.123	0.112	0.103	0.094	0.086	0.079	0.072	0.066	0.061	0.056
12	0.102	0.092	0.083	0.076	0.069	0.063	0.057	0.052	0.047	0.043
13	0.084	0.075	0.068	0.061	0.055	0.050	0.045	0.040	0.037	0.033
14	0.069	0.062	0.055	0.049	0.044	0.039	0.035	0.032	0.028	0.025
15	0.057	0.051	0.045	0.040	0.035	0.031	0.028	0.025	0.022	0.020

APPENDIX 3

ANNUITY FACTOR TABLE

Present value of an annuity of 1, i.e. $\dfrac{1-(1+r)^{-n}}{r}$ *Where r is the discount rate and n is the number of periods.*

Discount rates (r)

Periods (n)	1%	2%	3%	4%	5%	6%	7%	8%	9%	10%
1	0.990	0.980	0.971	0.962	0.952	0.943	0.935	0.926	0.917	0.909
2	1.970	1.942	1.913	1.886	1.859	1.833	1.808	1.783	1.759	1.736
3	2.941	2.884	2.829	2.775	2.723	2.673	2.624	2.577	2.531	2.487
4	3.902	3.808	3.717	3.630	3.546	3.465	3.387	3.312	3.240	3.170
5	4.853	4.713	4.580	4.452	4.329	4.212	4.100	3.993	3.890	3.791
6	5.795	5.601	5.417	5.242	5.076	4.917	4.767	4.623	4.486	4.355
7	6.728	6.472	6.230	6.002	5.786	5.582	5.389	5.206	5.033	4.868
8	7.652	7.325	7.020	6.733	6.463	6.210	5.971	5.747	5.535	5.335
9	8.566	8.162	7.786	7.435	7.108	6.802	6.515	6.247	5.995	5.759
10	9.471	8.983	8.530	8.111	7.722	7.360	7.024	6.710	6.418	6.145
11	10.368	9.787	9.253	8.760	8.306	7.887	7.499	7.139	6.805	6.495
12	11.255	10.575	9.954	9.385	8.863	8.384	7.943	7.536	7.161	6.814
13	12.134	11.348	10.635	9.986	9.394	8.853	8.358	7.904	7.487	7.103
14	13.004	12.106	11.296	10.563	9.899	9.295	8.745	8.244	7.786	7.367
15	13.865	12.849	11.938	11.118	10.380	9.712	9.108	8.559	8.061	7.606

ANNUITY FACTOR TABLE (continued)

Discount rates (r)

Periods (n)	11%	12%	13%	14%	15%	16%	17%	18%	19%	20%
1	0.901	0.893	0.885	0.877	0.870	0.862	0.855	0.847	0.840	0.833
2	1.713	1.690	1.668	1.647	1.626	1.605	1.585	1.566	1.547	1.528
3	2.444	2.402	2.361	2.322	2.283	2.246	2.210	2.174	2.140	2.106
4	3.102	3.037	2.974	2.914	2.855	2.798	2.743	2.690	2.639	2.589
5	3.696	3.605	3.517	3.433	3.352	3.274	3.199	3.127	3.058	2.991
6	4.231	4.111	3.998	3.889	3.784	3.685	3.589	3.498	3.410	3.326
7	4.712	4.564	4.423	4.288	4.160	4.039	3.922	3.812	3.706	3.605
8	5.146	4.968	4.799	4.639	4.487	4.344	4.207	4.078	3.954	3.837
9	5.537	5.328	5.132	4.946	4.772	4.607	4.451	4.303	4.163	4.031
10	5.889	5.650	5.426	5.216	5.019	4.833	4.659	4.494	4.339	4.192
11	6.207	5.938	5.687	5.453	5.234	5.029	4.836	4.656	4.486	4.327
12	6.492	6.194	5.918	5.660	5.421	5.197	4.988	4.793	4.611	4.439
13	6.750	6.424	6.122	5.842	5.583	5.342	5.118	4.910	4.715	4.533
14	6.982	6.628	6.302	6.002	5.724	5.468	5.229	5.008	4.802	4.611
15	7.191	6.811	6.462	6.142	5.847	5.575	5.324	5.092	4.876	4.675

ANNUITY FACTOR TABLE (continued)

Discount rates (r)

Periods (n)	21%	22%	23%	24%	25%	26%	27%	28%	29%	30%
1	0.826	0.820	0.813	0.806	0.800	0.794	0.787	0.781	0.775	0.769
2	1.509	1.492	1.474	1.457	1.440	1.424	1.407	1.392	1.376	1.361
3	2.074	2.042	2.011	1.981	1.952	1.923	1.896	1.868	1.842	1.816
4	2.540	2.494	2.448	2.404	2.362	2.320	2.280	2.241	2.203	2.166
5	2.926	2.864	2.803	2.745	2.689	2.635	2.583	2.532	2.483	2.436
6	3.245	3.167	3.092	3.020	2.951	2.885	2.821	2.759	2.700	2.643
7	3.508	3.416	3.327	3.242	3.161	3.083	3.009	2.937	2.868	2.802
8	3.726	3.619	3.518	3.421	3.329	3.241	3.156	3.076	2.999	2.925
9	3.905	3.786	3.673	3.566	3.463	3.366	3.273	3.184	3.100	3.019
10	4.054	3.923	3.799	3.682	3.571	3.465	3.364	3.269	3.178	3.092
11	4.177	4.035	3.902	3.776	3.656	3.543	3.437	3.335	3.239	3.147
12	4.278	4.127	3.985	3.851	3.725	3.606	3.493	3.387	3.286	3.190
13	4.362	4.203	4.053	3.912	3.780	3.656	3.538	3.427	3.322	3.223
14	4.432	4.265	4.108	3.962	3.824	3.695	3.573	3.459	3.351	3.249
15	4.489	4.315	4.153	4.001	3.859	3.726	3.601	3.483	3.373	3.268

APPENDIX 4

SOLUTIONS TO REVIEW QUESTIONS

Chapter 2

Solution 2.1

Though governments would like to provide for their citizens' total welfare needs they are unable to do so. The following factors are examples of circumstances that have impacted on the government's ability to find a welfare provision which provides financial security to individuals throughout their lives:

- People are living longer, hence state pensions have become more costly.
- Birth rates are low – this means that fewer employees will be available to pay social security contributions and the government will be reliant on immigration to make up the deficit.
- Contributions to social security are dependent on the economy. In a boom economy, there are higher levels of contributions relative to when there is a recession.
- The population's demands are increasing all the time. What is regarded as a reasonable standard of living now would have been luxurious 50 years ago.
- Technological advances have meant that governments have to invest heavily in expensive equipment to provide the service demanded by the public (hospital scanners, etc.).
- Governments have borrowed heavily over the past few years to reduce the impact of the financial crises and to bail out banks.

The result is:

- A move towards private health care, private dental care, private pensions and encouraging individuals to save for their own retirement.
- Cuts in public services.
- A change in the state pension which will mean it is less attractive in future years.
- Higher taxes, new taxes, lower public sector wages and lower welfare benefits.

Solution 2.2

Most people have debt. When interest rates increase, the cost of debt increases and individuals' disposable incomes falls. This may impact on their quality of life and their ability to save, to fund investments and to make provision for their retirement. In the more extreme cases, where the individual has debt levels that are very high, financial distress may result. In the worst cases, where the individual can no longer meet the higher debt repayments, bankruptcy will occur.

Solution 2.3

The surge in oil prices caused inflation to increase. Energy cost impacts on virtually every product that is bought or sold, as most are made with machines that are, directly or indirectly, dependent on energy. Even goods that are not manufactured are affected – fruit and vegetables have to be transported, which requires oil. It may be that the increases in oil prices will result in more domestic sourcing of perishable goods, etc. Inflation has the same impact as interest rate increases, it increases the amount that individuals have to spend each year, which reduces the amount of disposable income available for savings, investment and pension investments.

Solution 2.4

Northern Ireland
- ISAs
- Tax breaks for pension fund contributions

Republic of Ireland
- PRSAs
- Tax breaks for pension fund contributions

Solution 2.5

The banking and economic crises have caused a reduction in the wealth of most individuals and households. Unemployment has risen, house repossessions are up, salaries have fallen, house prices have plummeted and banks have become tighter with their lending policies. The result is that many individuals/households are experiencing liquidity problems and some are experiencing financial distress, while others have seen their income levels fall with the result that spending, saving, debt management and investment are more of a challenge. The economic crises also impacted on the financial markets and exchanges, hence pension funds have fallen in value affecting many individuals.

Solution 2.6

- Tied advisers work for and offer products from one company.
- Multi-tied advisers offer products from a selection of companies.
- Independent financial advisers offer products from the whole of the market.

Tied and multi-tied advisers are typically paid for their advice from commissions received from the companies that they promote. Independent financial advisers must provide the option for the individual to pay for advice with a fee, or commission.

Chapter 3

Solution 3.1

The key factors that should be considered in a financial plan include the following (as a minimum):

- *Profile* – obtain background information about the individual: age, employment, contact details, tax status and dependants.
- *Key objectives* – identify the primary financial objectives of the individual and his/her secondary financial objectives.
- *Determine the net cash flows* – identify areas where savings could be made if need be.
- *Consider debt management* – mortgage deal, credit card interest rates, loan rates, savings, set-off being used in the bank, etc.
- *Investments* – what are they for, when are they expected to crystallise? If there are future commitments (i.e. education); consider investment options to suit the future needs.
- *Taxation* – consider the influence of income tax, capital gains tax and inheritance tax on the current financial set-up and the impact on tax of any advice given.
- *Consider risk* – what are the current insurances; do they cover death (life cover), critical illness, unemployment (payment protection)? Are income levels protected?
- *Retirement* – the plan should refer to the needs of the individual when they retire, summarise the current steps taken and advise on whether there is a shortfall and the steps to take if there is.
- *Education planning* – where there are children – determine the extent of support the individual is willing to give; assess the current steps taken to achieve this, highlight any shortfall and recommend action to alleviate the problem.
- *Care* – determine if the individual has, or will have, to care for themselves or for another party (disabled child, elderly parents, ageing self).
- *Succession* – consider the steps taken to ensure wishes on death are known (will). Advise on the tax implications of the current will and suggest more tax efficient methods, if relevant.

Solution 3.2

Financial strategies to achieve financial independence might include the following: starting to budget and manage money; debt reduction/rescheduling; develop a savings plan; invest in equity shares or bonds; purchase property for investment purposes; invest in tax efficient savings products; invest in a pension.

Solution 3.3

Risk in personal financial planning is the chance that the individual's actual cash flows and life expectancy turn out to be different to what was predicted in the financial plan.

Solution 3.4

Statement of affairs for the businessman at the start of the period:

Assets	€/£
Main family residence	400,000
Investment property	150,000
Credit union share account	3,000
Deposit account	35,000
ISA	15,000
Current account	15,000
Motor vehicle	18,000
Share portfolio	18,000
	654,000

Liabilities	
Mortgage	(180,000)
Vehicle loan	(18,000)
Credit card	(12,000)
	(210,000)
Net worth	444,000

In addition, the businessman has a pension fund of €/£45,000 (this is untouchable until he is retired). Taking this into account his net worth is €/£489,000.

Solution 3.6

Most marketing people use affordability as a marketing ploy to entice people to purchase products/goods/services. People will think a product is good value if it can be obtained by paying out a small amount on a regular basis, preferably monthly/weekly. If people have to pay one large bill, they would be a little more wary about spending money.

The cash budget can be used to determine the actual spend on items in yearly terms. It can make individuals more aware of the consequences of not keeping control of their money. Most people consider their income in yearly terms and, even though they are often well paid, cannot accumulate wealth, because they let the Pounds/Euros dribble away all year. For example, a coffee in Renoirs (a café beside the university I work in) is £1.70. Assume a person purchases one coffee every working week day (I generally do) – this means that the person will spend £8.50 per week on coffee. In yearly terms (assume the person works 47 weeks of the year), this person spends £399.50 in cash, each year, just on coffee! This sort of spending is no problem at all, so long as the person is in line with their finances to achieve their objectives (sufficient retirement fund, savings, paying debt, etc.). However, if the person is living beyond their means or is not going to achieve their financial objectives (for example, building up a deposit to purchase a house, or building up a good pension fund), then this budget can be used to highlight unnecessary expenditure. The person can then take steps to reduce their expenditure. For example, they could decide just to have coffee two days a week – saving £239.70 per year.

Another saving might be to decide that one phone will suffice, where an individual has both a landline and a mobile phone. They could decide that the satellite and cable channels are not worth it, etc. These are all luxury expenditures that should be curbed when a person is living beyond their means.

Solution 3.7

(i) Preparing a monthly budget can help an individual achieve financial security by making the individual more aware of their cash inflows and outflows; thus helping them to make better cash allocation decisions.

Chapter 4

Solution 4.1

(a) Students typically have little income. They should try to ensure that they leave college with the lowest level of debt that they can. Therefore, the focus of their financial plan should be on analysing expenditure and minimising debt. When analysing expenditure the focus is on reducing non-necessary expenditure and making the student aware of the amount they spend on various consumables. Whereas a budget for experiencing the 'student life' should not be ruled out, a limit should be placed on it.

Minimising the exposure to debt is very important. Student loans are available and these, apart from loans from family members, should be the first source of debt finance. Student loans typically charge inflation rates only, so will be the cheapest source of funds available. Students should be made aware of the pitfalls of using credit cards and other sources of bad debt.

(b) Retired individuals will have two key areas that become more important than others. The first is structuring their investments, savings and pension funds in such a manner that they receive a suitable level of cash to maintain the lifestyle they planned for. This will involve making an estimate of life expectancy. The second is succession planning. A will should already have been created in earlier years. However, now is the time to update the will to reflect their wishes. It is recommended that individuals, who plan for succession, make their heirs aware of their wishes. This is something that retired individuals might want to consider.

Solution 4.2

A 30 year-old person is likely to be employed, to have some savings, some debt, maybe own a house (with a mortgage) and a few assets. They are likely to have been paying into a pension scheme in their work and to have a reasonably high consumable spend. Given that the person is married, a premarital agreement is too late. The focus now should be on whether to integrate the couple's assets, or to keep them apart. If both parties own a property then the decision may have to be made to sell both and purchase one together, or to sell one, or rent one. Getting the documentation, deeds, etc., changed to include both names is important if the decision is made to merge assets.

Other issues, less immediate, might include:
- Both parties should get together and revisit their financial plans, creating a new one between them.
- New objectives should be set.
- The couple should decide whether or not they are going to have children. The likely number of children, etc., should be considered.
- Estimates for the cost of this should be factored in, including whether they are going to pay for their child/children's education.
- Insurance will also have to be reviewed and the partner included on insurance policies.
- The pension company will need to be made aware of the spouse.
- Joint surplus funds can be determined and suitable investments reviewed.

Solution 4.3

The immediate issues to be dealt with are the redundancy money, the mortgage and the pension.

If the redundancy money can cover the mortgage, and Percy has no other debt and has a savings buffer until he secures new employment, then this would be one approach that could be taken. It would reduce Percy's financial risk in the future, as the fixed mortgage repayment would not need to be made.

As Percy has worked for the same company for 20 years, he has probably built up quite a pension pot. He would need to get information on his options in relation to the pension. To remove pension funds before retirement is costly. The company seems strong – hence it might be better to leave the pension in the company until retirement (more detail would be requested).

Pensions can no longer be solely relied on to provide for an individual when they retire, Percy will need to look at his assets (savings, other investments, etc.) to see if they are sufficient to provide him with an income when he retires.

Other factors need to be considered. Has Percy a partner who is earning? Is it likely that Percy will get another job? Is the company offering retraining? How is Percy's health, etc.?

The financial plan will have to be completely changed to take account of the new cash flows, the risks reassessed and the objectives revisited.

Solution 4.4

The list might include information on the following:
- Life insurance policies taken out by the husband
- Pension scheme paid into by the husband and Mary's rights, if any to these funds (sometimes this will pay out on the death of the pension fund member)
- Qualifications, if any
- View on working
- Health
- Debt
- Savings
- Mortgage (life insurance)
- House
- Investments
- Ages of children
- Views on education of children
- Support for caring for children (parental support)
- Cash inflows expected from any source
- Benefits being received/possible financial help
- Views on downsizing property
- Number of vehicles in household (sell one?)

Solution 4.5

Being frugal is recommended in a person's early financial lifecycle, as money has the greatest value to that category of person. When a person gets established, they naturally spend more, as the foundation blocks of their wealth have been created. When a person is being frugal they are more likely to build up a deposit for a house and also may be able to purchase a motor vehicle for cash. This immediately impacts on their net worth, as properties usually increase in value each year and, the earlier an individual starts to pay off their mortgage, the quicker that property will be repaid before retirement. When an individual purchases a car using funds saved, not borrowed, they do not have monthly car repayments with interest to cover. This provides them with cash flexibility. Being frugal will also be interpreted in a positive light by the bank when an individual goes to obtain credit, even initial credit. Banks and other financial institutions consider people who have a strong savings record in a far better light. They are classed as being low risk and are likely to be able to negotiate a low rate for the debt they are seeking.

Solution 4.6

Comparison of financial goals and positions

Likely position:	*Father*	*Son*
Age	52	22
Income	High	Low/nil
	Surplus income	Income deficit
Dependants	Spouse	None
	Children	
	Parents	
Assets	Property	Nil
	Investments	
	Pension	
Liabilities	Debts (probably low)	Student loans

Likely goals:	*Father*	*Son*
	Educate children	Reduce debt
	Low-risk pension	Full-time earnings
	choices/planning for	Deposit for property
	retirement (c. 10 years	purchase/rental
	to retirement)	Car purchase
	Reduce debt	Holidays/Travel
	Adequate insurance (life,	Unlikely to have much
	health, disability).	interest/priority yet
	Investments to be tailored	in pension/investments
	with short-/medium-term	Critical illness insurance
	access in mind and probably	
	low risk given age profile	

Solution 4.7

(i) Death – the individual has to consider the financial impact on the surviving dependants and value of the estate. Some issues to consider might include:

- Loss of earnings – only investment income (if any) continues.
- Dependants/survivors may not have sufficient income.
- Dependants may be unable to pay outstanding debts which could lead to a forced asset sale.
- If non-earning spouse dies, then survivor may have substantial increase in costs e.g. childminding costs.
- Survivor – single tax status may increase tax payable and thus reduce net income.
- If no dependants, then no financial obligations beyond funeral and related costs.

(ii) Disability – the individual has to consider the change in their circumstances which may include the following:

- Loss of earnings from employment.
- If self-employed, the potential loss of profits in business or even the possible loss of the business.
- Disabled person becomes a dependent person.
- Evaluating how to pay outstanding debts.
- Determining the additional costs for medication, care and possible alterations that may be required to the house.
- Reviewing state benefits and allowances available and determining whether these are adequate.
- Childcare costs may increase if the non-earning spouse becomes disabled.

(iii) Retirement – the individual has to consider the change in their circumstances which may include the following:

- Loss of earnings, which are only partially replaced by pensions (state and personal).
- Difficulty in borrowing money. Therefore expensive items are usually financed by the disposal of other assets.
- Inflation may progressively reduce real income (particularly where the return from the investment does not exceed the inflation rates).
- Increase in medical costs.
- Benefit from decreasing number of dependants, no mortgage, etc.
- Too late to boost pension or other income at this stage.
    (Source: Chartered Accountants Ireland, CAP 1, Summer 2009 (Extract from Q7))

Chapter 5

Solution 5.1

Insurance refers to policies that insure against the risk/chance/likelihood of something happening, like a nature disaster, or accidental death during the term of the policy. Assurance refers to policies that provide for something that is going to happen. The best example is death.

Solution 5.2

For some life assurance policies death does not have to occur during the term of the policy – **whole-of-life policies** pay out on the death of the policyholder. These policies are more expensive than term assurance policies as the company providing the policy definitely has to pay out on death. A policy which only pays out on death within the policy term is called a **term policy**. There are two types of whole-of-life policies. One involves the policyholder paying premiums for a set term after which the policy is treated as being paid up. The lump sum will be paid on death afterwards. The other option involves paying contributions for the rest of the policyholder's natural life. Whole-of-life policies might be used to cover expected inheritance tax liabilities on the individual's estate.

Solution 5.3

The most important insurance for a family man with three children is income protection both during his life (if he loses his job) or on his death. The policy should provide enough cover to keep the wife and children in their current lifestyle, at least until the children are educated and ready to leave home. By protecting current income, this should also cover debt repayments, so the family's home should not be at risk because they are unable to pay their mortgage. A life assurance policy is also of high importance.

Solution 5.4

(i) A term policy covers the individual during the term of the insurance. A whole-of-life policy extends up to death, so inevitably a benefit will be received by dependants. However, it is more expensive than a term policy due to the higher risk involved.
(ii) The young married couple have two major insurance requirements:
 (a) protection of the decreasing mortgage liability; and
 (b) long-term provision for their incapacitated child.

Decreasing term mortgage protection is usually good value as it will leave a debt-free asset for dependants if either spouse dies before the loan is repaid. It is recommended, subject to affordability, that a decreasing term mortgage protection insurance be obtained despite limited income at present, this will help to ensure that there is capital available for the long-term care of their child, in the event of either parent's death. (The property can be sold to contribute to the child's care costs.)

Chapter 6

Solution 6.1

The annual percentage interest rate is: $(1 + 10\%/12)^{12} - 1 = 10.47\%$

Solution 6.2

Any debt which is used to acquire an appreciating asset, or which improves overall financial health, is generally regarded as **'good debt'**. Any debt that is used to finance items that depreciate in value, or are consumed, is considered **'bad debt'**. This type of debt will lead to an unhealthy financial position and may cause financial distress.

Solution 6.3

(a)   The monthly interest rate is calculated as follows:

$$(1 + r)^{12} - 1 = 24.8\%$$
$$1 + r = \sqrt[12]{1.248}$$
$$r = 1.863\% \text{ per month.}$$

(b)   The current interest being charged per month is €/£5,000 × 1.863% = €/£93.15. As Fernando pays the minimum repayment amount of €/£300, this means that €/£206.85 (€/£300 − €/£93.15) must represent Fernando's monthly spend on consumables.

(c)   As a first step Fernando should use the €/£2,000 that he has built up in his current account to reduce this credit card debt. This is probably earning very little interest, but the bank manager would see it as a good financial move if it were used to reduce the expensive credit card debt. This will leave Fernando with no emergency funds but he has the opportunity to re-use his credit card if need be, so he will be able to pay for unexpected cash outflows. This is only recommended for a very short period of time and it is assumed that Fernando's job is secure.

Fernando will be receiving an additional €/£500 cash inflow each month from now on. He should stop spending on consumables using his credit card. If these expenditures are necessary he should now pay for them in cash. This will mean that €/£206.85 of his additional salary per month will be used to purchase consumables, leaving a balance of €/£293.15 for debt management. As Fernando does not wish to be left with any current liquidity issues (he may have no savings) it is recommended that only €/£250 of the surplus funds should be used to pay off the credit card each month. The remaining €/£43.15 should be accumulated in a savings account, as evidence to the bank manager that Fernando can save and is serious about improving his financial position. If his spending habits increase in line with his pay increase, this will send out a negative signal to the bank manager. Indeed, if Fernando is able to reduce his spending on consumables and to increase his savings per month this will provide an even stronger signal when his application for a mortgage is being assessed.

The new credit card monthly repayment will be €/£550 (the original €/£300 + the additional €/£250). The card will not be used to purchase anything again. Following this repayment schedule, Fernando should be able to repay this debt in six months.

Balance	Interest (1.863%)	Repayment	Closing balance
€/£5,000	€/£93.15	(€/£2,550)	€/£2,543.15
€/£2,543.15	€/£47.37	(€/£550)	€/£2,040.52
€/£2,040.52	€/£38.01	(€/£550)	€/£1,528.53
€/£1,528.53	€/£28.48	(€/£550)	€/£1,007.01
€/£1,007.01	€/£18.76	(€/£550)	€/£475.77
€/£475.77	€/£8.86	(€/£484.63)	–

(Cut up the card)

On viewing this, the bank manager will be able to see that Fernando is able to service debt at the rate of €/£550 per month. This will help him/her to determine how much Fernando will be able to afford to pay each month – which will influence the amount of debt the bank is willing to offer.

At this point, Fernando will also have amassed at least €/£258.90 (€/£43.15 × 6) in his bank account as well as any other monthly surpluses (that he used to have before) and in the six months following this, the balance should increase to a minimum of €/£3,817.80 (€/£258.90 + ((€43.15 + €/£550) × 6)).

Solution 6.4

The advantages of an IVA(NI)/FSA (ROI) are as follows:
 (i) Not all creditors have to agree (60% will do for a FSA).
 (ii) All interest and charges are frozen.
(iii) Once agreed to, the creditors cannot change their minds, as they are legally bound by the agreement.
(iv) Some of the debt may be written off.
 (v) It is based on affordability, not what an individual owes.
(vi) An individual can manage their finances better as they just have to pay one monthly repayment, which is affordable and they know when the debt will be cleared.

Solution 6.5

The individual should pay off/reduce his credit card debt of €/£8,000 first. Then, assuming the four options are the individual's only debt and assuming that he does not wish to purchase a car, etc., it is recommended that the remaining €/£7,000 is used to reduce his mortgage debt. This depends on whether there will be penalties for doing this.

Solution 6.6

The individual with quite a bit of debt who missed one repayment two years ago is likely to have the poorest credit rating and as a consequence will only be offered higher priced debt.

Solution 6.7

The best way to manage credit card debt expenditure is to pay the full balance off each month.

Solution 6.8

Monthly rate = $(1+r)^n - 1 = 12\%$ Where n is 12 and $r = \sqrt[12]{1.12} - 1 = 0.9489\%$
It is an annuity so you need to solve the equation (see Appendix 3):

You need to find out the payment multiplied by the annuity factor that gives the present value of the loan which is €/£16,000

Monthly payment x annuity factor = €/£16,000

The annuity factor will not be given in the tables (Appendix 3) as it is for 60 monthly periods, so you will have to use the formula to work it out.

$$\frac{1 - (1 + r)^{-n}}{r}$$

Where r is 0.9489% per month and n is 60 (5 years $\times$ 12 months)

$$\frac{1 - (1.009489)^{-60}}{0.009489}$$

$$= \frac{0.4326}{0.009489}$$

$= 45.590$

Monthly payment $\times$ 45.590 = €/£16,000
Monthly payment = €/£350.96

Solution 6.9

Total Income	€/£
Barbara Scratchet's monthly salary	2,600
Rent – gross	600
Deposit interest ((6,000 x 1%)/12)	5
	3,205
Total payments on debt	
Rental property – mortgage repayments	800
Residence	900
Credit card minimum payment	300
Bank loan – car	380
	2,380
Montly Surplus	825

Debt to Income ratio: 2,380/3,205 = 74.3% (before insurance)

(b) Barbara Scratchett is over-borrowed with too much debt. She is in a risky situation, e.g. a rental void for one month − €/£600 − would leave her with less income to cover debt payments and she may have to deplete her 'emergency' savings of €/£6,000.

She has very little disposable income left after servicing debt to pay for living expenses or savings/investments.

The use of monthly insurance premium payments of €/£213.24 would further reduce her disposable income.

With present low interest rates on mortgage loans together with the investment nature of such spending they could be regarded as 'good debt', whereas the borrowing for consumption (credit card) and depreciating assets (car) is expensive bad debt.

Priority would be to eliminate credit card debt and then the car loan if necessary by reducing emergency savings. (Good) debt to income (€/£1,700/€/£3,205) = 53% is still higher than a normal benchmark of 36%. It may be that to avoid financial difficulty - Barbara needs to reduce her costs. The large discretionary items are the car loan and insurance €/£593.24 (€/£380 + €/£213.34). Perhaps replacing her car with a significantly cheaper second-hand car of less value with only third party rather than comprehensive car insurance would be worth considering.

(c) The yearly rate of interest is €/£213.24 × Annuity for 12 months (x) = €/£2,400
     x = €/£2,400/213.24 = 11.255. Using the annuity tables this equates to 1% per month, which is 12% per year or more accurately $(1 + 0.01)^{12} - 1 = 12.68\%$ p.a.

Chapter 7

Solution 7.1

Transactions motive refers to the holding of cash to cover day-to-day operating expenditure, such as buying petrol for the car, groceries for the house, clothes, etc.

Precautionary motive refers to the holding of a cash buffer to cover emergencies. It is sometimes referred to as an emergency fund. Unexpected emergencies may include the car breaking down or losing your job. The level of funds held for precautionary motives depends on the risks associated with an individual's income. For example, an individual who has a secure job, is in good health and has a new car can afford to hold less cash for precautionary motives.

Speculative motive refers to the holding of cash to make money on opportunities that may arise, such as buying goods in bulk to achieve a cheaper price, paying for insurance up-front to reduce interest charges on any finance that is offered for spreading the payments over the period, or paying for goods up-front in cash to avail of a discount.

Solution 7.2

A current account deals with all the daily transactions affecting an individual. It normally has a cheque book and a debit card/bank card facility. In addition, several standing orders, or direct debits can be set up for a fee. Wages are normally paid into a current account and expenses, credit card instalments and loan repayments are paid out of it.

A deposit account is more like a savings account. Some offer instant access. This means that they may have a bank card which allows the account holder to withdraw funds from an automated teller machine (ATM). Instant access accounts can also be set up to receive regular direct debit transfers from the current account. Transfers in can also be set up and instigated using internet banking. They do not have a cheque book, or a debit card and the interest received is usually higher to that received on a current account. Term deposit accounts are more restrictive. Money is lodged and cannot be touched for the term agreed. Though inflexible, this type of account normally provides a higher rate of return.

Solution 7.3

ROI

- National solidarity bonds
- Savings certificates (NTMA)
- Savings bonds (NTMA)
- Instalment savings scheme (NTMA)
- Prize bonds (NTMA)
- Up to €635 of the interest received on a long-term Special Term account, and up to €480 interest received on a short-term Special Term Account.
- All savings products for individuals who are over 65 years of age and who earn under €18,000 per annum.

UK

- Dividends received on credit union share accounts
- ISAs
- Premium bonds
- Index linked savings certificates
- Fixed interest savings certificates (no longer available)
- Children's bonus bonds
- Child Trust Funds
- Junior ISAs.

Solution 7.4

The best place to invest emergency funds is in an instant access deposit account.
Compounding $= PV(1+r)^n = FV$

Solution 7.5

a) $\unicode{x20AC}/\pounds1,000(1.08)^2 = \unicode{x20AC}/\pounds1,166.40$
b) $\unicode{x20AC}/\pounds1,000(1.08)^4 = \unicode{x20AC}/\pounds1,360.40$
c) $PV(1.08)^2 = \unicode{x20AC}/\pounds1,000 \quad PV = \unicode{x20AC}/\pounds857$
d) $PV(1.08)^4 = \unicode{x20AC}/\pounds1,000 \quad PV = \unicode{x20AC}/\pounds735$

Solution 7.6

(a) $\unicode{x20AC}/\pounds10,000(1.05)^{10} = \unicode{x20AC}/\pounds16,289$
(b) $\unicode{x20AC}/\pounds5,000(1.10)^{10} = \unicode{x20AC}/\pounds12,968$

Chapter 8

Solution 8.1

Bonds are traded debt. When a company or the government wishes to borrow funds, they can issue bonds. What they are selling is the promise to pay the holder of the bond a fixed amount of interest, called a coupon, periodically (every six months or every year) and a set payment (usually €/£100) to redeem (repurchase) the bond at a set date in the future. These streams of future cash flows are bought and sold in the bond markets. The interest is guaranteed (so long as the company does not go into liquidation) and the redemption amount is also guaranteed. Indeed, a company must pay what they owe in bond interest before they can pay a dividend, so from an investor's viewpoint they are less risky than equity.

Equity shares are different. The holder of an equity share might get a dividend and can sell the share. It is not redeemed as such. When an individual purchases an equity share they become an owner of a portion (a share) of the company. Though the holder of the share is an owner and is entitled to vote at shareholder meetings, their power is restricted in respect of dividend distributions. Directors decide what dividends to pay. Shareholders can only reduce this at a shareholder meeting, they cannot increase it. Directors may decide not to pay a dividend at all and they must honour the bond interest before they pay any dividend. The value of an equity share typically moves with the value of the company; when the company performs poorly, or the economy experiences a downturn the value of equity usually falls; when the economy does well and the company is successful, the value of equity increases (share price increases). When the company performs poorly the directors may not pay any dividend. However, when it does well the level of dividend can be very high.

Solution 8.2

A risk-free investment is an investment that is virtually free from risk, such as gilts. It is very unlikely that the government will not be able to honour the coupon and redemption values (the risk-free status depends on the country).

Solution 8.3

The periodic payment can be calculated using the following formula:

$$P = \frac{M \times r}{1-(1/(1 + r)^t)}$$

Where P is the periodic payment (to find)
M is the initial size of the mortgage (€/£280,000)
t is the number of payments 180 (15 × 12)
r, the periodic interest rate, is 0.4167% (5%/12)

Therefore
$$P = \frac{€/£280,000 \times 0.004167}{1 - (1/(1+0.004167)^{180})}$$

P = €/£2,214.28

Solution 8.4

(a) The interest payment each month to the bank will be
€/£1,166.67 ((€/£280,000 × 5%)/12).
The periodic payment to the endowment can be calculated using the following formula:

$$M = \frac{p((1 + y)^t - 1)}{y}$$

Where M, the target maturity amount, is €/£280,000
p is the periodic payment
t, the number of periods, is 15, and
y, the rate of return expected to be earned by the fund, is 7%.

$$€/£280,000 = \frac{p((1 + 0.07)^{15} - 1)}{0.07}$$

$$€/£280,000 = p \times 25.129$$

$$€/£280,000/25.129 = p$$

$$€/£11,142.50 = p$$

Therefore the monthly payment to the endowment policy will be €/£928.54 (€/£11,142.50/12).

The total monthly payment will be €/£2,095.21 (€/£1,166.67 + €/£928.54)

(b) When the calculations from **Question 8.3** and part (a) above are compared it would seem that Geoffrey would be better off going for the endowment mortgage. He stands to gain €/£116.07 every month as the payment required is lower (€/£2,214.28 + €/£2,095.21). This money could be invested monthly and would accumulate to a good amount by the end of 15 years.

However, there are risks associated with endowment plans. They typically invest funds in the stock market and therefore are exposed to risk. In addition the management fees and transaction fees have to be covered. To estimate a return (net of all these costs) of 7% might be deemed to be unrealistic. Over the past 20 years endowment mortgages have been receiving bad press as many of them did not mature at the value expected. The return earned had been overestimated in most instances. Though rare, endowments could outperform their initial predictions.

The option to take-up will depend on Geoffrey's attitude to risk and his views on how the equity markets will perform over the next 15 years. If he feels that they will perform strongly, and he wants to take the chance, then this product is fine for him.

Geoffrey's views on interest rates will also impact on his choice. If an endowment mortgage is selected, the outstanding capital balance will not reduce at all over the 15 years. This means that interest rate changes will change Geoffrey's repayment amount. Most fixed interest rate products are only available for short periods (typically up to five years), which means that Geoffrey is exposed to interest rate risk. Therefore, if Geoffrey were to opt for the endowment mortgage it might not be a bad idea to also take steps to repay some of the debt on a periodic basis to reduce his risks.

Solution 8.5

Unit trusts are funds that are operated by fund managers (banks, brokers or insurance companies). Investment trusts are companies that specialise in investing in shares in other companies.

A unit trust does not have shares. An investor who wants to invest in an investment trust has to purchase its shares in the stock market, usually from other investors.

Unit trusts are open-ended investments. An investor in a unit trust purchases units from the fund manager, increasing the size of the fund. When the investor sells units the fund manager decreases the size of the fund (sells underlying investments). Investment trusts are closed-end. When an investor invests in an investment trust they purchase shares in the company, the value of the underlying investments remains the same. When they sell their shares, another investor purchases them and there is no impact on the underlying investments held by the company.

The value of a unit trust is directly related to the underlying value of the investments the fund holds. The value of an investment company is influenced by this, but is also influenced by the demand for the investment company's shares in the stock market. For example, if the directors have a good track record, it may be that the market will value the investment company's shares higher than the value of the underlying investments, as equity holders anticipate improvements.

Investment trusts can raise debt to expand the investment portfolio, while unit trusts have less scope to do this.

Solution 8.6

The benefits of investing in collective funds are that an investor is able to get access to a wide range of investments that they may not have been able to invest in on their own. Collective fund managers typically purchase a wide variety of equity shares, bonds, gilts and commercial property. This means that they hold a diversified portfolio of investments so return is not as risky as it would be if the investor only invested in equity. The investor probably would not have sufficient capital to invest in a commercial property so collective funds open doors to this type of investment.

Solution 8.7

$PV(1 + r)^n = FV$
Amount to invest $\times (1.07)^3 = $€/£25,000
Amount to invest = €/£25,000/1.225
Amount to invest = €/£20,408

Solution 8.8

(i) The scoring of each investment according to their performance, risk and liquidity is provided in the following table, where '1' is the worst score and '5' is the best score.

	Cash	Bonds	Equity	Property
Growth/performance	1	2	5	3
Security/risk	5	5	2	3
Access/liquidity	5	3	4	1

(ii) Equity growth is best in the long term when compared to cash, bonds and property. The above generally agreed ranking of the main categories of investment shows that growth may be the best in the long run for equities, but short-run volatility and the risk of losses is unacceptably poor for risk-averse investors or investors who have only a short-term investment in mind.

So an individual who needs to liquidate their investment soon would favour the low risk and high liquidity of cash or bonds.

The conclusion is that the statement is too simplistic. Growth/performance is only one important factor, security and liquidity also has to be considered.

(Chartered Accountants Ireland, CAP 1, Autumn 2009 (Extract from Q6))

Solution 8.9

(Use the gross redemption yield (given) to calculate the market value of the bond, then using the client's tax rate calculate the net interest receivable and the IRR of the cash flows to establish the net redemption yield.)

Year	Cash flow €/£	12% factor	Present value €/£
0	?	1.000	?
1-12	8	6.194	49.552
12	100	0.257	25.700
		MV of bond	75.252

Therefore the market price of the government bond will be €/£75.252.

Interest receivable by Mr. Black – after 25% income tax
€/£8 × (1−0.25) = €/£6

Year	Cash flow €/£	12% factor	5% factor	Present value (12%) €/£	Present value (5%) €/£
0	(75.252)	1.000	1.000	(75.252)	(75.252)
1-12	6.000	6.194	8.863	37.164	53.178
12	100.000	0.257	0.557	25.700	55.700
				(12.388)	33.626

Interpolation to find the after tax return rate (lies between 5% and 12%)

$$\text{IRR} = 5\% + \frac{33.626(12\%-5\%)}{33.626 + 12.388}$$

$$= 5\% + 5.115\%$$

Therefore the net redemption yield to a 25% taxpayer is 10.115%

(Chartered Accountants Ireland, CAP 1, Autumn 2009 (Extract from Q7))

Solution 8.10

Investing 100% in shares in a single company is excessively risky. Jim should look to diversify his investments and therefore his risk. With a unit trust, the value is a function of the value of the portfolio of underlying shares and is not affected by supply and demand.

The benefits of a unit trust are:

- Access to a wide range of investments (diversification)
- Expertise of fund manager with a large fund
- Spread of equity, gilts, bonds, property – which together lower risk
- Access to a proportion of otherwise unaffordable large investments.

(Chartered Accountants Ireland, CAP 1, Summer 2009 (Extract from Q6))

Solution 8.11

The indexed equity mutual fund is recommended as the period of time that Joan and Jim are talking about is 18 years and the equity markets in general are considered to provide the best return over this time period.

Solution 8.12

George should continue renting as buying and selling properties is costly and the investment is very illiquid. If George did not intend to leave Dublin, then purchasing may have been an option, particularly since house prices have fallen so much over the past few years. However, George may move to London and hence the property purchase is short term, so is not advisable.

Chapter 9

Solution 9.1

A pension is a steady income that is paid to an individual who is typically retired.

Solution 9.2

A public state pension is typically an inflation-indexed annuity that is set and paid by the government out of social security payments to people who are retired and who have paid social security for a minimum amount of years throughout their lives. This payment is mandatory. Individuals cannot opt out of paying their social security, though they have to claim the pension on retirement. Individuals do not have to pay social security when they are not earning.

A private pension is instigated by the individual. It is not mandatory. It is up to each individual to decide whether they want to have a private pension or not. To encourage people to contribute to a private pension, the government allows a tax deduction for contributions made to the pension scheme throughout the working life of the individual. There are limits on the amount that can be paid in each year. A private pension can be received in three ways, a lump sum, an annuity or a combination of both.

Solution 9.3

A personal pension is set up by an individual with an institution which specialises in providing pension policies. Most insurance companies offer pension schemes. The individual pays into the pension policy independently from their source of income. Their yearly contribution to the scheme is limited (see the chapter for details). All personal pension schemes are money-purchase schemes. This means that the risk associated with the pension not providing a reasonable source of funds in retirement lies fully with the individual.

The total value of the fund on retirement will depend on the contributions made to the pension provider and how well the fund has performed (this will be linked to the stock markets and the economy). The pension provider will charge for setting up and administering the pension, these charges are taken from the pension fund. The government provides tax relief on contributions made to personal pension schemes up to certain limits of net relevant earnings (see the chapter for details). The income received from a personal pension scheme is taxable on the pensioner.

Company/occupational pension schemes are set up by employers for the benefit of their employees. Both employees and employers contribute to the scheme. The employee gets a tax deduction for the amount of pension that they contribute – their income tax and social security payments are less. The company also gets a tax deduction for the pension contributions they pay for the employee. There are two types of company pension scheme: defined contribution and defined benefit. These are discussed in the solution to the next question. The income received from a company pension scheme is taxable on the pensioner.

Solution 9.4

A defined contribution scheme is a money-purchase scheme. This means that the company does not guarantee a minimum pension. Both the company and the employee pay into the scheme. The pension received depends on the performance of the scheme assets and the amount of contribution paid in, net of scheme charges. This type of scheme is regarded as more risky than a defined benefit scheme.

A defined benefit scheme is also known as a final salary scheme or a salary scheme. In this situation the company guarantees the employee a set pension, usually a percentage of the final year salary (or an average of the salary received over a number of years). The percentage paid is usually related to the number of years' service given to the employee.

The company absorbs all the risk in this type of scheme – where the pension assets fall below what is required to meet future pension commitments, then the company has to make up the difference from its reserves.

Contributions to both types of scheme are treated the same way for tax purposes. A yearly contribution is tax deductible up to a certain percentage of the employees net relevant earnings (there is an overall ceiling level also – see chapter for details).

Solution 9.5

All annuity pension income (public and private) is taxable on the pensioner. The tax paid will depend on whether the individual is a lower or a higher rate taxpayer. Retired individuals do not have to pay social security. If the individual has a private pension and opts to receive a 25% lump sum on retirement, then this lump sum is tax-free. If the individual withdraws over 25%, the surplus is taxable at the individual's marginal rate of tax (up to a limit of €200,000 in the ROI and a limit of £375,000 in the UK (25% of the Lifetime Allowance)). It may also incur a Lifetime Transfer Charge/Crystallisation charge if the total pension fund is worth more than £1,500,000 (UK)/€2,300,000(ROI).

Pensioners in the ROI have a €18,000 annual income exemption and do not have to report their income if it is below this threshold. A retired couple has a €36,000 threshold.

Solution 9.6

(a) Thomas will pay €/£400 each month into the pension scheme (€/£4,000 x 10%). This means that Thomas will only be taxed on €/£3,600 (€/£4,000 − €/£400). Therefore, the tax relief is given at source (PAYE only).
(b) The total contribution to the pension scheme each month on behalf of Thomas is €/£520 (€/£400+(€/£4,000×3%)).

Solution 9.7

(a) Thomas' annual pension can be calculated using the following formula:

$$\frac{\text{Years and days/365}}{80} \times \text{pensionable salary} = \text{Annual pension}$$

$$\frac{22 \text{ plus } 304/365}{80} \times €/£48,000 = €/£13,700$$

This equates to a monthly pension of €/£1,141.67 (€/£13,700/12). This is subject to income tax.

(b) In addition Thomas will receive a lump sum equal to:
    €/£pension × 3 = €/£lump sum
       €/£13,700×3 = €/£41,100

Solution 9.8

Determining the annual pension for Thelma

Assuming a final salary of €36,000 per annum (€/£3,000 x 12)

€/£36,000 x 28/80 = €/£12,600 per annum (€/£1,050 per month)
Pension lump sum = €/£36,000 x 28 x 3/80 = €/£37,800

Chapter 10

Solution 10.1

The steps an individual might take when they believe they have been given advice negligently include the following:

Initial contact: Contact the entity who sold the product, explain any concerns and state clearly the remedial action required.
Formal complaint: If the problem is not resolved, contact the firm in writing with a formal complaint. Include all details and specify the outcome required.
Ombudsman: When unhappy with the response received from the firm contact the relevant ombudsman (independent complaint scheme that is free of charge for consumers). The ombudsman can recommend a solution, or pay out compensation.
Courts: When unhappy with the decision of the ombudsman, an individual can appeal their decision in the High Court.

Solution 10.2

ROI
The Central Bank of Ireland (CBI) is responsible for the regulation of all financial services providers in Ireland under the terms of the Central Bank Reform Act of 2010. The aim of the CBI's regulation is to promote a safe and fair financial services market for consumers, and to promote sound and solvent financial institutions, thereby giving depositor and other consumers of financial products confidence that their deposits and investments are safe. The CBI regulates the activities of credit institutions, investment intermediaries, stockbrokers, financial exchanges, collective investment schemes, funds, investor compensation and related consumer issues, life insurance, general insurance, insurance-related consumer issues, money lenders, mortgage and credit intermediaries and related credit consumer issues and credit unions (citizensinformation.ie, 2012).

The CBI monitors and enforces the consumer protection guidance, conduct of business and the prudential requirements of financial institutions as set out in the CBI's codes of practice. The codes of practice require financial institutions to act in a fair and transparent manner and to act in the best interests of their customers. The CBI also audit and monitor the practices of financial service firms and take punitive action if required.

UK

The current regulatory body in the UK is the FSA (though this will change soon and, therefore, you should revert to the latter part of the chapter when answering the question).

The Financial Services Authority

The **Financial Services Authority** (FSA) is an independent non-governmental body. It is a company limited by guarantee and financed by the financial services industry. It is accountable to Treasury Ministers and, through them, parliament. It regulates the financial services industry in the UK. All firms that wish to undertake financial service activities have to be registered with the FSA. Indeed, it is a criminal offence to give advice without being authorised by the FSA. Financial advisers must demonstrate competence (hold a relevant qualification), honesty and be financially sound. If a financial adviser is called 'independent' they must advise across a range of providers (**depolarisation**).

The FSA has four statutory objectives under the Financial Services and Markets Act (2000):
* to maintain confidence in the UK financial system;
* to contribute to the protection and enhancement of stability of the UK financial system;
* to secure the appropriate level of protection for consumers; and
* to reduce the opportunity for regulated business to be used for a purpose connected with financial crime.

To assist individuals, the FSA provides information on all the financial products that are available in the UK and will also provide advice/guidance when an individual considers that they have been treated negligently by a financial adviser.

BIBLIOGRAPHY

Bank of England, (2009), Quarterly Bulletin: Household Survey: www.bankofengland. co.uk/publications/documents/quarterlybulletin/qb090302.pdf, accessed July 2012.

Bloomberg, (2012), Irish Stock Exchange Overall Index, www.bloomberg.com/quote/ ISEQ:IND/Chart, accessed July 2012.

Bawden, A., (2002), Personal Finance: Tangible Assets with less of a Sting Attached, FT.com site.

Berry, S., Williams, R., and Waldron, M., (2009), 'Household Saving', Bank of England Quarterly Bulletin, Vol. 49, Issue 3, pages 191–201.

Central Bank of Ireland, (2012), Central Bank of Ireland's Registers, www. registersfinancial regulator.ie/, accessed July 2012.

Citizens Advice Bureau, (2010), Options for dealing with debt, www.adviceguide.org. uk/, accessed July 2010.

Cortavarria, L., Gray, S., Johnston, B., Kodres, L., Narain, A., Pradhan, M., and Tower, I., (2009), Lessons from the Financial Crisis for Future Regulation of Financial Institutions and Markets and for Liquidity Management, Monetary and Capital Markets.

Department of Social and Family Affairs, (2012), SW 19 'Payments for Retired or Older People, DSFA.

Directgov.com, (2012), Money, Tax and Benefits, http://direct.gov.uk/en/ MoneyTaxAndBenefits/, accessed July 2012.

Financial Services Authority, (2011), Enforcement Annual Performance Account 2010/11, www.fsa.gov.uk/pubs/annual/ar10_11/enforcement_report.pdf.

Financial Services Authority, (2012), About the FSA, www.fsa.gov.uk/.

Finfacts Ireland, (2012), Irish Economy: Irish House Prices Fell by 16.4% in the Year to April 2012, 24 May, www.finfacts.ie/, accessed July 2012.

Glennon, D., (2008), Investment Outlook 2008, Business Matters: A Newsletter for Chartered Accountants in Business, February 2008 edition.

Hall, J., (2012), UK Pension Performance among worst in Developed World, The Telegraph, 11 June 2012, www.telegraph.co.uk/news/9325041/uk-pension-performance-among-worst-in-developed-world.html.

Harrison, D., (2005), *Personal Financial Planning: Theory and Practice*, FT Prentice Hall, England.

Harvey, R., (2004), Comparison of Household Savings Ratios: Euro zone/United States/Japan, Statistics Brief, OECD.

Heartwood, (2006), Fine Wine – liquid gold? *Horizons*, Winter 2006, page 5, www.heartwoodwealth.com

HM Treasury, (2012), Reforming UK Financial Regulation, www.hm-treasury.gov.uk/fin-stability-regreform-structure-htm, accessed June 2012.

Hosking, P., (2009), OECD Blames Weak Bank Regulation for Financial Crisis, *The Sunday Times,* January 9, 2009.

International Monetary Fund, http://www.imf.org/external/.

Irish Life Website, (2008), Pensions and PRSA, accessed 16 January 2008, http://www.irishlife.ie/pensions/prsa/employer.html

Ivory, J., (2007), Hugh Grant Sells Warhol Portrait of Elizabeth Taylor, efluxmedia website, 14 November 2007, http://www.efl ucmedia.com, accessed 26 March 2008.

Maastricht Return, (2012) March Return, Department of Finance, www.finance.gov.ie/documents/publications/economicstatsetc/infonotemaastrichtmar2012.pdf, accessed July 2012.

Mortgageguideuk, (2012), Ratio of House Prices to Income, http://www.mortgageguideuk.co.uk/, accessed June 2012.

Nationwide seasonal regional quarterly index, (2010), http://www.nationwide.co.uk/hpi/historical.htm, accessed July 2010.

Nationwide seasonal regional quarterly index, (2012), http://www.nationwide.co.uk/hpi/historical.htm, accessed July 2012.

Northern Ireland Executive, (2012), Enterprise Minister introduces Debt Relief Bill, http://www.northernireland.gov.uk/news/news-deti/news-deti-march-2010/news-deti-090310-enterprise-minister-introduces.htm, accessed July 2012.

Northern Ireland Statistics and Research Agency (2011), Divorce Rates in Northern Ireland, www.nisra.gov.uk/, accessed June 2012.

Office of National Statistics (ONS), (2011), 'Life Expectancy at Birth Remains highest in the South of England', News Bulletin, Office of National Statistics, 19 October 2011.

Redhead, K., (2003), *Introducing Investments: A Personal Finance Approach,* FT Prentice Hall, England.

Revenue, (2012), Tax Relief for Mortgage paid on a Home Loan, Revenue Irish Tax and Customs Website, accessed June 2012.

Turner, Lord, A., (2009), The Turner Review: A Regulatory Response to the Global Banking Crises, March 2009, Financial Services Authority.

Vina, G., (2010), UK Scraps FSA, Reversing System Set up by Brown (Update 2), *Bloomberg Businessweek*, 17 June 2010, http://www.businessweek.com/news

Williams, B., Hughes, B., and Redmond, D., (2010), Managing an Unstable Housing Market, Working Paper Series NII 10.02, UCD Urban Institute Ireland, www.ucd.ie/uii

MEETINGS NOT STARTING WITHOUT YOU

Chartered Accountants work at the highest levels in Irish business. In fact six out of ten Irish Chartered Accountants work at Finance Director level or above.

Discover our flexible training options:
CharteredCareers.ie

Chartered Accountants Ireland